THE HUMANE SOCIETY OF THE UNITED STATES

COMPLETE GUIDE TO
HORSE
CARE

ERIN HARTY AND THE STAFF OF
THE HUMANE SOCIETY OF THE UNITED STATES

HUMANE SOCIETY PRESS

Erin Harty is a freelance writer and former moderator/administrator of *The Chronicle of the Horse*'s online discussion forums, which have more than 32,000 registered members. She received her B rating from the United States Pony Clubs and competes in eventing.
The Staff of The Humane Society of the United States contributors were Keith Dane, Eric Davis, D.V.M., Holly Hazard, and Deborah Salem.

First edition
ISBN 798-1-934785-00-3
Library of Congress Cataloging in Publication Data
Harty, Erin.
   The Humane Society of the United States complete guide to horse care /
Erin Harty and the Staff of the Humane Society of the United States.
      p. cm.
   Includes bibliographical references and index.
   ISBN 978-1-934785-00-3
1. Horses. I. Humane Society of the United States. II. Title.
   SF285.3.H36 2008
   636.1'083–dc22

                                                        2008001876

Printed in the United States of America

Humane Society Press
The Humane Society of the United States
2100 L Street, NW
Washington, DC 20037

Printed on 100% post-consumer recycled paper, processed
chlorine free and FSC certified, with soy-based ink.

Contents

Foreword

WHEN OUR ANIMAL WELFARE PARTNERS at The Humane Society of the United States (HSUS) told us about plans to write and distribute its *Complete Guide to Horse Care*, I was delighted. Much-needed attention is being paid to the plight of America's horses, and I know how many people have stepped in to help, with everything from donations to legislation to adoption and fostering.

This project brought back a lot of memories from decades ago of our work to help people care for their dogs and cats. For twenty-five-plus years much of our mission has been to provide information about pet overpopulation and the numbers of companion animals being sacrificed because of a lack of good homes. Happily, animal welfare advocates spurred people to adopt dogs and cats for the first time or to add to the numbers of pets who were already family members. That meant we had many people who either had little or no experience caring for companion animals or were faced with new challenges as more animals were added to the family. We mobilized as information providers, with vehicles such as call-in help lines and newspaper columns. The HSUS's earlier guides for cat and dog guardians were extremely helpful and are great templates for the necessary information this book provides about caring for horses.

Now, even with some seven million horses in the United States, there is a general lack of knowledge about how to help and care for these special animals. People are concerned, but they do not know what to do. Fortunately, The HSUS is stepping in to provide another worthy public service, this time for our horses.

The Doris Day Animal Foundation was invited to help fund *The Humane Society of the United States Complete Guide to Horse Care*, and it was a privilege to say yes. This is a wonderful educational project. We know that, with the right information, people will be better equipped to care for their horses. Our message—that caring for horses, like caring for dogs and cats, is a lifetime commitment—will reach those interested in caring for horses.

Both novice and experienced horse caretakers will benefit from *The Humane Society of the United States Complete Guide to Horse Care*. It's a beautiful book with vital information, and it will be a great source of information for years to come. We're proud to be involved.

Doris Day

Acknowledgments

The authors are grateful for the support of Wayne Pacelle, president and CEO of The Humane Society of the United States, and The Doris Day Animal Foundation and for the contributions of Stacy Segal (research), Paula Jaworski (art direction), Jean Bernard (copyediting), and Fran Jurga and Amy Kolzow (photography).

CHAPTER 1

The Mystique Versus the Reality

FEW AMONG US LIKELY REMEMBER OUR FIRST introduction to a dog or a cat. But a horse? If you don't recall every detail of the encounter, there's almost certainly a photograph tucked away somewhere in a family album that memorializes it. Perhaps you were riding a pony at a birthday party, patting a police horse on a busy city street, or perching on an equine retiree on a neighbor's farm.

The moment's significance stems from the fact that horses aren't common fixtures in the lives of modern-day Americans, so meeting a horse tends to be pretty memorable. But there's more to it than that. You can see the emotions writ large on the face of a child who's meeting his first horse—it's a mixture of wonder, awe, and curiosity, with a dash of trepidation thrown in for good measure.

Horses are big. Very, very big. Bigger than most animals we encounter in daily life. That's the first thing most people notice as they cautiously inch toward a new equine friend. Horses are also strikingly beautiful. Those large, expressive eyes exude a depth of character and intelligence, even in the plainest of horses. The powerful and fluid way a horse moves almost demands admiration and seems to embody the phrase, "poetry in motion." Horses are just different. While cats and dogs, wonderful creatures in their own rights, trigger our "Aww!" response, horses truly inspire *awe*. And, of course, a little bit of "Aww!" as well.

Although humankind has forged many friendships across the divide that separates us from the rest of the animal kingdom, our relationship with horses is unique, as are the animals themselves.

In the beginning, the relationship was a utilitarian one. Generally docile and relatively easy to domesticate, horses were used as beasts of burden and machines of war. We human beings harnessed their strength to plow fields and pull heavy loads, and we carried out on their backs our quest to explore and expand our horizons.

As our knowledge grew and technology advanced, horses were replaced with machinery that could transport human beings faster and carry heavier loads. Our relationship changed from one of necessity to one primarily of recreation.

Most horses still have "jobs," however, and are expected to earn their keep in some fashion, whether it's as a backyard pony who gives rides to the grandkids or as a stakes-winning racehorse with millions of dollars in earnings. For many people, the relationship between an owner and a horse may mirror a boss/employee relationship: human beings, as the "bosses," are the authority figures. Owners expect their horses to behave as they've been trained to do and to follow human beings' instructions. They select horses for their "job openings" on the basis of the animals' qualifications and potential, much as an employer selects a new employee. And owners expect their horses to try hard to succeed in those jobs.

There is a dichotomy in this relationship, though—one with which numerous horsemen struggle. In the past, horses have been thought of primarily as tools, as a means to an end. That mindset has evolved gradually to the point where many of us also consider our horses to be companion animals. Their value isn't solely dependent on what they can do for us; as with our pet dogs and cats, we also enjoy their company and personalities, and we simply love them and care about them. They are important to us because of who they are, not just because of what they can do.

So how to reconcile the roles of working animal and companion animal? Horses don't fit neatly into either category, and the responsibilities and expectations of each may sometimes compete or outright conflict. Most of us consider ownership of a cat, dog, or other pet to be a lifetime commitment, yet horses may have half a dozen owners (or more!) in their lifetimes. Is that wrong? Is it fair to use a horse in a manner that might cause him to become injured, such as racing or jumping? Can a horse be happy kept in a stall, considering that he's a creature found in nature roaming the plains?

One reason we have written this book is to try to help you answer these questions. Our perspective is that of an animal protection organization with fifty years of experience in dealing with the best—and, unfortunately, the worst—of what horses experience in the modern world. We are also longtime horse owners ourselves.

Horsemanship is an ancient art, and one that has remained largely unchanged—the skills that made someone a good horseman five hundred years ago are just as applicable today. But circumstances change, and the ways in which we keep, use, and think about horses are constantly evolving. To be the best custodians of our horses, we sometimes need to rethink old habits as well as constantly reassess our own personal situations to be sure everyone's needs are met.

Think of your experience with your horse or horses as a series of crossroads: you will make decisions that will influence your life and the life of your horse in ways that reflect your view of animals and their role in the world. Your views will come into play when you acquire a horse; when you solve any behavior, training, or medical problems that may arise during your life together; when you decide your horse's future with or without you; and when you decide how your old friend and partner will end his life.

If you're reading this book, it's because these unique and amazing animals have captured your heart. The more time you spend with them, the more fully you will realize that horses are always teaching and challenging you, and, no matter how experienced you are, a horse can always add to your enjoyment and appreciation of life. If you keep in mind that awe and reverence of your first introduction to horse-kind, you'll be well equipped to make the best choices for your equine friends.

There's just something about horses that makes an impact—whether you're a small child stroking a pony's velvet-soft nose for the first time or an adult marveling at polo ponies on a polo field pounding by at top speed. Horses embody traits that humans admire and want to emulate. It's not solely what they can do that draws us to them; it's also what they symbolize.

The Allure of the Horse

Whether nature or nurture is to blame, you'd be hard-pressed to find an elementary-school-age munchkin who wouldn't do *anything* for a pony. In some families, the obsession with horses pops up out of the blue— no one in the family is "horsey," nor has anyone gone out of his way to introduce Susie to the wonderful world of equines. It may start with a pink plastic My Little Pony, then interest may turn to the long-running Saddle Club series of books and progress to television shows and movies about horses. Soon it's a full-blown obsession that can only be appeased with riding lessons, living in real life the adventures of the Saddle Club's hero and heroines, who learn to ride at Pine Hollow Stables.

Although little boys aren't immune, females are definitely afflicted more frequently by the horsey disease. About 92 percent of the more than twelve thousand members of the United States Pony Clubs, a youth organization dedicated to teaching English riding and horse care, are female.[1] The majority of the thirty-one thousand youth members at the American Quarter Horse Association, a breed organization with a focus on Western riding, are also female.[2] Some of the inclination toward horses may be innate. Girls tend to include nurturing in their play and may enjoy caring for horses as much as they enjoy riding them.

The benefits of being around these creatures are easy to document. Riding can be a tremendous boost to self-esteem—in fact, horses are often used as therapy animals, not just for riders with physical handicaps, but also for those with emotional issues. Riding therapy has been used to treat everything from eating disorders to attention deficit hyperactivity disorder (ADHD).

Let's not completely overlook the boys, however. The attraction is just as real—if, perhaps, less frequent—for them, as are the benefits! In the western United States, the cowboy culture is the norm and is more male-oriented than is the formally attired gentility of English-style riding sports. At the highest levels of virtually all English and Western competitive riding sports, men often outnumber women, although both sexes compete in the same events on equal terms—a rarity in modern competitive sports. *The Man from Snowy River*, Kentucky Derby-winning jockey Edgar Prado, or the legendary western trainer Ray Hunt might be a boy's role model.

Adults, of course, are far past the point of youthful infatuation. (Well, mostly.) We're too mature to want to live our own versions of *Black Beauty* or *The Black Stallion*. (Mostly.) But there is still somewhat of a fairy-tale allure...after all, this is the "sport of kings" and of cowboys, too. Think of Prince William and Prince Harry of England on their polo ponies, or John Wayne galloping across endless cinematic deserts of the Southwest.

The so-called English riding sports embrace the stately image whole-heartedly. The competition "uniforms" for many English sports look nearly identical to what riders wore two hundred years ago—highly polished boots, crisp breeches, and smartly tailored hunt coat topped off with a velvet cap, and the horse decked out in spotless tack, his mane and tail neatly braided. A horse and rider ready to show look like they've just stepped out of an eighteenth-century English painting. Having "the look" is part of the fun of showing.

The Western disciplines call to mind a different fairy tale: the simpler times and romantic cowboy folklore of the American Old West. Don a pair of jeans and cowboy boots; add a pair of chaps, gloves, and a cowboy hat; swing up into a comfy Western saddle aboard a smart and willing Quarter Horse; and you're ready to ride all day on the plains working cattle.

The Reality

In the abstract horses occupy an exalted position in our society. In reality, however, they're not always so lucky. As their champions and caretakers, we bear the responsibility for ensuring that every horse—from a stakes-winning racehorse to a child's pony—enjoys a life befitting the horse's stature in our culture.

Although it's an uphill battle for animal advocates to secure conscientious treatment for all species, horses present a special challenge. For any domestic animal, life is something of a roll of the dice: the quality of his care depends on the resources—and the intentions—of the person he draws in the human lottery. A dog or cat usually only has to take a chance once or twice, since most people who bring pets into their home keep them for the duration of the animals' lives. But every time a horse changes hands, his fate hangs in the balance.

(A note on terminology: Throughout this book, we refer to the person with legal ownership of the horse as the horse owner, by far the most common noun used to describe the relationship between horse and human being. We define the word in our own terms, however: the horse owner to us is also a caregiver, advocate, partner, and guardian—a safeguarder of the horse's well-being, and a conscientious steward.)

Consider this hypothetical example: a Thoroughbred colt is born on a farm in Kentucky, sired by a prolific winner on the track who has just recently retired to stud. The breeder, Owner #1, has carefully matched the stud with a lovely mare and is hoping for the best.

Owner #2 purchases the colt as a yearling for a considerable sum in the hopes that he will have a stellar career on the racetrack.

As a two-year-old, however, the colt's performances are nothing special. Owner #2 sells him (at a considerable loss) to Owner #3, who races horses at the smaller tracks against less talented company. The colt earns his keep, but at the end of his three-year-old year, the owner decides the horse just isn't cut out to be a racehorse.

The colt is gelded and finds himself with Owner #4, a young, professional horseman who specializes in buying horses off the track, retraining them, and selling them to new homes as show horses. The gelding spends six months with Owner #4, learning his new job under this horseman's careful tutelage. The gelding proves to be an amazingly talented jumper, and Owner #4 is thrilled to have found such a diamond in the rough. The gelding is sold to Owner #5, who puts him in training with a professional show jumping rider, looking for a grand prix superstar.

The gelding begins his show career in the lower jumper divisions, rising up through the levels as he gains experience. He wins frequently and shows great promise. He is brought along slowly and carefully, so as not to overface him or cause an injury.

The gelding spends several years with Owner #5 and the professional rider. He makes it to the grand prix classes, the top level of show-jumping competition. He earns a few ribbons at this level, but he seems to have reached the limits of his abilities.

The gelding, now seven years old, is sold to Owner #6, a teenage girl with high aspirations seeking a horse with talent. The pair begins in the children's jumper divisions, eventually moving up into the juniors. The gelding is well within his comfort zone and is able to teach the girl and "forgive" her mistakes.

The two compete together for several more years, earning ribbons and accolades, until it comes time for the girl to go to college. She won't have time to ride, so she sells the gelding to Owner #7, a teenage boy who needs an experienced, talented horse on which to learn to ride. The boy and the horse do extremely well for several years.

By this time, the horse is in his mid-teens and has logged many miles in the show ring. His body is starting to show the signs of this wear and tear. He comes out of the stall stiff some days, and jumping is more of an effort for him than it used to be. The gelding is ready to start slowing down, but the boy has advanced (thanks to his horse's experience) and is ready to move up to the next level.

The gelding is sold to Owner #8, an older adult who competes at a few shows each year but mostly likes to ride at home, take lessons, and go on the occasional trail ride. The workload is a little lighter for the gelding, who is still happy to work but needs a more forgiving job. His owner enjoys the benefit of a well-traveled, older horse who can handle just about anything, but the owner also has to be mindful of the horse's aches and pains and limitations.

Unfortunately, after a couple of years of happy partnership, the owner loses her job to corporate downsizing and needs to limit her expenses. She sells the gelding to Owner #9, an experienced horsewoman whose husband has decided he'd like to ride with her occasionally. As a "husband horse," the gelding goes on trail rides, taking care of the new-to-horses husband.

This arrangement works well for several years, until the gelding, now about twenty, develops a lameness. The owner works with her veterinarian to treat it, but the gelding just never seems to recover fully and isn't sound enough for steady work.

Owner #9 knew this day could come when she purchased the gelding. Some horses remain rideable until the day they die; others develop conditions that don't interfere with their everyday comfort, but are enough to keep them from being ridden. The owner is prepared to let the horse live out his days on her farm and to be the horse's final owner.

With so many years of service and instruction to so many different riders, the gelding deserves to retire in comfort at the end of his serviceable years.

Changing Hands

The above hypothetical example is a best-case scenario for a horse who changes hands over and over again. A well-bred, well-mannered horse had a couple of different "jobs" early on until he found the one for which he was best suited. He was served well by horsemen who trained him expertly, giving him a good chance at a long, healthy, and productive life in service to the human beings crossing his path. These horsemen kept the horse's well-being in mind and found him a career where he could use his talents to their fullest. Although various circumstances led to the horse's being sold many times, his owners took care to find him suitable homes. When he was no longer sellable, he had a conscientious final owner who assumed responsibility for caring for him for the rest of his natural life.

But there were a number of crossroads in this horse's journey where he could have been sent down a much different path. Each time he changed hands, the old owner was putting his fate in the hands of the new. If just one of this horse's nine owners had not had the horse's interests at heart, his life story might have turned out dramatically different.

The horse industry in the United States is vast and varied. According to the American Horse Council, there were approximately nine million horses in this country in 2003, the most recent year for which figures are available. There is no central equine registry, no universal identification number for a horse. Even those horses who are registered with various individual organizations often don't keep the same names throughout their lifetimes, making it very difficult for former owners to keep track of them. On equine discussion forums on the Internet, one can often find people looking for a horse they owned years ago, wondering where he is and how he's doing, if he's still alive, even regretting that they sold him and wanting to buy him back.

There's nothing intrinsically wrong with selling a horse. After all, most people buy their "horse of a lifetime" from someone else—knowledgeable and talented breeders and trainers develop these horses for the rest of us. But the process is also fraught with uncertainty, and there are horror stories aplenty.

As our example demonstrated, there are countless reasons why people decide to sell their horses. Sometimes it's a matter of choice, and sometimes it's outright necessity.

Growing Pains

There's no such thing as a "one size fits all" horse. The perfect horse for a beginner isn't always perfect for an advanced rider. The tiny pony who's well suited for a small child becomes much less suitable when the child is taller than his parents. Riders who have outgrown their horses—in either size or talent—account for many of those "for sale" fliers hanging on tack shop bulletin boards.

This is especially true for the littlest riders. Many budding equestrians begin their riding careers on ponies, who are easier for those with small hands and short legs to manage and much closer to the ground (in the event of their riders' inevitable falls).

But if you think keeping a sprouting child in clothes that fit is frustrating, imagine the difficulty in keeping that child appropriately mounted. The pony likely doesn't care (an old rule of thumb dictates that most equines can comfortably carry 20 to 25 percent of their body weight). Long before a child is too heavy, however, her feet will dangle well below the pony's belly. From such situations was born the phrase seen in many advertisements for horses for sale: "sadly outgrown."

It's not just physical growth that can end a partnership, however. Riders grow in their abilities as well.

The horses who taught most of us to ride are saintly creatures, perhaps not fancy or much to look at, but invaluable for their patience and forgiving natures. These horses tolerate inadvertent jabs in the side or bumps in the mouth from unsteady new riders and tread carefully so as not to squash the feet of humans who haven't yet learned to move out of the way. Above all, these horses take care of the riders until the riders are able to take care of themselves.

As riders advance, however, and want to learn new skills or compete in a chosen sport, they may believe they need a horse with different qualities from those that make a horse an excellent teacher for beginners. It's a conundrum that an ambitious rider can encounter as well while aspiring to be a better—or more competitive—participant. Some equestrians are fortunate enough to find a horse whose interests and talents dovetail with their own and with whom they can advance in tandem. Others, however, have to face the choice between sticking with their partner and following their own goals as riders.

Reaching this crossroads isn't indicative of a failing in the horse. Quite the contrary: often, a horse has done his job so well that the pupil has surpassed the teacher. Some horses are best suited to activities requiring only moderate athletic skill; others have talent and potential limited only by their pilots' aptitudes. In some instances a horse may not be able to perform at as high a level as a rider wishes—he might be capable of completing a twenty-five-mile endurance ride, but not a fifty-miler.

Outgrowing a horse can be really heartbreaking—for many riders, that close partnership between human and horse is what attracted them to riding in the first place, and it's sad to have to close the book on a relationship with a particular horse.

When all parties involved handle the situation responsibly, however, it can actually be a happy and exciting, if bittersweet, time. A horse or pony can use his talents to help another rider learn and advance, while a rider can use the skills imparted by a treasured old friend to reach new goals. Ideally, both horse and rider go on to shine in their now-separate roles.

Changing Priorities

Sometimes the circumstances that lead a horse and rider to part ways aren't foreseen as easily. It may seem incomprehensible to those of us who have been smitten with horses for decades, but people—especially children and young adults—*do* lose interest in horses and decide to follow other pursuits.

Being a dedicated rider is *hard* work. For every hour spent riding, there might be two or three hours of grooming, tacking up, cooling down, and commuting back and forth to the barn (if you aren't fortunate enough to be able to keep horses at home or nearby). Riding isn't a twice-a-week sport if you have your own horse. Your horse needs to be ridden almost daily. There's no "off season"—even if a horse is given some time off, he still needs grooming and other attention. It's a lot of responsibility for a young person, and a huge time commitment during a period when most kids are hanging out at the mall or instant messaging their friends.

So the choice is made to move the horse to a new home. With luck, these situations work out better for all parties involved: the horse can enjoy the attentions of someone who makes him a priority and his skills can be put to good use, and the previous owner is free to pursue other interests.

Younger riders aren't the only ones who find that life's changes force a reevaluation of their life with horses, of course. The trappings and responsibilities of adulthood bring their own challenges and tough decisions.

Sometimes, the decision to put a horse up for sale isn't made willingly, but is forced by finances. Drastic changes in one's circumstances—losing a job or going through a divorce, for example—may lead to drastic reevaluation of priorities and to selling a horse who might otherwise never have been for sale.

A Good Beginning Doesn't Guarantee a Good Ending

In an ideal world, when horses are sold, they are passed from home to home like treasured family heirlooms. Each owner treats the horse gently and lovingly, caring for him attentively so that he can go on to be enjoyed by yet another family if circumstances require it.

When responsible and caring owners decide to sell, certainly they *hope* the new home will be just as good as, if not better than, the current one. But do they ever entertain the possibility that it will be worse?

 Ignorance is bliss. Everyone prefers to focus on the positive and minimize the negative. But when another living being's life is in your hands, you don't have the luxury of sticking your head in the sand and simply trusting that everything will turn out okay. As difficult as it may be, owners need to be aware of what *could* happen, and weigh the risks and take steps to minimize them, before handing over the lead rope to someone else.

Is it frightening and depressing to consider such worst-case scenarios? Absolutely. If doing so makes you afraid to sell a horse at all, you're not alone. Although some people claim that buying and selling is simply part of owning horses, there are plenty of individuals in the horse world who eschew that businesslike approach for a very simple reason: they don't want to take the risk, however small, of their horse's landing in bad situations.

Let's look at another hypothetical "life story." A young Quarter Horse foaled on a Plains state ranch is started under saddle by a good, low-key horseman, then ridden on the ranch for everyday work for five years. He learns useful skills such as loading in all kinds of horse trailers, standing like a stone while being mounted or tied, and acclimating himself to pretty much any experience the West can offer. At age nine, he is purchased by a horse trader who makes up truckloads of horses sent east to be sold as quiet trail horses or "kid horses" through a network of horse dealers. Our horse is in good health, about fifteen hands tall, but nothing fancy to look at and with no particular aptitude other than his quiet nature. A young, intermediate-level rider in Pennsylvania who is looking for a safe horse to ride, but without many lessons under her belt, buys him. All goes well for a few months, until a motorcycle backfire startles the horse while they are crossing a road. He bolts down the trail for a few hundred feet before his rider can manage to stop him. This shakes her confidence. She begins to grip her reins rigidly every time she rides outside the riding ring, making the horse more and more tense, until, instead of walking quietly under saddle, he develops a jiggy little trot step to get away from the pressure of her heavy, unyielding hands. Rather than consult a trainer or instructor to help her fix her problem (which is a direct result of her own riding inexperience), the owner begins to ride less and less. She eventually sells her horse through a local newspaper ad to a young man who doesn't mind the jiggy trot. In fact, he likes it, gunning the horse forward on every ride, only to jerk him to a halt like cowboys do on TV—twenty times a ride. This treatment basically deadens the horse to the rider's cues and makes him so nervous and jumpy that he becomes a real challenge to ride. In a year the so-called cowboy has lost interest and sends the horse to a local auction. An experienced trainer could retrain this horse into a safe, enjoyable riding animal, but Quarter Horses without such "issues" can be had for six hundred dollars apiece. Why should the trainer put the time into this eleven-year-old? At the auction the local equine rescue volunteer has to pass him up (too many horses, too little cash); the owner of a lesson barn thinks he is too difficult for her beginner students to ride, and the only bidder is the local "killer buyer." The horse is loaded on a truck with a bunch of other unwanted horses destined for a slaughterhouse somewhere, only halfway through what should have been his normal life span, and that's the end of the story.

What Can Go Wrong

Such an ending is shocking and dramatic and deeply unsettling. But it's not the only unseemly end our old friends may encounter, and when horse slaughter is successfully outlawed in the United States, even that milestone won't guarantee safety for our horses.

No, there are much more mundane dangers out there, such as simple lack of food and improper care. Every year there are highly publicized incidents where dozens of horses are found starving in a field, in horrible states of neglect. In some cases the owners simply don't care; in others they have good intentions, but are either uneducated and don't know any better or are overwhelmed and have been unable to stop their horses' downward spirals toward ill health. In the happier instances, animal-control officials step in before the situation becomes too dire, but often, such cases only come to officials' attention when horses are near death.

Neglect usually arises from ignorance. Sometimes owners aren't aware that most horses can't simply subsist off the land year-round and fail to provide enough hay when pasture isn't adequate, or they don't provide horses with appropriate shelter from the elements. They might not be aware that horses' teeth need periodic floating, or that their hooves need regular trimming.

Despite their size and strength, horses are relatively fragile creatures, and certain horses are especially so. If a horse who tends to be a hard keeper becomes slightly underweight as winter sets in, her condition can deteriorate rapidly during cold weather when she's burning calories just to keep warm. And if the mare's uneducated owner doesn't know that a heavy winter coat can hide protruding ribs that would be easily seen in summer, the mare could be in a shocking state by the time she sheds out in the spring.

Although the results may not always be as obvious as when horses who are starving to death, lack of knowledge is usually at the root of most horses' suffering, both on the ground and in the tack.

Ignoring the importance of proper grooming can lead to thrush in the hooves (and, likely, lameness) or painful cases of rain rot, an infection of the horse's skin. Asking a horse to perform strenuous work that's beyond his level of fitness can lead to injuries, colic, or tying-up. Ill-fitting tack can lead to painful rubs and sore backs and mouths. These issues are easily prevented (or, if discovered early, quickly remedied), but if an owner doesn't know better, the horse will suffer.

All horse folk start out knowing nothing: being a new horse owner doesn't automatically make one a *bad* horse owner. The problems arise when owners don't realize how much they *don't* know and don't seek guidance or education.

A lack of education in the saddle can lead to problems as well. The idea is to learn and improve throughout the process, ideally with the help of a qualified instructor. When riders don't continue along that learning curve, their horses are sentenced to a life of amateur mistakes—caught in the mouth by the bit because of a rider's uneducated hands on the reins or thumped endlessly on the spine by riders who haven't developed a balanced, educated seat. While the horse might not suffer much physically from this behavior compared to other abuses, such repeated injustices take a mental toll and lead to horses who have soured on their jobs and no longer enjoy their work.

Abuse and mistreatment aren't solely the domain of the uneducated. They're there—in subtle and blatant forms—at all levels of horsemanship. Selling your horse to a well-known show barn or a "big name" trainer doesn't guarantee she'll be treated well. It could be argued that the unscrupulous horsemen who perpetrate abuse in the name of competition or a quick sale bear more responsibility than their lesser-educated counterparts, because the former know better and do it anyway.

Some of the most egregious examples have actually occurred at the highest levels of the competitive equestrian world. In the 1990s several prominent riders and trainers in the hunter/jumper world were convicted of charges related to having their horses electrocuted by a killer-for-hire to collect on the horses' insurance policies.

Other practices of unscrupulous individuals on various show circuits include withholding water to make a horse quiet, tying a horse's head up high all night so he will carry it low during competition the next day, administering pain-masking drugs so an injured horse can continue competing, and shooting off fire extinguishers at a horse when schooling at home to encourage an "up" look in the ring.

Clearly, the ribbons hanging on the tack room wall don't always signify how well the horses are treated.

THE HUMANE SOCIETY OF THE UNITED STATES COMPLETE GUIDE TO HORSE CARE

Horse Trading Roulette

It's rare to be able to track a horse throughout her lifetime and all her various homes. More often, former owners are left wondering "what-ever happened to...," and new owners are in the dark about their horse's history.

Buying and selling will always be a part of the horse world. But just because it is common doesn't mean horse folk should be cavalier about it. If your horse spun the new owner roulette wheel, how would you feel about her chances of landing somewhere that would provide her with the same kind of home you do? What about her second, third, and fourth spins of the wheel after that? Would her luck run out at some point?

Although the majority of horsemen are good people who try to do right by their animals, there will always be exceptions. There will always be facilities that you drive by and shudder to think about the lives of the horses there, or the riders you can't bear to watch. Sadly, many of those horses likely have former owners somewhere who would be equally appalled on behalf of their old friends, if they had any idea where they were.

CHAPTER 2

The Species

IN THE WORLD OF HORSES, SIMPLY KNOWING
how to ride or professing a love of horses doesn't make
you a horseman. That badge of honor comes from
knowing a horse inside and out: knowing how he thinks,
how his body works, and how best to work in harmony
with the often-puzzling qualities that make horses...
well, horses. The very qualities that attract us to these
unique creatures can also be the downfall of many
an inexperienced trainer or caretaker.

Those who do understand equine behaviors learn to love their horses all the more for them. Often, our horses do the opposite of what instinct tells them they should do, simply because we ask them to and they trust us. It's a covenant that every horse owner should understand and respect.

The essence of "horseness" comprises two parts, the mental and the physical. To be a real horseman, you need to know the depths of the equine body and soul.

When you consider a horse's physical being—his body—it's truly an example of a living machine that is perfectly adapted to its environment. The equine is a highly effective grass-to-manure conversion factory with a sensitive surveillance system, all wrapped up in a sleek, aerodynamic package that can travel at speeds of nearly fifty miles an hour.

Thanks to a remarkably complete fossil record, we can see exactly how today's horses came to be the creatures they are. Scientists can trace the evolution of the horse from *Eohippus*, the fox-size "dawn horse" of fifty-five million years ago, all the way to modern-day *Equus caballus*, who first appeared in the last million years. Over the millennia, horses have grown taller and longer-legged, presumably because the added speed and agility made them better able to elude the predators that evolved along with them. Horses' teeth also changed, becoming better equipped for grinding as their diet came to consist more of grasses than of vegetation and fruit. Most notably, their multiple toes evolved to become a single hoof, corresponding with their adaptation from being a forest-dwelling creature to one that roamed open plains.[3]

Likewise, understanding the horse's mind comes from knowledge of the way the horse lived in the wild, how she interacted with others, how she spent her days, and how she stayed out of the clutches of predators and lived to reproduce another day.

Does this seem like ancient equine history? Although pampered show horses and sedate trail buddies might seem far removed from the wild horses who roamed the plains, knowing where horses come from is integral to understanding the way they are today. Domestication is only a very recent development: horses are the way they are because they were required to be that way to survive in the wild for millions of years. Keeping the equine "design plan" in mind helps to make sense of the things horses do and what they require to be happy and comfortable.

A Day in the Life of a Horse

Most horses live their lives on a schedule their human beings set for them. Eat, go out, come in, eat, get ridden, eat, go out—that's pretty much the schedule. But what about horses left to their own devices? How do they spend their days when they, not human beings, decide how their time is spent?

Whether horses are wild and free-roaming, or domestic and confined to pasture, they exhibit similar preferences for how they spend their time when given their own free will. The vast majority of a horse's day is spent grazing. That single activity occupies 50 to 80 percent of his time over a twenty-four hour period. Horses graze in spurts throughout the day and night, although a number of factors can influence when and how long they graze. Horses spend more time grazing when forage quality is poor or when their nutritional needs are increased (such as when pregnant or nursing a foal). They may alter their grazing patterns due to weather or biting insects, choosing to stand in the shade during the hot, buggy times of the day. But, despite day-to-day variations, the one constant is that the horse spends most of his day eating.

When horses aren't grazing, they're usually sleeping, either dozing lightly or sacking out for deep sleep. Horses don't take a long, uninterrupted period of sleep as humans do. Rather, they sleep for short periods of time throughout the day and night, with the cumulative amount varying from day to day and horse to horse, depending on weather and other factors. Horses who are stabled tend to sleep more than those who are at pasture, but still only sleep for a few hours each day—much less than the eight hours human beings sleep or the ten to twelve hours dogs and cats enjoy.

The horse is aided in this endeavor by a unique system of tendons and ligaments known as the "stay apparatus," which allows the horse to lock his legs, relax his muscles, and sleep lightly while remaining standing up. The horse stands with one hind leg cocked and resting, his head hanging low, ears and lips drooping, and his eyes fully or partially closed.

Horses do sleep lying down as well, some more than others. Most lie down for at least a brief period once daily, either flat out on their sides or propped up on their chests with their legs folded beneath them. Due to horses' large body mass, lying down is actually less relaxing for them than sleeping standing up; the weight of the horse's own body puts pressure on internal organs when he is lying down and may cause additional stress on the heart and lungs.[4] Horses only lie down for short periods, which is also why it is so difficult for horses to recover from severe injuries like broken legs. A human is laid up in bed for six weeks while such an injury heals, but this simply isn't physically possible for a horse.[5]

Like humans, horses experience different stages of sleep, characterized by different brain-wave patterns (measured by an electroencephalogram). In slow-wave sleep, brain activity is much slower than it is in an awake animal, but the quality of sleep is relatively light and the animal can be roused easily. In paradoxical or REM (rapid eye movement) sleep, the brain is more active. It is during this period of sleep that humans, and presumably animals, experience dreams, but the muscles of the body are very relaxed. This is a much deeper period of sleep from which it is more difficult to awaken.

Because of the state of muscle relaxation that occurs, horses must be lying down to experience REM sleep. It is possible for horses to become sleep deprived if they are unable to lie down, and thus unable to partake of REM sleep, for extended periods.[6]

Dealing with the Elements

A horse's day-to-day behavior can be summed up as an endless cycle of "eat, sleep, repeat," but keep in mind that this year-round proposition requires seasonal adjustment. Horses aren't able to dig burrows or create nests or other shelter to protect them from the elements, whether it's summer's heat or winter's chill. They have to make do with windbreaks provided by hills or stands of trees, shade where they can find it, and the heat their own bodies can generate. Through a combination of physical attributes and instinct, however, most horses are ably equipped to handle whatever Mother Nature sends their way.

Horses generally are able to handle extremes of both cold and heat, although there can be great variation among breeds and individuals. For example, an Arabian, with his desert heritage, is better equipped to handle oppressively hot weather, while a Shetland pony, whose ancestors hail from the harsh islands of Scotland, is more impervious to bitter winter chill. Individual horses also have the ability to adapt to their own surroundings, however; so an Arabian who was born and raised in Ontario might actually fare better in a harsh winter than would a Shetland pony raised in Florida and abruptly moved north.

To stay warm in the colder months, horses begin growing a long winter coat (replacing their sleek summer one) when the days begin to shorten. The length of hair itself does its part to keep the animal warm, but horses (and other animals) are also equipped with muscles under the skin that cause the hair of the coat to stand on end when the animal starts to get cold. This traps air in the now-fluffy hair coat, which adds another insulating layer. (This phenomenon is also responsible for human goosebumps, although it does little to keep us warm.)

Horses are often quite comfortable outside in cold temperatures or wintry conditions and can continue grazing rather than seek shelter. More bothersome than the thermometer reading is the wind and wet, so savvy equines seek shelter in the form of buildings, hills, or stands of trees, turning their tails to the wind and standing in close proximity to one another to take advantage of neighbors' body heat.

Horses are also able to shiver to generate heat, and the action of digestion generates heat to help keep them warm as well.

A horse's primary defense against the heat is to sweat. Glands in the skin release sweat to the skin's surface, and the action of evaporation helps to cool the body. (The process of sponging a horse off with water after a ride does the same thing.) Horses are quite proficient sweaters, giving rise to the phrase, "sweating like a horse."

An additional aggravation for horses in warm weather is bothersome biting insects. At best, they annoy a horse and distract him from eating or sleeping; at worst, insects can draw blood with painful bites and can harass a horse to the point of making him frantic for relief.

Horses are equipped with subcutaneous muscles that can make certain portions of skin twitch rapidly in an attempt to dislodge insects. If that and a swishing tail are insufficient, a horse usually retreats to a less buggy spot and waits out the pests.

Form Follows Function

It's important to understand the way horses were intended to live in the wild, because that's the lifestyle for which their bodies were designed. Domestic life is quite different. Often we ask a horse to live in a completely unnatural state, and doing so can have adverse consequences. A smart caretaker keeps in mind the way horses are *supposed* to live and tries to tailor the horses' barn-kept lifestyle to approximate it.

Perhaps nowhere is this more important than when considering the equine digestive system. Of the myriad things that can go wrong with horses, digestive tract problems are responsible for considerably more than their fair share.

If you think about a horse's diet and eating habits, it should be immediately apparent that his digestive system is somewhat different from yours, as an omnivorous human being, and different from your carnivorous cat or dog's. Horses are herbivores; their diet is comprised entirely of plants, so their digestive system is geared toward using those foods. And while carnivores spend their days hunting and eating a large meal when they make a kill, herbivores spend their days grazing: a "meal" is an hours-long event.

Keeping those differences in mind, let's take a look at the equine digestive tract. We begin at the very beginning, with the horse's mouth. Horses have agile, expressive upper lips, capable of wiggling gate locks open and offering the goofy equine equivalent of a smile. Study a horse as he grazes sometime, and you'll see that lip in action in its natural environment. Seeming to have a mind all its own, it ferrets through the densest vegetation in search of the good stuff and ably steers those choice bits into the horse's mouth. Once the grass is guided into the mouth, the horse's teeth—adapted over millions of years for this specific diet—tear it off and chew it.

When the horse swallows, food moves down the horse's esophagus via a process called peristalsis, a wave of contractions in the muscles ringing the esophagus that pushes the food along, in much the same way you squeeze the last bit of toothpaste out of a tube. You can actually see the wave of muscle action move along the bottom of a horse's neck when he swallows.

The esophagus empties into the stomach, and here we find one of the oddities of the equine digestive tract. The muscular valve found at the junction of the esophagus and stomach allows only one-way passage. This means that horses are unable to vomit (or burp), except in very rare circumstances that involve very severe digestive illness. If you've got unpleasant memories from a recent bout of the flu, not being able to vomit might seem like a good thing, but it means that a horse is unable to resolve simple cases of digestive upset by expelling whatever is causing the problem. This is why equine digestive problems are considered so serious and are quite frequently life-threatening.

Herbivores are classified by the way they digest plant material; they are separated into ruminants and nonruminants. Cattle, goats, and sheep are ruminants, meaning they chew a cud and their stomachs have four compartments. Horses are nonruminants and thus have a simple single stomach, as do humans, dogs, cats, and pigs.

The equine stomach is small relative to the animal's overall size. Its maximum capacity is about four gallons, but it functions best when it contains about two and a half gallons of food. It's designed to handle small amounts of food at frequent intervals (which, considering the natural state of grazing in the wild, makes perfect sense).

The stomach fills up as the horse eats, and when it's about two-thirds full, digested food begins to exit (via another muscular valve) into the small intestine to make room for more food coming in. If a horse consumes a large amount of food at one time, however, material must be rushed out of the stomach before it has been digested properly to make room for additional food coming in. The process is designed to accommodate the leisurely eating habits of a grazing animal and is disrupted when a horse consumes food in a less natural manner.

In the small intestine, various enzymes act on fat, protein, and carbohydrates to break them down into the basic components that can be absorbed through the intestinal wall and into the bloodstream to be used by the body. The system is designed for a grazing animal and is optimized for frequent, small deposits of digested material. When a horse consumes very large meals, certain enzymes are not as effective.

Muscle contractions move the contents, mostly fibrous material and water by this point, through the small intestine and into the large intestine. This portion of the digestive tract has a large capacity and is relatively slow, as the bacteria in the gut need ample time to ferment and break down the fiber that comprises a great portion of the horse's diet.

As digestive material nears the end of the large intestine, most of the useable nutrients and water have been absorbed; what's left is formed into fecal balls and exits the horse's body. At this point, it becomes a matter for you and your pitchfork!

So why is understanding this anatomy important? Because today's horses often aren't kept in the manner for which they were designed and often don't eat the diet they were intended to eat in the way they were intended to eat it.

As the human population expands and more land is developed, there's less room for farms and pastures. Even those folks lucky enough to have some acreage often don't have the amount necessary to keep horses out grazing twenty-four hours a day, seven days a week. Instead, many horses find themselves in a completely unnatural environment, spending a good portion of their days in stalls and eating highly concentrated sources of energy in the form of grain rather than their natural staple of roughage.

Deviating too far from the horse's natural diet and way of eating can lead not only to inefficient use of nutrients (which means a good portion of the expensive grain you're feeding is going straight from the feed bucket to the manure pile without benefiting your horse), but also to severe digestive problems that can affect performance or require dangerous and expensive surgery. It can even be fatal.

The most common digestive issue in horses is colic, an all-encompassing term used to describe most any kind of abdominal pain. (We examine colic more thoroughly in chapter 10.) Horses can colic from eating too much grain or from not having enough roughage in their diets, among many other causes. Severe colic cases often require surgery (which is a risky proposition in itself) and may result in the horse being euthanized. In fact, colic is considered one of the leading causes of death in adult horses.[7]

Gastric ulcers are another common digestive ailment, frequently found in high-performance show and racehorses. Ulcers can have many causes, but a diet that includes large quantities of grain is considered to be a contributing factor.

Proper management is no guarantee against colic or other digestive ailments, but it minimizes the risk considerably. Try to imitate the natural diet as much as possible, relying on roughage (hay or pasture) for the lion's share of the horse's daily calories. The age-old feeding mantra is "little and often," meaning small amounts of food at frequent intervals. Grain should be fed only as necessary and doled out in multiple small meals (two or three times daily) rather than in one big one.

Avoiding Becoming a Lion's Lunch

There's much to be gleaned from understanding the way various equine bodily systems work and the many practical applications to everyday horse-keeping. Equally important is an understanding of the equine mind, and to delve into this, we once again consider the way horses exist in nature.

The horse is a prey animal, meaning that large carnivores like wolves or mountain lions are quite happy to eat the horse for lunch. His survival depends on being alert to any approaching predators and his ability to get away before it's too late.

Thanks to Mother Nature, the horse is well equipped for this. The horse's eyes are placed along the sides of his head, rather than in the front, as they are in humans, dogs, and cats. This gives the horse a field of vision of about 330 degrees—almost a complete circle around his body—without even moving his head. Since he's blessed with a long neck, he's able to turn and look directly behind him, expanding his field of vision to a full 360 degrees. Without moving his feet or twisting his body at all, the horse can see easily in all directions. His vision is quite good, compared to that of other non-primate mammals; it's better than a dog or cat's and almost as good as a human being's.

Couple those two attributes with the horse's keen senses of smell and hearing, and his ears that can swivel to and fro like little satellite dishes, and you have an animal who is extraordinarily tuned into his surroundings. A crackle in the brush in the distance? Head is up, ears are cocked toward it, and he's assessing the situation to see if there's any danger. Something moving across the field behind him? He's seen it without even having to turn around.

Of course, noticing an approaching danger doesn't do a horse much good if he's just going to sit there and wait for it to arrive. Contrary to cinematic depictions of stallions fighting to the death, when it comes to the age-old question of "fight or flight," horses usually choose flight. They don't even consider their options—they just run. Speed is a horse's ally, and it's better for him to run away from nothing than to end up as a mountain lion's lunch because he paused to think about it.

You don't need to observe horses in the wild to see this instinct in action. In fact, if you've spent much time around horses at all, you've likely experienced the phenomenon of the "spook," when a horse spots some kind of equine-eating monster (invisible to everyone else, of course) in the most innocuous of places and takes off in a panic. Usually the culprit is something like a blowing plastic bag, or an overturned bucket, or…anything, really. That's the point. Instinct tells the horse that he should simply run away from anything he finds suspicious, rather than investigate to find out that, yes, it really is just a bucket.

Although it's no fun to fall off when your horse spooks at a lawn chair and spins out from underneath you, it's important to understand that this is something intrinsic and central to a horse's very being. After all, natural selection favored the horses who ran away instead of those who stood their ground to sniff the mountain lion! The flight mentality is a tendency that can be a little more or a little less prevalent in any individual horse, but it's there in all of them.

Good horsemen and trainers help horses learn to overcome this innate fear through careful engineering of good experiences, desensitizing, and establishing trust. When a young horse is taken to a local schooling show just to hang out and see the sights while munching grass, this introduces in an unthreatening way the concept of showing and all the hoopla that goes with it. The horse leaves the show with nothing but a pleasant, relaxed memory, rather than a sense that there's something to fear.

When working at home with a young horse, a thoughtful rider doesn't punish a spook, but recognizes it for what it is, the horse's natural reaction to a frightening situation. Imagine a young Quarter Horse who's just getting started under saddle with arena work. She's convinced that the new tractor parked outside the arena will eat her if she gets too close. Her handler calms and steadies her, lets her study the tractor from a distance, and then slowly and quietly leads her gradually closer, and closer, and closer until she's near enough to sniff the tractor with a carefully outstretched nose and see there's nothing to fear. Her handler leads her back and forth in front of the tractor several times, praising her for being brave, until she's calm and even bored with the situation. Then it's back to work, with nary a worry about the "horse-eating monster" in the corner.

Thanks to that good training, the mare can go on to have an impressive reputation for quiet behavior, giving hardly a thought to scary things like wind-whipped flags around an arena or raucous crowds, because she's been taught to trust in her human rider and focus on her job.

The extent to which horses can learn to suppress their flight instinct through proper training and trust in their handlers is remarkable, really. So much of what we routinely ask horses to do goes against their better judgment—getting into small, confined spaces like horse trailers; jumping huge obstacles without being able to see where they'll land on the other side; standing in the middle of busy traffic on a crowded city street. Not all horses are able to overcome their natural fears to such a degree, of course, but careful training and understanding the way the equine mind works can help almost any horse learn to cope with scary situations.

Ignorance of the horse's natural instincts can lead a handler to assume a horse is misbehaving when she's simply frightened and to punish a horse inappropriately, creating an even less trusting animal.

The Herd Mentality

Although horses are well equipped to be on high alert for danger, no animal can maintain that state of readiness all the time. They have to sleep, after all. Horses, like many other prey animals, find safety in numbers. The herd is an insurance policy—if one horse is dozing and doesn't hear the approaching wolf, another horse might, and his hasty departure will alert the other horses to the danger.

Wild herds usually include three to twenty horses, and are either a "bachelor" band of young stallions or a harem of mares and their offspring led by a mature stallion (who is continually challenged by younger stallions seeking to take over his harem). The mares within a herd usually stay there, although their offspring leave the band when they're old enough, preventing inbreeding between a stallion and his progeny.

Domesticated horses don't need the herd's protection, but the instinct to stay together is still strong. Horses are social creatures. They enjoy company, primarily that of other horses, but in a pinch, even a goat or a donkey is an acceptable substitute. They generally graze in loosely knit groups rather than strike off on their own. They develop friends within the herd, often engaging in mutual grooming or fly-swatting. And when separated from their herd, they can get anxious and upset, calling back to the group and pacing nervously. A horse who is extremely herd-bound can be difficult to work with and to train, as he is distracted and nervous whenever away from his friends.

The equine herd is a complex social structure in which each member is keenly aware of his place. The highest-ranking horses have first priority for resources, such as food, water, or the choice shady resting spot. Horses who are lower in the hierarchy simply yield to those who occupy a higher social position.

In wild herds, the stallion is usually in charge, with other members sorting out their places by virtue of age and the length of time they've been in the herd. An older mare assumes the role of "alpha," leading the band on its travels to water sources and grazing areas, while the stallion drives the herd from behind. The stallion occasionally is challenged for control of his harem by younger stallions; if the younger horse wins the battle, he assumes the leadership position in the herd, and the former leader, vanquished, must find another herd.

In a herd of domestic horses, the roles are not defined so rigidly. There's generally no de facto leader, unlike the stallion-led wild herds; in domestic herds, the horses simply sort out who the leader is among themselves, independent of age, sex, size, or length of time in the herd.

If you've ever seen a new horse turned out with an established group, you've seen how this process works. The squealing and posturing, the laid-back ears and bared teeth, the double-barreled kicks, all are acts of aggression that horses use to sort out a dominance hierarchy among themselves. It can be a little hair-raising to watch sometimes, and, of course, human beings should stay nearby to separate horses if need be. But generally, after lots of squealing and some nicks and scrapes, the newly reordered hierarchy is set and everyone coexists peacefully. If a horse ever forgets his place and oversteps his bounds with a horse above him in the hierarchy, the more dominant horse needs only to threaten to bite or kick to put the submissive horse back in line—there's no need to go through the whole production again.

The dominance hierarchy gives the group stability. It can change over time, or if one horse is removed from the group and later reintroduced. But for the most part it stays relatively constant. Even when horses are moved to a new herd, they often adopt similar positions. Certain horses always tend to try to occupy the "alpha" position, while others are content to submit and be lower-ranking members of the herd. And the alphas might not be who you would think—mares can be dominant over geldings; small horses can be dominant over large ones.[8]

Although we humans tend to anthropomorphize—feeling pity for the horses who are lower in the hierarchy, or feeling that higher-ranked horses are being "mean" to their subordinates—it's important to remember that this is a natural behavior for horses, and that a stable hierarchy prevents constant squabbling over position and access to resources. It may seem unfair that certain horses have a lower social position than others (some owners blanch to see their "expensive" show horse submit to a scruffy pony), but horses shouldn't be punished simply for acting on their instincts to establish peace in a group situation.

In some cases, though—say, when herds have two very "alpha" horses constantly fighting with each other for supremacy—a stable hierarchy may never be established (or the horses' owners might simply lose patience with the ongoing fighting). In these situations, it might be best to rearrange the herds if possible, splitting a large group into two smaller ones and putting the alphas in separate groups, for instance.

While horses should be allowed to sort differences out among themselves, there should always be one leader in the "herd" whose position is

Ears pressed back, an angry horse turns to defend himself from a pursuing dog.

unquestioned—the human handler. Learn to understand the equine body language that depicts aggression, like the flattened ears and bared teeth that signify a horse is threatening to bite, or the rump turned toward the handler with a leg cocked, threatening a kick. Horses should never be allowed to show aggression toward any human being. If such behavior is allowed to continue, the horse might become dangerous to handle, and certainly difficult to work with and train. Humans should always be unchallenged in their position at the very top of the hierarchy.

Humans use their superior reasoning ability, knowledge of equine behavior and of their own equine herds in particular—not kicks, whips, or nearby farm implements—to maintain respectful order on the ground, of course. Horses who push past human handlers to charge into the field ahead of them; who won't stand still to be mounted or administered to by a veterinarian or farrier; who crowd handlers while being led, need some lessons in horse/human etiquette. Manners are a wonderful gift to a horse.

A Very Different Environment

When considering all the aspects of horses' behavior, it's striking to realize how dramatically different we have made their lives in domestication. Rather than slowly ambling along an open plain all day, a horse might be cooped up in a twelve-by-twelve box for all but an hour a day. Instead of constantly nibbling grass, a horse might get a tub full of highly concentrated grain to devour in a few minutes and a paltry flake of hay to occupy him the rest of the day. Rather than enjoying the social camaraderie of a herd, horses might find themselves isolated in individual turnout paddocks, unable even to sniff noses with a friend across the fence.

These substantial changes in a horse's lifestyle can have physical consequences, as in the case of colic, as well as psychological effects. Imagine a horse who bares his teeth and lays back his ears whenever someone opens his stall door. He's incorrigible to handle, nipping whenever he gets a chance, and bulldozing his way down the barn aisle with no respect for his handler's tugs on the lead shank. Under saddle, he bucks and tries to take off. And on top of everything else, he has just about destroyed his stall, gnawing away giant portions of the wooden boards.

Would you buy such a horse for your young child? Or would you consider him dangerous and disagreeable?

Imagine the same horse after some significant management changes. Instead of being allowed fifteen minutes of turnout daily in a small dirt paddock, he now goes out in a large field for twelve full hours with a group of other geldings and has a chance to play and "get his bucks out." Instead of a huge portion of sweet feed, he now receives a much more modest serving of a pelleted feed and plentiful helpings of hay. The increased turnout, combined with a more reasonable diet, diminishes his nervous energy, and he's now pleasant and able to focus under saddle. He no longer acts aggressively toward his handlers or misbehaves on the ground because he no longer is trying to act out his unhappiness.

The cribbing has all but gone, now that he's getting an ample oral workout from grazing and his hay.

When uneducated horse owners fail to recognize the effects of an unnatural lifestyle, their horses are blamed for acting out when it's really no fault of their own.

Fortunately, in most cases, a happy medium can be struck between what the horse needs and the realities of suburban horse-keeping. But it falls on the caretakers to recognize the unnatural demands that can be placed on their horses in these situations and to examine possible causes and solutions before blaming the animal.

CHAPTER **3**

Horses and Humans

IN THE BEGINNING, HUMAN BEINGS AND HORSES
were adversaries—the hunter and the hunted.

Archaeological records suggest that, beginning about
fifty thousand years ago, wild horses were a primary
source of food for early human beings. (These early
horses were generally the size of ponies, not the larger
animals we know today.) Historians speculate that
human beings scavenged the remains of horses who
were killed by other animals.

Eventually hunters learned to drive horses into confined areas where they could be killed with a club, or they simply drove them off a cliff and let them fall to their deaths. At one site near Salutre, France, the remains of some ten thousand horses have been recovered at the base of the cliffs.

But at the same time, and perhaps as a portent, horses appeared in cave paintings as objects of both prey and admiration. Obviously these early hunters not only depended on horses for meat but also admired them for their beauty and fleetness of foot.

From those humble (and somewhat violent) beginnings has emerged a long partnership that has forever changed both species. Human beings owe much of their early progress to the domestication of horses, which allowed them to travel, work the land, and haul goods more easily. Among our relationships with domestic animals, the one we have with horses is unique because of how dramatically it has changed over the millennia—from prey, to beast of burden, to companion and athletic partner.

Domestication and Early Use

The layperson's impression of domestication is confining and taming a wild animal. But the proper use of the term refers to taming and changing an entire population of animals, not just a few select members.

To be truly domesticated, a species must be able to assimilate into human culture. When a species begins to be domesticated, the species itself begins to change and adapt. Some experts believe this is due to natural selection, in which the animals who are naturally inclined to be friendlier toward humans are able to be domesticated and thrive, while other animals are left to take their chances with nature. The changes may also be due to selective breeding. Those animals with traits that people want to keep in the population are bred, and eventually those traits become common.

Horses were among the later species to be domesticated, probably in about 4000 BCE.[9] The presence of fossilized animal remains among ancient human civilizations indicates at about what point the animals became part of human society, and physical changes (also observable in the fossil record) often accompany domestication and help differentiate these remains from those of wild animals.

Horses were likely first domesticated as production animals, kept in herds and used to provide meat and milk. Nomadic societies based around these herds migrated from area to area to provide grazing for their horses.

The transition to riding probably happened by chance, when some enterprising tender of a group of horses realized he could herd them more easily when mounted on one of them. Early bridles consisted of cheekpieces made of antlers or bone, and a soft "bit" made of rawhide, sinew, or hemp.[10] In Mesopotamia, a nose ring similar to that used on oxen was used for control instead of a bridle. What we know as snaffle bits first appeared in the Near East around 1500 BCE.[11]

The first saddles consisted of nothing more than a pad or piece of cloth, which likely explains why riders were just as likely to ride bareback—there wasn't much difference between the two. Saddles that actually aided a rider's stability didn't appear until the first century CE. These saddles had a wooden frame, or tree, which allowed construction of a deep seat that helped the rider stay on the horse. The later addition of stirrups further improved a rider's security, and made it much easier for him to wield a weapon in battle.[12]

It's interesting to note that rather sophisticated training and breeding methods also appeared during this time. The first recorded training plan for horses was written in 1345 BCE by Kikkuli, who was responsible for the Hittite king Suppiluliuma's horses. Written in cuneiform script on clay tablets, the "Kikkuli text" explained how to care for and feed the chariot horse. It used what is now known as interval training, specifying the distances and frequencies horses should be ridden. It also included regular swimming for conditioning and detailed instructions on feeding.

Xenophon, who lived from about 430 to 356 BCE, was a Greek soldier, historian, philosopher, and lifelong horseman, and was known as the father of classical equitation. He wrote the first fully preserved training manual for riding horses, *The Art of Horsemanship*. In this work, Xenophon became perhaps the first documented advocate of humane care and training for the horse. He emphasized the importance of gentle handling, good management practices, proper tack fit, and an understanding of the horse's mind.

> The one great precept and practice in using a horse is this—never deal with him when you are in a fit of passion. When your horse shies at an object and is unwilling to go up to it, he should be shown that there is nothing fearful in it, least of all to a courageous horse like him; but if this fails, touch the object yourself that seems so dreadful to him, and lead him up to it with gentleness. Compulsion and blows inspire only the more fear; and when horses are at all hurt at such times, they think what they shied at is the cause of the hurt.[13]

Horse sport was already flourishing at the time of Xenophon. The ancient Olympic Games, held every four years in Olympia, Greece, included four-horse chariot racing for the first time in 680 BCE, and two-horse chariot races in 408 BCE. Races on horseback also took place as far back as 648 BCE.[14]

It was the Romans, however, who elevated chariot racing to a national passion. Races were held at the Circus Maximus until 549 CE. Twelve races made up a day-long event, although at the height of the sport's popularity, as many as one hundred races were held in a single day.

The horses used in chariot racing were treasured and carefully trained. They were introduced to harness at the age of three, but were not raced until they were five. At one point, the Romans kept a stable of fourteen thousand chariot horses.[15]

Human Beings' Use of Horses

It's difficult to imagine how different our history would have been without horses. Horses allowed humans to travel farther and faster than they were able to before, enabling separate cultures to meet, interact, and exchange ideas (or to invade and conquer each other, depending on the culture).

In more modern times, horses were as indispensable and ubiquitous as cars are today. They were part of all aspects of culture, working alongside humans to till the soil, log forests, and build roads; providing transportation, not just to town or to church on Sunday, but also across countries and continents; and providing a form of entertainment and sport.

There's seemingly no aspect of modern human life to which horses have not contributed in some manner.

Warfare

One of the first uses of domesticated horses was to assist one tribe in attacking another, and horses continued to be used in battle up through World War II.

The Hittite empire, which existed from about 1800 to 1200 BCE, used chariots very effectively. The Scythians, a nomadic tribe of marauding horsemen who harassed the Persian Empire, were expert archers who let loose volleys of arrows while galloping at full tilt. The Parthians, descendents of the Scythians, developed a highly effective maneuver: they would feign retreat, then fire arrows back at their enemies over their horses' tails while galloping away.

The Greeks and Romans used chariots and mounted soldiers in war, although primarily as support for foot soldiers. The cavalry scouted ahead of main armies, while draft horses were used to move supplies. The Macedonians used both light and heavy cavalry, the former being lightly armored units that were more mobile and could carry out reconnaissance and raids, and the latter being heavily armed and armored, often used to mount a fearsome charge at opposing armies.

The cavalry truly rose to prominence with Charles the Hammer's defeat of the Moors at the Battle of Poitiers in 732 CE. The Moorish armies relied on light cavalries, using small, agile horses in loose formation. Charles amassed a heavy cavalry, which was able to withstand the Moorish attacks, then decimate their armies with a forceful charge.[16] Their success convinced Charles to use heavy cavalry more extensively, and his armies—and those throughout Western Europe—were transformed to rely on mounted soldiers, a tradition that continued through medieval times.

Later armies returned to the light cavalry tradition primarily, with riders swooping in to mount hit-and-run attacks while a battle was already in progress. As firearms became more prevalent, cavalry units were relegated to a mostly supportive role for the infantry. A role was developed for mounted infantrymen, who rode into battle, then dismounted to fight. Most cavalry use in the American Civil War was of this type.

Although cavalry units were still used in World War I, the advent of machine guns and tanks quickly made them obsolete in conventional warfare, and horses were used primarily to bring supplies to the troops. It's estimated that about six million horses were used in that war, and most of them were killed.

Today the U.S. Army maintains one detachment of horse cavalry for ceremonial uses, but the use of the horse in warfare still hangs on in other parts of the world, even in the era of "smart bombs" and laser-guided missiles. U.S. Army Green Berets rode horses in the rocky hills of Afghanistan in 2001 to conduct reconnaissance and scouting missions.

Transportation

Although the horse was not humans' first mode of transportation (other than their own two feet), until recently he was certainly the most effective one. Able to move along quickly when necessary, but also to cover great distances at a slower pace, the horse enabled early humans to expand their sphere of influence and travel almost anywhere.

During the Roman Empire, thousands of miles of excellent roads were built that allowed for easy travel by chariot. After the fall of the empire, these roads fell into disrepair; it wasn't until the late eighteenth century that a reliable system of roads existed again in Britain, for example, making it possible to use horse-drawn coaches for extensive travel.

As the Industrial Revolution took hold and railroads were built, the horse-drawn coach was no longer needed for long-distance transportation, but horses were needed by the hundreds of thousands to transport passengers, goods, and coal to and from the rail stations. Within growing cities, horses hauled trams, trash carts, fire engines, canal barges, cabs, and hearses.

It's estimated that New York City had between 150,000 and 175,000 horses in 1880, while a smaller city like Milwaukee (population 350,000) had about 12,500. In 1900 an estimated three to five million horses lived and worked in America's cities.

Communication

The Persians established post stations a day's ride apart in the third century BCE. The Greeks, Romans, and Mongols had similar arrangements.

Centuries later, fledgling postal services operated in the same manner in the United States and Britain. Post riders began carrying mail between New York and Boston (a distance of 250 miles) in 1673.[17] Mounted "post-boys" were also used in Britain (from them comes the term "posting," as they invented the practice of rising in their stirrups on every other beat of the trot to make their mounts' rough gaits more comfortable to ride over long distances).[18]

The Pony Express route traversed 1,966 miles, from St. Joseph, Missouri, to Sacramento, California, from April 1860 until October 1861. Riders covered seventy-five to a hundred miles apiece at a fast clip, switching to a fresh pony every ten to fifteen miles, then handing the saddlebag specifically designed to carry mail to the next rider at the end of a run. The development of the telegraph doomed the Pony Express, although it lives on in lore.

Farming

Until the 1700s, oxen were preferred for the mundane work of plowing fields. Agricultural technology began to improve during this time, making the work of farming faster and more productive. This new emphasis on volume and speed ushered in the use of the horse, who was capable of doing more work more quickly than oxen.

The early agricultural machinery had to be pulled by teams of horses. As the machines got larger and heavier and they became more complex, even more horses were required. (By 1890 the combine harvester was forty feet wide and required forty-two horses, controlled by six drivers, to pull it.)

In the United States, agriculture was booming at the end of the 1800s, and the horse population was booming right along with it. In 1860 there were about seven million horses in the United States.[19] In 1915 their numbers reached an all-time high of almost 26.5 million.

Just as quickly as the horse population had exploded, it was decimated. The proliferation of the tractor and internal combustion engine spelled the end of the widespread use of horses in agriculture. By 1935, there were just over 16.6 million horses, 10 million fewer than there had been twenty years earlier. By 1950 the population was only 7.6 million, and by 1960, there were only 3 million horses in the United States.[20]

Horses and other equines, such as mules and donkeys, are still used for agriculture in some parts of the world, and in the United States as well, in small numbers, by the Amish and other small-scale farmers.

Ranching

Cattle ranching was brought to North America by the Spanish conquistadors, and the same population pressures that brought the agriculture boom in the early 1800s also led to a great demand for beef. The wide-open plains of the American West were ideal for raising cattle, although it was not an easy existence for the cowboys who tended them, or for their horses.

A cowboy of Native American ancestry rides the country of his forefathers.

ISTOCK / JULIE VADER

Early cowboys rode Indian ponies or wild mustangs, but the capable Quarter Horse soon supplanted those breeds. The cow ponies were used to move cattle on the range and to cut individuals from the herd when necessary. The ponies were sturdy and hardy; they were also adept at managing the herds and provided able assistance when a cowboy needed to rope a steer.

Horses are still the preferred means of moving cattle today, as they're able to traverse any kind of terrain and are nimble and fast enough to keep up with a herd without spooking the cattle.

Mining

Coal was needed to fuel much of the new machinery that was developed during the Industrial Revolution. Ironically, old-fashioned horsepower helped provide much of this coal.

Horses were used aboveground, turning giant winches that hoisted loads of coal from the depths below. They were also used below ground to pull cartloads of coal up from the depths. Known as "pit ponies," these hardy animals (Shetlands in America and Welsh ponies in England) lived and worked underground for most of their lives. They needed to be sturdy, muscular, and sure-footed, so they could traverse the steep, rocky grades within the mines while hauling loads of coal up toward the surface.

Mining was a dangerous occupation for these ponies. They suffered injuries from accidents, eye and breathing problems caused by coal dust, and hearing loss caused by loud equipment. According to mining lore, the ponies were sometimes able to sense roof collapses before they occurred and would stop in their tracks and refuse to budge, thus saving themselves and the miners working with them.[21]

Entertainment and Sport

Equestrian sports have been part of humans' relationship with the horse from the very beginning.

Polo, one of the world's oldest horse sports, was played in Persia and China in the first millennium BCE. The first recorded match was between the Turkomans and the Persians in 600 BCE.[22]

In ancient Rome horses didn't just pull chariots in the circus; they also participated in gladiatorial mounted fights against animals such as bulls and elephants.

In medieval times, the tournament became a source of entertainment. These war games likely originated in France in the eleventh century and later became elaborate events that drew knights from many different countries. The main feature of a tournament was the mêlée, a battle (using real weapons) between knights who had been assigned to one of two sides. Jousting also took place at these tournaments.

By the end of the thirteenth century, rules for tournaments had been established, changing them from all-out brawls to organized spectacles with a strict code of chivalry. Jousting and riding at the rings (galloping at a series of suspended rings with a lance, spearing them one by one) eventually replaced the mêlée tournaments. These sports remained popular until the seventeenth century.[23]

Hunting on horseback was another popular pastime. The tradition began in France and was introduced in Britain, the country with which it is most associated today, in the eleventh century. At the time, the quarry was usually a stag or boar, but as the number of those species dwindled in the fifteenth century, the fox and the hare became targets.

Although the sport had a practical, if inhumane purpose—foxes were considered vermin and were fond of helping themselves to a farmer's chickens—it became a sport of the aristocracy. The sport was introduced to the United States in 1650, and many of the founding fathers, including George Washington (who had his own pack of hounds) and Thomas Jefferson, enjoyed it.[24] Although thirty-five states have recognized hunt clubs, foxhunting is popular in only a handful of states. Many horseman and landowners find the chasing and occasional killing of foxes repugnant, and real estate development has limited the activity's growth as well.

The Impact of Domestication

Historians believe that there were four types of primitive horses: the Forest Horse, a very heavy animal (similar to a smaller version of today's drafts) that lived in northern Europe; the Asian Wild Horse; the Tarpan, which was found in eastern Europe; and the Tundra Horse, which lived near the Arctic Circle. The first three of these primitive horses are believed to have developed into the more modern types—pony-size animals who lived in the cold, wet climates of Europe and Asia, and lighter desert horses who were found in the hot, arid areas of central and western Asia. (The Tundra Horse is not thought to have contributed significantly to the development of modern horses.)[25]

Domestication allowed for the increased movement and mingling of these early horses, leading to crosses between types and the creation of distinct breeds. The modern horse is found in a nearly mind-boggling array of breeds that are vastly different, ranging from ponies to massive drafts and displaying an enormous variety of coat patterns and colors. These modern breeds owe their existence to selective breeding (see chapter 7).

Amid the flurry of new breeds, however, the primitive types mostly disappeared. Only one has survived in its original form, the Asian Wild

Horse, also known as Przewalski's horse, which was almost hunted to extinction, but survived in zoos and was reintroduced to the wild in its native Mongolia.[26] The wild horses in other parts of the world, such as the mustangs in the American West, the ponies who live on Assateague Island off the coast of Virginia, and the brumbies in Australia, are actually feral horses, descendants of domesticated horses who escaped or were turned loose.

Horses accompanied humans on their early travels, allowing the species to be reintroduced in North America, where it had become extinct some eight thousand years ago for unknown reasons. Hernán Cortés brought sixteen horses with him when he landed in Mexico in 1519; from these animals and later imports from Europe, North American equines were repopulated.[27]

Domestication ensured that horses, as a whole, proliferated and thrived, even though certain breeds and types died out. But the effects of domestication and selective breeding were not always beneficial.

Although certain cultures have cherished horses and treated them well, horses have been considered expendable property. Untold millions died accompanying humans into war, and many more were worked to death in cities, where cab and coach drivers were more concerned with making a living themselves than with feeding or caring for their horses. Legislating humane treatment for animals is a relatively recent development (Britain passed its first law in 1822), and it is still a foreign concept in many developing countries.

Although selectively crossing horses has produced both remarkable individuals and wonderful breeds, it has also created its share of problems. Breeders often pursue fads to the detriment of horse health or breed horses with significant flaws in favor of more marketable qualities. For example, in Thoroughbreds, the trend has been toward breeding sprinters, since there are more races for sprinters at racetracks nationwide. Sprinters tend to have a slighter body type than do more substantial horses who are capable of longer distances. Although sprinters are able to run at faster speeds at two and three years of age, they often don't stand up to continued hard work later in life.

In the Quarter Horse breed, there has been criticism of horses who are bred specifically to show in halter (classes where horses are judged on looks and conformation, not on movement or performance), because the fad in recent years has been toward very heavy, muscular horses with very straight legs and small feet. Although this type of horse may win lots of halter ribbons, his legs and feet can absorb less concussion, a harbinger of problems later in life.

The Modern Horse Industry

When horses ceased being used for agriculture, the government no longer closely tracked their numbers, so there is no single definitive "horse census" of precisely how many equines live in the United States. Various groups do attempt to estimate the number of horses as well as their uses. The American Horse Council (AHC), a national group dedicated to the promotion of equine-industry interests, conducted a survey that estimated the American horse population to be 9.2 million in 2003, up from 6.9 million a decade before. The horse population has been climbing steadily since the precipitous decline in the mid-twentieth century, with the advent of mechanization, but it still pales in comparison to other farmed animals (there are about one hundred million cattle in the United States at any given time) and is also dwarfed by the populations of household companion animals (seventy-three million dogs and ninety million cats).

The majority of today's horses—about 42 percent—are used for recreational purposes, with 29 percent used for showing or competition, and 9 percent in racing. Texas has the most horses of any state in the Union, according to the AHC—just shy of one million in 2003. California, Florida, Oklahoma, and Kentucky round out the top five. But raw numbers don't tell the only story, as the smaller states in the Northeast can assert. Maryland is actually tops for the number of horses per square mile of land area, followed by New Jersey and Connecticut, then Florida and Kentucky. Still another measurement is the number of horses compared with the number of humans, a metric in which Wyoming claims top honors, with 5.1 people per horse, followed by South Dakota, Montana, Idaho, and North Dakota. While there might not be very many residents in those states, those who do live there are much more likely to be "horsey" than anywhere else.

The Quarter Horse has enjoyed undisputed dominance in the United States for decades. It remains, as popularly billed, "America's horse," with approximately 40 percent of the overall equine population. The Thoroughbred is next most common, at around 10 percent.[28]

Many horse owners joke that they try never to calculate exactly how much money they spend on their horses, for fear of what the amount is. Considering the cost of basic care (boarding, bedding, feed), veterinary care (vaccinations, emergencies), tack and equipment, show and/or training fees, the investment can be quite significant (see chapter 4).

According to the AHC, the horse industry is a $39-billion-per-year business and has a $102-billion impact on the U.S. economy, when spending by industry suppliers and employees is factored in. Of this $102 billion, racing contributes about $26.1 billion to the gross domestic product, showing about $28.7 billion, and recreational pursuits around $31.9 billion. (In other words, "recreational" riding is actually big business.)

About 4.6 million people are involved in the horse industry in some fashion. Two million actually own horses, while others are employees, service providers, or volunteers.[29]

A Horse's Many Jobs

Today horses exist in pockets, appearing wherever there is enough land to keep them comfortably and affordably. They are part of niche sports and recreational endeavors that are, for the most part, out of the mainstream. The industry itself is so varied and fragmented, one where those with different interests tend to travel in discrete circles that may not often intersect with others, that even the individuals who are part of the horse world may not be aware of all its aspects.

A Recreational Partner

For the majority of riders, their horses are primarily pleasure mounts. This designation can include horses whose only work is a slow monthly trail ride and those who are ridden, conditioned, and trained just as diligently as any show mount. Some of these "recreational" horses work pretty hard, being loaded up on trailers and hauled off near and far to attend clinics, ride in parades, trail ride in different locales, or participate in demonstrations at expositions. Clearly, no two recreational horses have the same job description.

A Competition Partner

There are horses everywhere who, along with their riders, lay their skills on the line in competition. The lifestyle of an elite equine athlete rivals that of any NFL or NBA star, replete with whirlpool baths for their legs and massage therapy for their aching backs. These horses travel across the United States and the world, earning Olympic medals or millions of dollars in purses for their owners.

Racing is the sport with which most people are familiar, and, indeed, more equine athletes are in use in this sport—whether racing in harness, on the flat, or over steeplechase or timber fences—than in any other, but there are literally dozens of other sports that involve horses regardless of age or breeding. Although some horses are bred specifically for a certain sport, others are simply pressed into service in whatever discipline appeals to their riders at the time. Since racing is a sport for professionals (there are very few amateur riders, although they do exist in steeplechasing), we explore other competitive athletic activities open to amateur as well as professional riders in chapter 6.

Horses may be moved from sport to sport (with the same or different riders) before one is found that best suits their talents. Thoroughbred racehorses in particular often find a second career when they retire from the track (because of injury or lack of speed or competitive spirit), and may end up excelling in sports their breeders might never have imagined.

A Working Partner

Horses who truly work for a living are definitely in the minority, usually falling under the heading "other," which claimed 19 percent of the horse population in 2003, according to the AHC. They work on ranches, as lesson horses, or in a number of other pursuits.

Police horses are still in wide use in the United States, in both major metropolitan areas and national parks. These well-trained horses are most often pressed into use for crowd control, thanks to their imposing size, but are also used in routine patrols and for ceremonial duties.

At the opposite end of the spectrum from the formidable police mounts are therapeutic riding horses, who are called on to bolster the confidence of people with physical or mental disabilities. They are a unique subset of "lesson" or "school" horses, who also qualify as "working horses," since their services are paid for.

Therapeutic riding, sometimes also called hippotherapy, has been used since the 1950s with often amazing results. Disabled riders are mounted on horses (carefully selected for their quiet and unflappable demeanor) and led around at the walk, generally with an assistant walking on each side for safety and another leading the horse. The movement of the rider's body in the saddle is similar to the movement of walking, and riding often leads to improvements in the rider's balance, flexibility, and strength.

A Friend and Companion

Finally, some horses are the equine equivalent of the retiree. They may have been used previously for sport or recreation. They may have sustained an injury early in life that precluded any kind of athletic career. Their owners and riders may have lost interest in actually *riding*, but continue to keep horses as companions, fulfilling their responsibilities to their "companions for life."

Humorously referred to as "pasture puffs" or "lawn ornaments," these horses live out their days under their owners' watchful eyes, receiving the same dutiful care as any competition horse. In some cases, it's the conclusion of a long partnership, where the owner is rewarding the horse for efforts from his younger days. In others, the owner might never have known the horse in his previous life, but perhaps rescued him from a slaughter pen or took him in to be a companion for other horses.

Riding is just one aspect of our relationship with horses, and nowhere is it written that a horse must be ridden to be useful or live a valuable life. It can be incredibly rewarding to provide a safe and happy home to a horse with no expectations for anything in return.

Should You Get a Horse of Your Own?

EVERY LONGTIME HORSEMAN HAS A PERSONAL highlight reel filed away in his memory bank—moments spent with horses that have special meaning or poignancy. They might include competitive successes, such as winning a prestigious event, or training milestones, like starting a young horse under saddle for the first time.

Among those public and private victories, however, are scattered other memories that are much smaller and more personal—a shared moment in the stall late at night, when a horse nickers softly and snuffles through jacket pockets for carrots; a pause while on a trail ride to admire the scenery, perfectly framed through a horse's pricked ears; watching a future competitive partner first raise his wet head from the straw after foaling. These moments are snippets of joy gleaned from a life with horses, born from the sense of connection fostered through partnership with these great creatures.

You don't need to own a horse to appreciate them, but nothing compares to the kinship experienced in a long-term equine-human relationship. It's simply not something that can be experienced on an hour-long guided trail ride or occasional lesson on a rotating cadre of school horses. It's no wonder that many equestrians yearn for a horse to call their own, a familiar face peering over the stall door—ears pricked and muzzle outstretched for a treat—day after day.

Buying a horse isn't an endeavor to take lightly. Our combined many decades of direct and indirect experience with hundreds of horse owners convinces us that the horse you buy will have an enormous influence on all of your subsequent experience with horses. Buying the right horse may spare you from having to learn some horsemanship lessons most horse folk could do without, such as how to catch a horse who runs away from you in the paddock, or how to manage a horse who won't allow his feet to be handled by the farrier. You might also avoid the tough decisions that come with owning a horse whose useful life has been cut in half by chronic health issues, or any number of other heart- and wallet-breaking problems.

Before you make the decision, be sure you understand all the pitfalls of the journey you're embarking on. Be honest with yourself regarding your abilities, your financial situation, your level of interest, and your time constraints. And most important, enlist a trusted horse-savvy friend or a professional instructor to help you make the decision and guide you through the purchase process.

An Expensive Hobby

For most prospective horse owners, the first perceived hurdle to horse ownership is financial. Horses are not inexpensive creatures, although purchase prices vary widely. Top competition horses routinely sell for several hundred thousand dollars, or even into the millions for racehorses. We're lucky that most of us don't need that kind of cash for an appropriate animal! But a well-trained horse, especially one suitable for a beginner rider, is likely going to be at least a moderate investment.

The purchase price of any individual horse is influenced by an array of factors, including the horse's level of training, age, breeding, conformation, competition record, rideability, ground manners— even color, breed, location, or gender.

The overall economy can also affect horse sales. Horses are considered "luxury items," and sales tend to suffer whenever the economy causes individuals to cut back on non-essential purchases. Prices are also influenced by the local market—horses with identical résumés can sell for vastly different prices in different areas of the country.

For most horse purchasers, the factors that influence an animal's price are much more concrete. A horse in the prime of his life—old enough to be ridden but not yet so old as to be developing physical limitations—will be more expensive than will a very young or very old horse. An attractive horse with pretty markings will be more expensive than a plain horse who's nothing special to look at. For horses who compete, as show mileage increases, so do their purchase prices.

Buying the horse isn't the most costly part of this endeavor—it's *keeping* the horse that proves pricey. Consider the recurring costs for even very basic horse-keeping—board, farriery, and routine veterinary care. Add the cost of lessons and entry fees, if you plan to compete, and all the new horse's accoutrements: tack, blankets, boots, and so on. Then factor in the unexpected, yet inevitable—an emergency veterinary call for a serious wound or colic episode, for example (see the table on page 68).

What horse owners spend varies tremendously from person to person. At the cheaper end of the spectrum might be the casual trail rider who keeps her easy-keeping Appaloosa gelding in a small field at home and leaves him barefoot. The polar opposite is the dressage rider in full training at a fancy show barn whose Danish Warmblood schoolmaster needs joint supplements, corrective shoeing, and massage treatments to stay comfortable and perform well at the many shows in which they compete. The difference in these two riders' monthly expenses can easily be thousands of dollars.

Since expenses for the same services can differ greatly depending on where you live, the best way to estimate how much it will cost to own a horse in your area is to talk to other local horsemen. Ask what they pay for routine vaccinations, farrier work, or lessons. Check the bulletin board at local tack shops or scan local equine publications to see what different local barns charge for board.

You'll usually find that you get what you pay for when it comes to horsey goods and services. If you're on a budget, there's no reason to go for the Cadillac of boarding barns when the Chevy will do, but you are entrusting these professionals with your horse's health, soundness, and well-being. The farrier who charges half as much as all the others in the area won't turn out to be such a bargain if he causes your horse to go lame, nor will a dirt-cheap boarding facility be a good choice if your horse's stall never gets cleaned and your horse is fed moldy hay.

There are plenty of opportunities for cost-cutting in horse ownership, but they shouldn't be taken at the expense of the horse's care. When conducting your informal pricing surveys, don't count on being able to use whoever is cheapest; instead, plan your budget around the median prices.

Once you've got a good idea of how horsey services are priced in your area, you can estimate your routine expenses. But before taking the plunge, remember that horses don't always stick to the routine. What if your horse is kicked in the pasture and needs stitches on a Sunday afternoon? What if he develops a chronic condition that requires ongoing treatment? Can your pocketbook handle the unexpected expense of an emergency veterinary call or long-term medications?

It's important to confront all the financial realities before signing that bill of sale and taking responsibility for a horse's care. Sometimes owners may have to make tough decisions—for example, when facing an expensive colic surgery that may offer the horse only a slim chance of survival. It doesn't make one a "bad" horseman to factor cost into the decision-making equation; a horseman may decide against such a surgery because she simply can't take on such debt for an uncertain outcome. There's no shame in this, as long as the horse's suffering is not prolonged and, instead, is ended quickly and humanely by a veterinarian.

Although no one wants to think of the partnership ending before it begins, you should research the costs of euthanasia and body disposal as well. These are an inevitable component of the horse-human bond, and a responsibility you should be prepared to undertake no matter what the age of your horse.

Most veterinarians are sensitive to their clients' financial limitations; they often help owners minimize costs where possible, perhaps by starting with the most conservative method of treatment or by forgoing the more expensive diagnostics. It's also a good idea to look into medical and mortality insurance for your horse—while you'll have to factor the recurring cost of the policy into your budget, insurance can help minimize the financial impact of the more costly, nonroutine treatments.

More Than Money: It's Time as Well

You've crunched the numbers and determined that you can financially handle the addition of a four-footed family member. You're not done yet—you also have to evaluate whether you can budget the *time* you'll need to devote to your new charge.

Take a good look at your schedule and your responsibilities. Consider where your horse will be kept, and how long it will take you to get there from home or work. Then take inventory of your goals. What do you see yourself doing with your new horse? What do you want to accomplish?

Consider two riders who have very different sets of goals. Rider A is an amateur eventer with lofty competitive ambitions. She is single with no children and works full time. She rides six days a week, either before or after work, spending two to three hours at the barn each day. She takes two intensive lessons per week with a trainer and spends many weekends at competitions.

Rider B is a recreational rider and a stay-at-home mom with two kids in elementary school. She usually rides once a week (twice if she's lucky), on the weekend, when her husband can watch the kids. Her rides are leisurely trail rides, maybe an hour or two long and purely for fun. She also tries to stop by the barn once or twice during the week, with children in tow, just to groom and say hello to the horse and let the kids take a pony ride.

These two riders with very different ambitions and lifestyles have tailored their riding around their responsibilities. They represent opposite ends of the amateur rider spectrum.

There's no "right" amount of riding time; it varies with each rider and horse, the situation, and the rider's goals. You need to take stock of your goals *and* your available time and judge whether the two are compatible.

Unlike other hobbies, riding isn't something you can shelve for several weeks or months when something else comes up. While the staff at a boarding barn will see to your horse's basic needs—feeding, stall cleaning, turnout, etc.—everything else is usually up to the owner. You're the one your horse looks to for individual attention, treats, and grooming. Most boarded horses really do notice when their owners go AWOL for any length of time.

If you're planning to keep a potential new horse at home and care for him yourself, then it goes without saying that you can't simply "take a break" from taking care of him—your horse counts on you to be there daily for feeding, watering, turnout, and mucking duties (or to delegate those duties to someone else).

Consistent riding is important for fitness and safety. You can't give a horse a month off and then pull him out of the field to go on a three-hour trail ride, for example—he won't be fit enough for it and will be at risk for fatigue-related injuries. Consistency is also important for the continued progression of horse and rider. You both need to practice the skills you've already learned and work on adding new ones to your repertoire.

For most people who are bitten by the horse bug, that daily trip to the barn is part responsibility and part play—you *need* to go to further your training and keep your horse in shape, but you also *want* to ride because you enjoy it. There are certainly days when it's very hot or very cold, you're tired or busy, or the alarm clock just seems to be going off too early, and that trip to the barn can fall by the wayside. When those days become the rule rather than the exception, it's the horse who suffers as he sits idly in his pasture or stall. The time to think about this is before you take on the responsibility for a horse's life, not afterward.

So before you make the decision to buy your own horse, honestly assess your time and your level of motivation. Be sure it's something you really want. (If you do decide you cannot commit to horse ownership at this stage of your life, lessons at training barns, "catch riding" for horse owners, or volunteering at equine-assisted therapy classes allow you to get your horse "fix" while improving your horsemanship skills.)

Responsibility

Taking the horse ownership plunge is unique in one very important way—a horse will eventually reach the end of his "serviceable" life, when he can no longer be ridden or driven, however lightly. At this point, which may or may not be anywhere near the end of a horse's actual life span, he will no longer be of use in his original capacity—or, perhaps, in *any* physical capacity. Since most people who own horses do so because they enjoy riding or driving them, this situation poses a bit of a dilemma.

When a car reaches the end of its serviceable life, we trade it in on a new one. But a horse is not an inanimate object that can be replaced if it wears out. He's a living, breathing, feeling being.

When you purchase a horse, you're taking responsibility for another creature's life—a particularly fragile creature, prone to perplexing injuries and accidents, and one who, at some point, will no longer be able to perform a job. You hope, of course, that this point comes after many years of happy partnership and at a ripe old age. But that's not always the case.

Consider this scenario: you purchase an eight-year-old gelding, in the prime of his life, and plan to compete on the local hunter circuit in the adult amateur classes. All goes swimmingly for a year or two, but then the horse becomes lame. Your veterinarian diagnoses ringbone, advising you that the lameness will only worsen if you continue to ride him in the same capacity. That means no more jumping or showing, but the good news is that he can still live a long and comfortable life, and perhaps enjoy a few more years of light work, if managed properly.

Suddenly, your dream horse is no longer able to perform the job for which he was purchased, and your promising show partnership has come to a crashing end. You adore your horse, but you also love to train and show and aren't really interested in simply going on trail rides. The lameness renders your horse unsellable; basically, you are now the owner of a very large and expensive pet.

This is a crossroads every horseman dreads encountering, but it's hardly a rare occurrence. Lameness, injuries, illness, freak pasture accidents all can signal an abrupt end to a horse's riding career. What then?

The path chosen in these unfortunate instances is what separates those who consider themselves mere owners of a piece of property from those who think of themselves instead as guardians of another living being. Rather than dumping a horse at a sale or with a dealer—the equine equivalent of a used car lot—and leaving his fate to chance, these caretakers keep their end of the bargain and do right by their friends.

If you're going to purchase a horse, you should do so with these kinds of situations in mind, because your responsibility doesn't end when a horse's career does. Sometimes a horse with lameness issues can be given (or free-leased) to a home where he can be ridden more lightly or can provide companionship to another horse who would otherwise be living alone fretfully. If the horse is a mare worthy of being bred, she might find a home as a broodmare. The owner might be able to find a retirement farm where the injured horse can live out his days as a pasture ornament. It might take a lot of legwork and networking, and it may mean paying expenses for a horse you can't even ride, but there are workable solutions out there for owners who care enough to look for them.

In the cases where no other solutions can be found, it is likely kinder to put the horse down than to let him take his chances at a sale, where he could wind up in unkind hands or on a killer buyer's truck.

To Lease or Buy?

If all this forethought has you feeling a little overwhelmed, there's another option available for those who want that one-on-one relationship with a horse but perhaps aren't ready or able to dive headfirst into horse ownership. Leasing a horse provides many of the benefits of ownership without requiring a lifelong commitment. It can be a good first step for many would-be horse owners.

Lease situations vary with the terms of the lease agreement, which can be written however the owner desires. In general, though, a lease transfers the day-to-day care and responsibility of a horse over to another party (the lessee), while the owner (the lessor) maintains ownership of the horse.

A lease might involve a fee, paid to the owner, for use of the horse (in the case of very talented horses), or it might be a "free lease," where the lessee takes over the horse's expenses but does not pay anything above that.

For owners, leases are often a good solution for temporary circumstances, saving the owner from having to make the rather permanent choice to sell a horse. A horse might be leased out while his owner is pregnant, for instance, or away at college. A lease might be a way for an owner to gain respite from a horse's expenses during a time of financial difficulty—after being laid off from a job, for example.

A lease can also be a long-term solution, a way to rehome a horse without the original owner giving up ultimate control and responsibility. For some owners it's an attractive alternative to selling a horse outright because it minimizes the risk of a horse ending up in a dangerous situation. For example, an amateur breeder might be trying for a homebred dressage star and instead wind up with a spectacular jumper. If the owner has no interest in jumping but doesn't want to sell the horse outright, he can be leased instead to a jumper rider for as long as the rider wishes to ride him.

In the case of a horse who would be difficult to sell, a lease eliminates the risk for the new "owner" and opens more doors for rehoming the horse. In the case of our hypothetical horse with ringbone, the horse owner might lease him to someone wanting a trail horse without asking that person to assume permanent responsibility for a horse with an uncertain future under saddle. While there would likely be little interest in buying such a horse, the horse can simply be returned to the owner if he becomes physically unable to perform the job for which he was leased.

For the lessee, leasing offers many of the benefits of horse ownership without much of the risk. There's no long-term commitment. If a rider's level of experience or interest changes, or if a young rider shoots up six inches over eighteen months and "outgrows" his mount, the horse can go back to his owner.

A lease carries its own risks—the owner can end it at any time, as long as it's in accordance with the terms of the lease agreement, and it can be heartbreaking to say goodbye to a horse who's become a friend when you're not ready to let him go. There can be misunderstandings over expectations, management, and workload. It's important to have a detailed written lease agreement that spells out each party's responsibilities to minimize potential conflicts. The lease should address worst-case scenarios—such as end-of-life decisions, liability for/collection of unpaid fees/bills, and insurance coverage—as well as boarding, travel, training, and care arrangements.

In well-thought-through circumstances, leases offer benefits to both the lessor and the lessee, and, most important, to the horse.

Taking Stock

Horse-shopping is a little bit like dating—you'll know you've found "the one" when the chemistry is right, you have common interests, you can tolerate each other's faults, and you work well together. Finding the right partner can take time, but it's better to wait for the right match than to settle for something that's less than perfect. (This is where a short-term lease may come in handy: preventing an "I've got to have a horse *now*" decision you'll regret later.)

Not every horse is right for every rider. Finding the one who is right for you begins with an honest assessment of your own abilities, strengths, weaknesses, and goals. Ideally, and especially if you're new to riding, you should also have a trainer, or an experienced and trustworthy friend who rides, to help in this process and provide an impartial opinion.

Perhaps the single most decisive factor is your own level of experience. There's more to riding than just "knowing how to ride." Only after years of experience does a rider learn the subtleties and nuances of this sport. That wealth of knowledge is what allows a rider to adapt to new horses and new situations, to know when to ask a horse to do more and when to quit for the day, and to solve training problems as they arise.

Experience isn't just the amount of time you've spent in the saddle, although that's an important part of it. It also comes from riding a variety of horses in a variety of situations and from taking lessons, reading, asking questions, and watching. Be humble in your self-assessment here— while you may be sure of your own abilities, compare what you've done to the résumés of other riders you know. If you find that yours is much shorter, that's a sign that you might not know quite as much as you think you do. Remember, this is a sport with a lifelong learning curve, and horses always come up with new lessons to teach.

There's nothing "wrong" with being light on experience, of course—even Olympic-level riders had to learn the basics at some point in their careers. The danger in overestimating your experience comes from having a horse who's not appropriate for your level. A horse with whom you're well-matched will teach you much more than a horse with whom you're in over your head.

Matching a green rider with a green horse is one of the most common recipes for producing an incompatible pair. Green horses are often less expensive than well-trained ones. They are enormously appealing, full of youth, energy, and bloom, and many parents are charmed by the idea of two youngsters (one a horse, the other a rider) learning together. Unfortunately, it's easy for an inexperienced rider to inadvertently create bad habits in a horse's under-saddle performance, or worse, frighten a young horse and undermine his trust in human beings. A green horse may also pose training dilemmas that a green rider is incapable of solving. While such combinations *can* be successful, the horse must be very honest and forgiving, and a trainer should be deeply involved every step of the way so small problems can be corrected before they become big ones.

An experienced horse can be one of an inexperienced rider's greatest teachers. She may not have the vigor and beauty of the youngster, she may be plain or big-kneed or even worn down by years of service. However, she's seen it all, with her cooperative, trusting nature still intact. One type of experienced horse—the "schoolmaster"—is always in high demand for new riders. These older, well-educated horses have kind temperaments, know what's expected of them, and are more tolerant of a green rider's mistakes than a less experienced horse would be. (Top schoolmasters are also sought after by experienced riders trying to break onto the national or international stage in their chosen sport. These elite horses often carry big price tags.)

If you're lacking in experience, you also want to keep in mind the types of horses you feel comfortable riding. A horse might be a wonderful mover and jumper, but if you can't sit her trot, or her exuberant jump jostles you loose from the saddle, she's not the right horse for you. You don't need to worry about having the best horse in the show ring—you just need to have the best horse *for you*.

You also want to assess your approach to riding. Are you a rider who enjoys being challenged, or do you prefer to operate within your comfort zone? Are you easily rattled by a spook or a buck? Do you get very nervous or even become crippled with fear?

If confidence is an issue for you, be honest with yourself about it. There are horses out there who can help you learn to trust your own abilities; if you don't acknowledge your confidence issues, however, you're more likely to end up with an unsuitable match who will only make the problem worse.

You should take into account where and how you will keep and ride your potential new horse. If your schedule is such that you're often away from the barn for days at a time, you need a horse who won't regress in his training every time he gets a few days off. If you live in an area where boarding facilities don't offer much turnout time, you want a horse who's emotionally and physically able to handle a more sedentary life, lived primarily in a stall. An older horse who might have some mild arthritis might not do well, nor would a very young horse with lots of energy.

Do you prefer mares or geldings? (Even experienced horse folk may prefer one or the other.) Large horses or small? Do you like a horse with lots of get up and go, or do you prefer one who is laid-back? You have to compromise somewhere, but it's important to know the kind of temperament you prefer, what you can tolerate, and what you can't.

TABLE 4.1

Budgeting for a Horse

Estimates are for one horse for one year.

Feed Costs	Quantity	Units	Cost per Unit	Median Cost	Total
Hay or Hay Pellets	7,300 lbs.	146 bales	$4.00–$18.00	$8.00	$1,168.00
Grain or Pellets	700 lbs.	14 bags	$4.00–$16.00	$10.00	$140.00
Minerals and Salts	30 lbs.	4 lb. block	$2.75	$2.75	$20.00
Horse Kept at Home— Total Annual Feed Cost Estimate					$1,328.00

Maintenance	Quantity	Units	Cost per Unit	Median Cost	Total
Bedding	15 yds.	Bulk	Less expensive	$142.50	$142.50
Farrier Service	8.6 times/ year	—	$45.00–$100.00	$75.00	$645.00
Worming	4 times/year	—	$5.00–$15.00	$12.00	$48.00
Vaccines (minimum)	2 times/year	—	Varies	$15.00	$30.00
Veterinary and Medicine	Varies	—	Varies	Varies	$375.00
Horse Care Products	Varies	—	Varies	Varies	$100.00
Miscellaneous	—	—	—	—	$50.00
Private Riding and/or Horseman- ship Lessons	2 times/mo.	—	$30.00–$75.00	$40.00	$960.00
Books/ Magazines/Info	—	—	—	—	$50.00
Maintenance, etc.— Total Annual Cost Estimate					$2,400.50
Total Estimated Annual Cost:					**$3,728.50**

(continued on next page)

Boarding Horse (Depending on locale and type of facility)

Boarding Costs	Quantity	Price Range	Average Cost	Total
Board	12 mos.	$150.00–$800.00	$300.00	$3,600.00

Notes:

- All costs vary tremendously from one area of the country to another.
- Hay or hay pellet quantities assume that a thousand-pound horse consumes 2 percent of his body weight daily.
- Grain/pellets are fed to the majority of horses, but some owners may disagree. This judgment may be based on the quality of hay available in their area and their feeding philosophy, etc.
- A bale of hay is calculated at fifty pounds, but like most things in this guide, it can vary. (Two-wire bales range from forty to seventy-five pounds; three-wire bales generally run ninety-five to a hundred pounds.)
- Salt and mineral consumption assumes 39 grams per day.
- Horse care products calculation includes hoof picks, brushes, shampoo, fly mask, fly spray, wound dressing, hoof dressing, scraper, and bucket.
- None of the estimates includes taxes, delivery charges, or personal vehicle expenses (e.g., picking up hay).
- No estimates for costs of land, equipment, insurance, or tack are included.
- The cost estimates used here are based on a pleasure horse: a horse used for recreational riding, trails, and general enjoyment. They assume the horse is not shown.
- Veterinarian estimates assume this horse has one or two minor injuries or illnesses during the year and may also get a minor checkup each year.
- Vaccine and worming estimates assume you, not the vet, do the worming and administer the vaccination.
- The boarding cost amounts used in this guide are based on a study done in 200l in the state of Arizona, adjusted for 2006.
- Boarding costs generally include feed only. Shoeing, vet, horse care products, worming, vaccinations, riding instruction/lessons are all extra.

Source: AllAboutHorses.com. Reprinted with permission.

CHAPTER 5

Finding Your New Horse

Finding Mr./Ms. Right

WHEN IT COMES TO ACTUALLY LOOKING AT horses and choosing the one who's right for you, you need to resist the urge to be influenced by the "in" breed, striking markings, or a pretty face. ("You can't ride the head!" old horsemen will tell you.) Instead, keep in mind what's really important—temperament, health, conformation, and experience. Only these qualities truly matter when you're in the saddle.

Horses are individuals. Although certain breeds tend to have certain qualities, individual horses are not necessarily defined by their breeds. (We explore the various breeds more thoroughly in chapter 7.) If you loved Walter Farley's book *The Black Stallion*, you might think an Arabian is the best horse for you, but don't necessarily discount the odd-sounding Tennessee Walker/Quarter Horse cross. Sometimes the perfect horse comes in a rather surprising package.

As you venture on your horse-shopping journey, think of yourself as someone conducting interviews for a job, where the horses are the job candidates. Write a mental job description for the position you're seeking to fill, whether it's for a trail/pleasure horse or a competitive mount. As you see and ride different horses, judge how they match up against the job description.

Perhaps the most important attributes to consider are the horse's age and experience, which usually—though not always—go hand-in-hand.

Young, green horses are usually less expensive, but it costs just as much to feed, board, and maintain a green horse as it does an experienced one. You won't have to fix as many problems as you might have with an older horse (a wily, hard-to-catch-in-the-field veteran can be frustrating, day in and day out), but you'll need a talented trainer to help you every step of the way to "make up" your green horse into the partner you want him to be.

Young horses can also be unpredictable—star pupils one day and troublemakers or class clowns the next. Two steps forward, one step back is typical with young horses, which can test all but the most patient of riders.

And although you (or your trainer) generally can get a good idea of where a young horse's talent lies, young animals are works in progress, and there are no guarantees. If your potential eventer won't get his feet wet, your dressage prospect turns ring-sour, or your trail-bound youngster hasn't seen a road he's liked yet, many months of hard work must be lost, chalked up to "experience." You may choose to send your youngster to a new home, putting you back at square one.

Older horses come with their own sets of benefits and drawbacks, of course. With experience can come some wear and tear. These horses are more likely to develop lameness-related issues or to need maintenance, such as joint supplements or injections. They also have fewer years left in their serviceable life span; while you can plan on being partnered with the four-year-old for two decades or more, that won't be the case with an eighteen-year-old schoolmaster. The older the horse, the more likely you'll be the one responsible for caring for him in his well-deserved retirement.

What older horses offer is a "been there, done that" attitude. They've been everywhere and seen everything, their behavior is predictable, and they know their jobs better than you do. The confidence these horses instill and the experience they can provide can be invaluable. They can be a true joy to ride, every ride, bringing you years of happy memories. For many owners, it's worth the higher purchase price and the responsibility of caring for the older horse in retirement.

Another important quality to consider is the horse's temperament, not just under tack, but also on the ground. It's a matter of compatibility—will your horse's personality suit yours? If much of the enjoyment you derive from being around horses comes from interacting with them on the ground, you're unlikely to enjoy owning a standoffish horse who doesn't want to be fussed with in his stall. If the herd clown's antics annoy rather than amuse you, you'll be better off with a horse with a less playful, less engaging personality.

Finally, you want to consider the horse's conformation—how he's put together. Form follows function, and conformation can provide important clues to the horse's future soundness and how well he'll be able to perform in a given job.

Here's where the educated eyes of a trainer or a veterinarian are especially helpful. What looks like an ordinary horse leg to you might make your trainer either gasp in horror or nod in approval. And the leg, arguably, is the key to an average horse's life as an athletic performer.

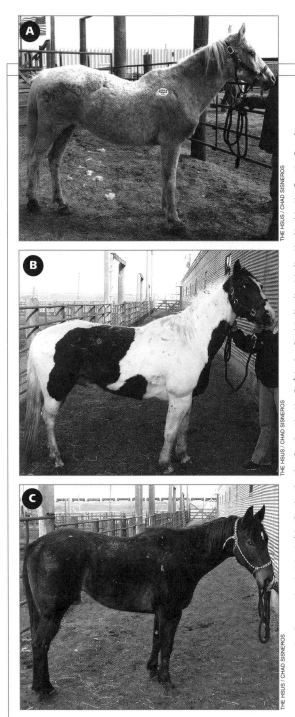

These three "Miracle Horses" were part of a load on its way to a slaughter plant when the plant was closed by legal action. In 2007 The HSUS cared for and placed all the surviving horses from this shipment in sanctuaries or adoptive homes. **Horse A** is a twenty-three-year-old Arabian mare. She has a beautiful head and gray color, but an injury or congenital malformation, evidenced by her swayback (the dip behind her withers), rendered her unrideable. Her set back front legs would place strain on their tendons, joints, and ligaments, so she was retired to an equine sanctuary after rescue. **Horse B** was a big, colorfully marked eleven-year-old paint gelding. Although he had a long back and thick, high-set neck—considered conformation faults in a top equine athlete—he had a successful career as a riding horse before an unrelated medical condition put him on the slaughter-bound truck (the condition did not respond to treatment after the horse was rescued, and he was euthanized to prevent his suffering). **Horse C** is a twenty-three-year-old Thoroughbred. He has an athletic build: a well-angled shoulder (facilitating a long, economical stride); well-set neck (and one neither too thick nor too thin); and well-proportioned back, when measured from withers to croup. His withers are slightly higher than his croup, and he has a deep girth area with well-sprung ribs, providing ample room for internal organs such as the heart and lungs.

These photos show that even unkempt horses can be evaluated for conformational strengths and weaknesses.

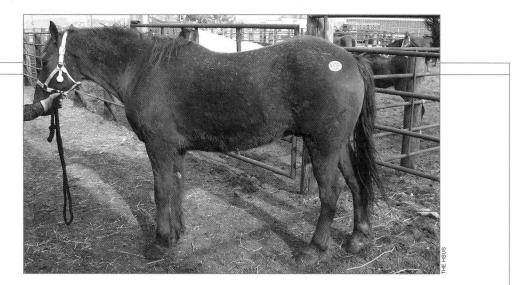

This twenty-one-year-old horse, also one of the slaughter-bound "Miracle Horses," has a more traditional Quarter Horse build, including a well-angled shoulder; larger rump, and well-set neck (although set lower on the body than is the Arabian mare A's, opposite page). This horse also has an attractive head. Western riders prefer a horse with a slightly higher croup-than-withers conformation, which provides greater power and more "stop."

The basic premise underlying conformation of the leg is that undue stress can lead to lameness. A horse with very straight, upright pasterns will have a more up-and-down, jarring gait. She is more likely to develop lameness that is exacerbated by increased concussive forces on the limb and joints. A horse with pasterns that are too long and sloping is at greater risk for bowing a tendon due to the increased forces created by the angle of the pastern. There's a small window that defines "perfect," and the ability to evaluate these qualities comes with experience, experience, experience.

The way your horse is built not only influences his soundness and the length of time he'll be serviceable for use in whatever discipline you choose, but also how good he'll be at it. If your goal is to do dressage, for example, a long-backed horse who's built slightly "downhill" (rump higher than his withers/shoulders) is likely going to lead to more frustration than success. Such a horse simply isn't built to carry himself in the way required for dressage. He can do it, and perhaps quite proficiently at the low levels, but it will be more difficult for him than for a shorter-backed, "uphill" horse, for whom the correct carriage is more natural.

Avenues for Horse-Shopping

By now, you've got a reasonably good idea of what you're looking for in your first horse. All that remains is finding your new Mr./Ms. Right.

Be forewarned that this can be a lengthy, time-consuming process, as well as an expensive and aggravating one. Your budget, your patience, and the amount of spare time you have at your disposal will likely influence how you shop. Fortunately, you have quite a few options.

Equine Rescues

The first place we recommend may be the last place you might think of otherwise: an equine rescue. Equine rescues have multiplied in the last ten years, and many horse folk have found them to be great places to go to adopt. Of all the players you will encounter on this important journey, from trainers, to dealers, to individual horse sellers, rescues and rehabilitation/retraining centers are the most likely to have the least reason to push you into a commitment that isn't right for you. It is just as important for them to be sure it's a good match as it is for you, because they deal with the outcomes of bad "fits" every day. Even if you end up not adopting from a rescue, the questions the rescue staff ask and the answers they provide will give you a good baseline for what to expect as you travel from barn to barn in your horse search.

In 2007 thirty-nine states had Internet listings for at least one equine rescue organization. Some states, like California and Texas, had more than ten such facilities. These organizations are all independent, with different criteria for accepting, rehabilitating, and adopting out the horses in their care. Many are non-profits; most require adoption fees, professional (veterinary) references, and/or pre-adoption barn inspections. Many also require, as a stipulation of their adoption criteria, that they be allowed to conduct follow-up visits for a time to ensure that your horse is well cared for. Others may place geographical limitations on adopters or specialize in one breed, such as Thoroughbreds or Arabians. In this way, they are similar to animal shelters and dog-breed rescue organizations.

Horses (including foals and in-foal mares) come into rescues at all ages and from all backgrounds. You may find a former show or race-horse or an untrained horse from a Native Nation in the Western states. Some rescues purchase horses at auction to keep them out of the hands of killer (slaughter) buyers; others may have been granted ownership of horses involved in animal-cruelty actions, including hoarding and starvation cases. Some may accept horses for which their prior owners could not find homes.

Typically a rescue evaluates each horse's soundness and suitability and tries to find a good match with a prospective adopter. Just as with sale horses, some horses may require an experienced rider; others may be beautifully trained. Some are suitable for light riding rather than heavy campaigning over jumps. Others may have been retrained for a particular job or discipline by rescue staff or volunteers. Many rescues have available horses profiled on their websites, and there are online search engines that allow you to view the horses available at rescues in a specific geographical area (the HSUS website *www.humanesociety.org* has a link to horses available for adoption.)

Rescue staff members want to find the best home for each horse, pony, donkey, or mule, so they will assess your level of experience to determine whether you are a good fit for the skills and temperament of the animal you want to adopt. Be prepared to be patient if the right horse is not available on the first try and keep checking back with rescues, as their inventory changes frequently.

Once you've identified a horse who matches your needs, you are required to complete an adoption application, provide references, and perhaps permit a site visit of the premises where you intend to keep your horse. You shouldn't view this as a challenge of your barn's horse-keeping virtues, but rather as a helpful way of assuring that your horse will receive the care he requires. Sometimes even experienced riders overlook simple horse care needs, and a trained rescue worker can point out deficiencies and give advice to ensure the best future for your horse.

THE HSUS / DEBORAH SALEM

Selling your horse should be a well-thought-out decision, and finding the right home should be a methodical process.

Private Owners

The vast majority of horse sales take place between individuals. An owner might decide to sell because she has outgrown the horse's abilities or because the partnership simply didn't work out. The loss of a job, a pregnancy, a cross-country move, or a divorce might force a sale. Perhaps the owner has decided to stop riding. However events conspire, the end result is that the current owner has decided a horse needs to move on to a new home. How do you connect with these sellers?

The primary route is via advertising. There are homemade fliers at horse shows and tack shops, classified ads in local equine publications, and listings on Internet websites, all offering horses for your perusal.

Horse-for-sale websites, the newest sales tool in a very old business, often offer the most selection and ease of use. These sites might be national or local, and depending on popularity, can have tens of thousands of horses listed, or just a few.

The larger sites offer sophisticated search engines that allow you to select various attributes you're seeking in your new horse; they then return a list of horses that meet your criteria. You can search by price, breed, age, sex, location, discipline, height, even color. Ads usually include photos and sometimes even videos.

In addition to the mega-size nationwide sites, there are lots of smaller online resources. Some serve only a limited geographical region, such as the Bay Area in California, or focus on a specific discipline, such as eventing. While these sites don't have as many horses listed and might not have search features, their parameters have already done a lot of the work for you if you're in their target audience.

Internet ads are easy to use and are instantaneous, but it can sometimes be difficult to narrow your search appropriately on the larger websites. If the type of horse you're looking for is relatively common, you'll be overwhelmed by a large number of ads that match your criteria. On the other hand, sometimes you can get so specific in your search criteria that you inadvertently eliminate horses that might be just about perfect for you, even if they're not *exactly* what you thought you were looking for.

Before the Internet, everyone advertised in the classified section of various publications, everything from national equine magazines, to breed-specific journals, to local general-interest newspapers. Many equine associations also include classified advertisements in their newsletters.

These publications are still an excellent source, and since many are local or serve only one particular discipline, the ads are more targeted. If you prefer scanning ads to see what catches your eye, you might prefer this method over a website search.

Regardless of the venue where the advertisement appears, remember that an ad is the seller's "pitch" to you—it's designed to make the horse sound as desirable as possible and is based on the seller's judgment of the horse's talents, which may or may not be particularly relevant or accurate. (One person's "dressage prospect" may be another's "trail horse.")

Then there is the old standby, word of mouth. Let everyone in your own horsey circles know you're shopping—your friends, other people at the boarding/lesson barn, the folks at the local tack and feed shops, veterinarians, farriers, and so on. One of them may have a horse for sale; if not, someone may know someone else who does. If you are taking riding lessons, your instructor may have contacts in the horse community or have seen horses at shows, clinics, or elsewhere who would be worth following up on. He may not be willing or able to evaluate the horse for you, but such information may still make an informal recommendation worth pursuing.

After exploring all these avenues, you are likely to come up with a list of potential equine suitors. Then you need to contact the owners of the horses to ask additional questions, and if a horse sounds promising, make an appointment to see and ride him.

This process can be time-consuming, and it can be frustrating to give up your weekends or take time off work to see horse after horse. If the kind of horse you're looking for isn't very common where you live, you may also find yourself doing a lot of driving. For this reason, many horse shoppers prefer not to deal with individual sellers, but rather go to venues where they have an opportunity to try multiple horses at a time.

Breeders and Trainers

If you know exactly what you want in a horse, sometimes it's worth going directly to the source. For horses, this means shopping with the people who breed horses for a living.

You'll encounter many horses on your search about whom little is known—the age and breed might be a guess, and the horse's previous history might be a complete mystery. When shopping with a breeder, though, you're talking to the person who was there when this horse took his first unsteady steps after being born. The breeder knows not only the horse's sire and dam, but also many other ancestors, going back multiple generations, as well as those horses' accomplishments, strengths, and weaknesses.

Based on knowledge of other members of the breed, a responsible breeder can make an educated guess about how the horse is likely to mature, what he'll be like to ride, and the disciplines in which he might excel. (There are no guarantees, of course!) Some breeders have decades of experience in their breed of choice and have studied genetics and

Choosing a Responsible Breeder

The Humane Society of the United States offers these tips to people choosing a horse breeder.

Responsible breeders:

- Have carefully bred their horses to minimize lameness or conformation issues and have started their horses slowly and correctly in their work.
- Are known to others in the local equestrian community for producing quality horses (and will provide references).
- Do not use feedlot, dealer, or killer-buyer auctions to dispose of unwanted breeding animals, including barren broodmares or unwanted/unsaleable young animals.
- Show a demonstrated commitment to breed improvement, through national breed associations as judges, instructors, competitors, or officials.
- Disclose any genetic health-related issues in the breed or the animal's bloodlines.
- Offer horses in good physical condition with complete veterinary histories.

equine conformation; others may be much less committed to improving the breed and more committed to improving their bottom line. Given the current overpopulation of horses, irresponsible breeders who dispose of unwanted/unsaleable animals should be avoided, regardless of the quality of the horses they offer (see sidebar).

Breeders typically offer for sale rather young horses—most don't keep their stock until maturity, so their animals won't have much experience under saddle. A breeder might have only one or two horses to show you or as many as several horses at once.

While breeders can offer horse shoppers an array of choices with potential, trainers can offer horses who are proven—they'll be in regular structured work and perhaps competing and demonstrating success in the show ring. Most trainers specialize in a particular discipline, either teaching students or bringing along horses (and sometimes both) in that sport.

The horses in a trainer's barn might be resale projects—horses with potential who were purchased with the intention of giving them additional training and selling them again at a profit—or they might be the horses of students who have decided they need a different mount. Trainers who specialize in sales will also likely have consignment horses who've been sent to their barns for the express purpose of being sold.

Buying a horse from a trainer will likely be more expensive than buying a similar horse from an individual, because the trainer charges a commission to the owner of the horse, which is generally included in the horse's sale price. You're also paying for the trainer's time, use of his facilities, and his expert opinion on the horse.

Trainers and breeders have hung out their professional shingles and should be known to others in your local equestrian community. They may have verifiable competitive or business histories. By doing a little research and asking for recommendations, you'll be able to determine which of these individuals is known for producing and representing quality horses and which should be avoided.

Auctions and Dealers

Anyone can call herself a horse breeder, horse trainer, or horse dealer. Unfortunately, there are no codes of conduct, licensing standards, or professional overseers of people involved in horse sales, other than those who enforce standard consumer-protection laws. It is pretty much caveat emptor throughout the horse industry.

There are two kinds of horse auctions, and although they operate along the same principles, they couldn't be more different.

Elite auctions are where horses are often pre-screened for bloodlines or conformation and only the "best" are accepted to be sold. American Quarter Horse or Arabian auctions are breed-specific examples, while premium sport horse sales, popular in Europe, attract buyers interested in the dressage and eventing prospects of several registered breeds.

At these auctions, you're usually provided with lots of information about the horses. A catalogue is generally available beforehand with photographs, pedigrees, and detailed descriptions. At some sales, veterinary reports and radiographs (X-rays) are available to buyers. These sales are designed to give buyers an opportunity to see a large number of horses for sale in one location and to give increased exposure to small-time sellers. The sales vary in quality: some have stellar reputations and are known as a source for premium horses. Others might not have quite the same quality of horses or enjoy the same level of respect.

The kind of auction most people are familiar with is the weekly or monthly livestock sale that takes place at a local fairgrounds or auction facility. Such sales might include other animals, such as cattle, pigs, and sheep. These kinds of events are intended for disposing of unwanted horses quickly and easily. Killer buyers and less-than-scrupulous folks who are interested in cheap horses frequent these sales, as do some private buyers.

You can look at the horses beforehand and perhaps watch them being ridden, but rarely are you able to ride one yourself at these venues. You won't usually have the opportunity to have the horse checked out by a veterinarian (except perhaps to draw blood for a Coggins test), and the horses are sold "as is"—if you get the horse home and discover an undisclosed physical problem, you rarely have any recourse.

Nice (that is, sound and well-trained) horses do go through these sales, and if you're educated enough to spot the diamonds in the rough, you can find a quality horse who might be down on his luck or must be unloaded very quickly by a cash-strapped owner. You need a very experienced eye; this isn't an endeavor for a first-time horse buyer.

Horror stories about unscrupulous selling practices at auctions abound. Horses may be drugged to mask serious injuries or behavioral problems. Their training and history may be grossly misrepresented. Because most auctions are so hectic and rushed, potential buyers have only the seller's "pitch" and their own quick observations by which to judge an animal.

While not quite as risky as auctions, horse dealers aren't necessarily suited for first-time buyers either. Dealers are professionals who specialize in buying and reselling horses in quantity. They tend to buy horses cheaply and resell quickly for a profit, large or small. Some dealers are more reputable than others, but in general their horses are likely to have less training and/or natural aptitude than those you would find at an individual barn. Dealers aren't likely to know much about the horses they're offering for sale, since they operate with a higher volume of horses, acquire them from a variety of sources, and don't typically hold on to them for long.

Dealers do offer the opportunity to try several equine candidates in one visit. Local dealers with good reputations for honest business practices—for example, trading a horse who does not work out for another who is more suitable (although not necessarily for the same price)—and have repeat, satisfied customers can offer a selection of good family horses but typically do not offer a wide selection of competition-bound horses.

Unless you're very experienced or have a trainer or other expert to assist you in your search, you might fare better shopping at another outlet.

How Not to Get Bamboozled

There's a reason why the term "horse trader" has negative connotations. For as long as horses have been bought and sold, the process has been fraught with dishonesty, deceptive practices, and outright fraud. Older horses with known lameness issues are presented as being young and sound. Horses with volatile temperaments are tranquilized to appear calm and sedate. A seller who only cares about getting a check for the horse will tell you just about anything to convince you to take the animal off his hands.

The horse you purchase isn't usually backed by a warranty. If you change your mind and decide you and the horse aren't a good match, you can't return him. Even if the horse is "defective"—he has a lameness or behavioral problem, for instance—you have only very minimal protection under the law.

Horse sales are conducted under the ancient edict "let the buyer beware." Legally, a seller is prohibited from actively and grossly misrepresenting a horse, but you're only protected if you can prove such deception. Let's say you look at a prospective Pony Club horse for your daughter. The mare is sweet and quiet, and the seller tells you that his child has ridden the horse with no issues. Your daughter and you both take trial rides on the mare and are enthusiastic about her. You purchase her and take her home.

Two weeks later, the mare's personality changes completely. She's aggressive and unruly. *You* won't get on her, much less your daughter. You call your veterinarian, who observes that sellers have been known to administer a long-acting tranquilizer to horses that, once it has worn off, reveals the horse's true demeanor. If you can prove this happened in your case and can document that the seller knew the horse was not at all suitable for a child, you have a viable legal claim against the seller. But how to get such proof? Did you ask for a blood test or even a rudimentary veterinary examination before you purchased the mare?

Although the legal protection for buyers is minimal, sellers may well be required to answer questions truthfully—if you ask if a horse has ever been lame, the seller can't lie and say no. The seller may have to be honest with the potential buyer about the horse's abilities, depending on state regulations. If you're shopping for a jumper and the seller's horse won't even step over a pole on the ground, the seller may have to disclose that fact to you. You may want to check with an attorney in your state if you believe the seller has misrepresented the facts in a sale.

Take Advantage of Others' Expertise

When buying a horse, your legal protection is skimpy at best, and you have to protect yourself by doing your own research, asking the right questions, and taking the time to judge the suitability of a horse under a variety of circumstances and conditions.

In most cases, as a first-time horse buyer, you simply don't know the questions you should ask or the potential problems for which you should look. Assessing the soundness of a horse or the control issues that are being "managed" with a harsh bit are tasks better left to experienced people. That's why we strongly recommended that you take advantage of the expertise of others so you can navigate the horse-shopping seas more safely.

If you've been working with an instructor or trainer, she may be an excellent resource to help you on your horse-shopping voyage. A trainer has likely bought and sold many horses and knows the ins and outs of the process (although a riding instructor may not have had as much experience in the marketplace as has a trainer). Ideally the instructor or trainer knows *you*, too, and can help assess which horse will best suit your ability level and needs.

You might want to leave the entire search up to your trainer, including finding appropriate horses to see and try. Or you might prefer to conduct a good portion of the search yourself, scanning the ads and finding horses who sound promising, perhaps even trying them for the first time on your own. If you find a horse you like, you can make a second appointment to go back and try him with your trainer or other expert present.

You'll need to pay your trainer for his time on these shopping excursions, but you're likely to find that it's a tremendous help to have an expert opinion on which to rely. Your trainer's experience can help prevent you from making the mistakes that are common to first-time horse buyers. If you don't have a trainer or instructor, a horse-knowledge-able friend or mentor may be able to offer some general help that will at least prevent you from buying a *completely* inappropriate horse.

The other expert advisor you want to rely on is your veterinarian. Your potential horse's soundness is extremely important, and although there are no guarantees—even a perfectly sound horse can be kicked in the pasture and go lame the day he comes home—you certainly want to minimize your risk as much as possible. One way to do this is via a pre-purchase veterinary exam.

Commonly referred to as a PPE, this examination should be conducted by a veterinarian of your choosing, *not* the seller's veterinarian. If you don't already have a relationship with a veterinarian, find a practitioner in the area who isn't associated with the seller. Although this can sometimes be a challenge if you're horse-shopping a considerable distance away from home, you want to use a veterinarian who represents your interests, not the seller's. (Although if the seller has veterinary records and is willing to make them available to you, those can be helpful.)

A PPE can be as cursory, or as thorough, as you're willing to pay for. A basic PPE includes a physical examination of the horse for any obvious issues, including an examination of the eyes and teeth. Your veterinarian will use the horse's teeth to gauge the animal's age—compare this estimate with what the owner has told you and what is stated on the horse's registration papers (if the owner has them).

This basic examination can often tell you a lot about the horse and her history. By looking at the teeth, your veterinarian can tell if the horse cribs. He can also spot certain old, healed injuries or surgical scars. If the seller hasn't been completely truthful with you, comparing your veterinarian's observations with the information the seller provides will raise a red flag, and you know to proceed with caution.

Your veterinarian will also want to watch the horse jog to see if there is any lameness and then perform joint flexions—individually flexing joints of the leg to stress them, and then watching the horse jog off again to see if he is still sound.

Flexions are not a foolproof indicator of lameness (try holding your own knee in a contorted position for a while and see how soundly *you* jog afterward). Some horses with known lameness issues don't flex "off" (lame), while other sound horses might, even though the joint in question doesn't seem to cause them any trouble during normal work. Positive flexions, however, can indicate that a joint might be a problem, and you and your veterinarian can decide if you want to pursue further diagnostics—such as a radiograph or an ultrasound—on any questionable joint.

Many owners who opt for a very thorough PPE have radiographs done on some or all of the important joints. These radiographs will show any arthritic changes or bone chips that might cause problems down the road. Radiographs are not a Magic 8 Ball, however. "Clean" films don't mean a horse is or will stay sound, and horses who show some trouble spots on their radiographs might stay sound forever.

Some veterinarians are hesitant to do PPEs because even though they stress it's an *opinion* based on observing the horse on one particular day, and not a guarantee, the purchaser may blame the veterinarian if the horse has a problem later. Don't expect the veterinarian to predict the future. You're asking for his assessment of the horse's *possible* physical issues and of how the horse *might* be expected to hold up for the job he's intended for.

PPEs, especially very thorough ones, can be quite expensive. Some buyers opt not to do them on very inexpensive horses, since the cost of the exam could rival the purchase price. But a basic PPE is quite affordable, and is an especially good idea for novice horse buyers.

One other expert whose opinion you might want to solicit is a farrier, especially if the horse you're considering wears special shoes or seems to have problem feet.

A farrier can tell you whether a horse's bad feet can be helped or how difficult any hoof problems will be to manage. Corrective shoeing can often be quite expensive, so it's good to know what you're getting into before you decide to purchase.

Trying a Sale Horse

If you're a first-time horse buyer, we strongly recommend that you take a trainer or experienced friend along on your first shopping trips, so you can rely on another knowledgeable person to guide you through this process and help you make your decision. But if that's not possible, we can offer some general guidelines and tips to help you navigate your way through the process.

Before going to see a horse, talk to the owner (either by phone or via e-mail) and ask some questions. Advertisements are usually short on details, so this is your chance to flesh out the minimal information you have about the horse and prevent you and the seller from wasting your time if the horse isn't what you're looking for.

You might want to ask for a more thorough explanation of what the horse has done so far—if he is in training for a particular discipline, what skills has he learned? If he has competed, how many times, at what levels, and with what placings? Is he reliable out on the trail? Will he go through water (some horses object to crossing streams, for example)? Does he load, clip, and tie? How is he with children? Tailor your questions to the particular horse and your own needs and interests.

If the horse sounds like a good candidate, make an appointment to see and ride him. Be courteous to the seller and make sure you keep the appointment and show up on time, dressed to ride.

The seller might have the horse all tacked up and ready to go, but if not, watch as the horse is groomed, saddled and bridled, and make note of how easy (or difficult) he is to work with. You can also use this time to ask the seller about any unusual tack the horse wears—a strong bit or other gadgets might clue you in to the fact that horse could possibly be difficult to control.

Have the owner or his agent ride the horse first—this will give you a chance to see the horse go at his best with a rider who's familiar with him. Watch everything the rider does and pay close attention to how the horse behaves. These moments are your brief glimpse into how easy this horse is to work with and what his personality is like. Does he lead willingly and politely? Does he stand quietly to be mounted?

Once the rider has mounted and warmed the horse up, ask him to show you everything the horse is capable of doing, whether it's simply walk/trot/canter in both directions or more complicated tasks commensurate with a higher level of training. Does the horse perform willingly with a happy expression, or does he misbehave and ignore his rider? If he behaves poorly, does the rider try to explain it away with excuses ("He never does this"), blaming the cold, blustery weather or the dog running around next door? Any horse, especially a young or green one, can have an "off" day, but misbehavior is a big warning sign.

After you've watched the horse in action, *and if you've liked what you've seen*, take your turn. Mount the horse unassisted, if possible, and ride in an enclosed area while the seller is present. Ask for—and follow—the owner's suggestions on how best to ride the horse. Take note of how well the horse responds to your aids, how comfortable he is to ride, and how much you enjoy the experience. (If the ride leaves you grinning, you've probably found your horse!) If you have determined that the horse is not suitable before riding him yourself, it is common courtesy to thank the owner and leave. Do not ride a horse you feel is beyond your skill level or is otherwise not a prospective purchase.

Try doing as much as you feel comfortable doing with the horse, being mindful of his own level of stress and fitness—being ridden thoroughly twice in a short time is a lot of work. Ideally, the horse goes as well for you as he did for the owner, but if not, it may be due to your unfamiliarity with each other, your nervousness, or your different level of experience. You have to use your judgment and decide if any issues are a matter of the two of you needing more practice together, or if this is a horse you're simply not going to be able to ride effectively.

If, at any time during the ride, you feel uncomfortable about the way the horse is behaving, stop and dismount if necessary. You're under no obligation to impress the seller or attempt more than you feel comfortable doing. Your own safety is the first priority.

A seller might also stop the trial ride if she doesn't think things are going well. If a seller says, "I don't think this is a good match," that's a polite way of saying that the horse requires more skill than you possess or that you're otherwise not suited to each other. Don't be offended—the seller is looking out for both you and the horse. The seller is doing you a valuable service by preventing you from purchasing an inappropriate mount.

With luck, however, you'll have a wonderful ride. If so, ask if you can come back for another ride, before which you can request to tack the horse up yourself, then ride him without the owner riding him first. (The owner should be present throughout the process, however.) This gives you more exposure to the horse's "out of the field/stall" behavior. A second visit is also a good time to ask the seller to show you that the horse loads on a trailer, longes, stands to be clipped and bathed, lifts all feet for the farrier, and can be caught in a field or paddock. Ask if you can participate in these activities, with the owner's supervision.

Take-Home Test

While your veterinarian, farrier, and trainer can all give their assessments of the horse, how *you* feel about the animal should be the deciding factor. Is this a horse with whom you'll enjoy working? Will you be able to ride him effectively? Does his personality suit yours?

These questions can be difficult to answer after only a half-hour test ride at an unfamiliar facility. If the seller is amenable to the idea, you may want to bring the horse home for a trial period before you buy. This gives you the opportunity to work with the horse on your own turf and without feeling self-conscious in front of the seller. You can ride the horse for several days in a row to see if the two of you get along. Most important, you can get to know the horse's personality. This is a partnership that will be years-long: you want to be sure you're really in love with this horse, not just "in like"!

Before taking a horse home on trial, you should have a very clear agreement with the seller about how long the trial period will be, where the horse will be kept, and what costs will be covered by the potential buyer. The seller might require you to take out a temporary insurance policy on the animal to protect both of you in case of an accident.

Some sellers may be reluctant to allow a horse out on trial, however. This doesn't automatically mean that a seller has something to hide; perhaps he just doesn't want to risk the horse getting hurt or having any training undone or has had bad experiences with trial periods for previous buyers. If a take-home trial isn't a possibility, the seller at least should be willing to let you ride the horse several times on different occasions. This can be a challenge if the horse is located some distance from your home, but it is well worth the investment in time and travel expenses.

Do Your Homework

There are many charlatans in the horse world who make a living preying on the naiveté of inexperienced buyers. Don't be afraid to insult a seller by asking questions. As long as you phrase them respectfully and don't accuse the seller of trying to cheat you, *any true horseman should be happy to provide accurate answers*. Good sellers are just as concerned about their horse ending up in an appropriate home as you are, after all.

Ask to see any documents that are available for the horse, including her registration papers, the current owner's bill of sale, and any previous veterinary records. Compare the information in the documents—such as the horse's age and breeding or previous veterinary issues—with what the seller has told you. Ask if the seller can provide you with contact information for the horse's previous owner. You can often backtrack through the chain of ownership and glean good information from a horse's previous owners.

If the horse has a competitive record, double-check the results. You can often find show results online or in various equestrian publications. If the horse is registered with a breed or sport association, ask the owner for his registration number, then contact the association in question and ask for a copy of his show record. (If the horse is an ex-racer, you can also get his racing record.) See if there are any long gaps in results that might indicate the horse was "out of commission" for a time and verify that the horse competed at the level the owner claims he did.

When you do decide to buy, sign a sales contract. If the seller provides one, *read* it thoroughly! If not, you can provide your own (many free

examples are available online that you can tailor to your needs).
Make sure any ownership papers are transferred to you when you take
possession of the horse. The vast majority of sales are straight cash
sales, but installment sales, lease-with-option-to-buy sales, and other
exotic options are available. The important thing to remember in such
transactions is to obtain a written agreement covering the horse's care
and the responsibilities and liabilities of all parties during the transition.

Buying a horse can be a complicated and sometimes stressful process,
but if you're careful, have competent people to advise you, and deal
with reputable sellers, the end result can be a wonderful new horse
you can enjoy for many years to come!

CHAPTER 6

Disciplines

English Versus Western

WHETHER YOU RIDE A PASO FINO, A PAINT, or a Welsh Pony, chances are you ride for pleasure. More horse owners in this country—about 42 percent, according to a 2005 survey by the American Horse Council—ride for pleasure than for any other activity. Only 29 percent show or compete.[30] Pleasure riding is typically defined as trail riding, and although it is not technically considered a riding discipline, trail riding is most closely associated with Western-style riding.

A horse in Western tack well equipped for the trail. The saddle's back belly band prevents the saddle's cantle from tipping up in steep terrain; the saddle pad is well fitted; the bridle is hooked over the horn since the horse is secured to his trailer by his halter.

Trail riding can offer the challenge of the unknown and an unmatched view of the terrain from between your horse's ears.

Whether you learn to ride English or Western (as defined by the two predominant and different saddle styles) depends most typically on how and where you learned to ride.

If you started riding by taking lessons at a local riding stable or lesson barn east of the Mississippi, you probably learned to ride in an English saddle, since most instructors at such barns have an English-riding background. If you started riding at a rental stable, dude ranch, on a family property, or west of the Mississippi, you may have learned to ride in a Western or stock saddle.

The various equestrian sports have more in common than they have setting them apart, and riders can—and do—cross freely between them. Many tend to call one sport "home," however, finding that it melds best with their personalities and goals. Each sport generates its own community as well, populated with trainers who specialize in the discipline, boarding barns that organize around it, publications that cover it, and tack shops that cater to its participants.

The vast majority of horses can be trained in either style of riding and can be ridden with either style of equipment. A number of horses can go both ways, adjusting their way of traveling to English and Western styles pretty effortlessly, depending on how they are ridden. Recreational riding is particularly democratic, and you are likely to see pleasure riders sporting a mix-and-match style of clothing and tack that reflects comfort, safety, and availability rather than the exacting standards of either the English or Western show ring.

That said, equestrian sports mostly fall under one main umbrella or the other, although a few pursuits don't fit neatly into either category. (We don't attempt to inventory and describe all equestrian sports here, but instead introduce some of the most popular activities.)

The two camps use different terminology and tack, they prefer different kinds of horses, and their style and dress couldn't be more dissimilar.

The most notable difference, and the one that allows any individual rider's "denomination" to be discerned at a glance, is in the tack. Western riders use a larger saddle with a deep seat and a horn and

A horse in English tack well equipped for the trail: the halter under the bridle provides a safe option for tying his head; boots provide protection from overreaching strides on rocky terrain; waterproof saddle bags are strapped securely to D rings at the front of the forward seat saddle. (Stirrups ideally should be run up the stirrup leathers, however, when the horse is tied so they do not bang the horse's sides or catch on trailer hardware—see photo A on page 256.)

generally use a bridle with no noseband, split reins, and a curb bit (one that acts via leverage on the horse's poll). The tack can be simple and plain or extremely ornate.

Those who ride English use a smaller saddle—flat, without a horn—usually with a snaffle bit (one with direct action on the bars of the horse's mouth), although curb bits are found and used frequently.

English styles of riding vary from the forward position of hunt seat to the deeper seat of dressage or saddle seat, but one commonality is that all English riders can choose whether to post or sit the trot, and most English sports call for both. Western riders use a deep seat almost exclusively, and riders do not post. Western riders also hold their reins in one hand and steer their horses via neck reining (the horse moves away from the light pressure of the rein on the side of his neck); English riders hold one rein in each hand and guide their horses with direct pressure on the rein.

Western riders tend to favor a smaller, stockier animal with a shorter stride and smoother canter, or lope, like a Quarter Horse, Appaloosa, or Paint. English riders tend toward taller, lighter horses, like a Thoroughbred or Saddlebred, and dressage riders strongly prefer a horse with an exaggerated overstep that yields spectacular, but often hard-to-sit, gaits.

English riders generally sport a hunt coat and breeches, although saddle seat showing usually dictates a saddle suit or riding habit (jodhpurs and a long coat—which may be either formal or informal, depending on the time of day—in conservative colors, paired with short jodhpur boots and a derby or top hat), and their horses "walk, trot, and canter." Western riders are typically in blue jeans and a cowboy hat, although dress can be considerably more ornate in certain segments of the show world; Western horses "walk, jog, and lope."

Despite outward differences, the same tenets of good riding apply across all disciplines—a balanced seat; educated, soft hands; and a finely tuned horse who's immediately responsive to any cue and happy in his work.

The English Sports

English is considered the "classical" form of riding: the result of the natural progression of horsemanship over time. As you might expect from the name, the English style of riding originated in Europe, emerging primarily from the military. Horses used in battle needed to be responsive, well trained, and agile. The Olympic equestrian sports—dressage, show jumping, and eventing—are English disciplines with military backgrounds.

One of the innovators in the English discipline was Captain Federico Caprilli, an officer in the Italian cavalry in the late 1800s who taught riders and horses the skills they needed in war. At the time, a deep seat was the only seat that existed. Even over fences, riders stayed seated on the horse, leaning backward, behind the natural arc of the horse's body, as the horse jumped.

Caprilli realized that this posture interfered with a horse's natural balance and movement, so he shortened his riders' stirrups and had them move forward, keeping their weight over the horse's own center of gravity in what became known as the forward seat. When it became apparent that horses were able to perform much better under Caprilli's system, it was adopted for the entire Italian cavalry and, eventually, throughout all of Europe.[31]

Show Hunters, Show Jumpers, and Hunter Equitation

When someone in the English world speaks of a "horse show," the person is usually referring to a competition featuring the three sister sports of hunters, jumpers, and equitation. The classes might look quite similar—in each horses and riders navigate a course of flower-festooned jumps in an arena—but they are judged completely differently.

Originally, hunter classes were intended to judge the horses that were best suited for a day in the hunt field. An ideal hunter had a tidy, efficient, jump; "daisy-cutter" movement on the flat, showing minimal knee action and a smooth, flat stride; and rideability with a calm demeanor. Competitors jumped courses of natural-looking obstacles on grass footing.

In the last several decades, however, "hunters" have evolved into a sport of their own, straying from the original intention of selecting horses for fox hunting. Today's hunters show a jump with tremendous bascule (the arc of the body over the fence) and are expected to be silky smooth and foot-perfect in the ring, right down to the number of strides between fences. The sport requires tremendous precision and attention to detail to be pinned by the judge. Professionals and amateurs generally compete in separate divisions.

The competitors are judged subjectively on the basis of the horse; the rider's job is simply to show the horse to his best advantage. Horses are also shown in an under-saddle class on the flat, and some shows include a "handy hunter" class, where the course is more complicated.

Although a horse's natural ability is ideally enhanced by a thoughtful and skillful rider, many hunter classes are so competitive that tiny disobediences can make the difference between first and tenth place.

While the hunters are about presenting a quiet and beautiful picture, the jumpers are about jumping error-free and fast. Jumper courses are exponentially more complicated than hunter courses, with tight turns, long gallops, and combinations of fences. Instead of the subjective judging found in hunters, jumpers are judged completely objectively. A knocked-down jump rail or a refusal incurs penalty points, as does exceeding the time allowed. The horse and rider with the lowest score win.

Show jumping features the tallest fences in all of horse sports. Most jumper classes feature an initial round with a time limit, followed by a jump-off course. The horse who finishes fastest with the fewest number of jumping penalties is the winner. Jumpers compete in a variety of other classes, including timed "speed" classes; gambler's choice classes, where each fence is assigned a point value, and the rider makes up her own course for the maximum number of points; and puissance classes, a high-jump competition with fences as tall as seven feet.

Hunter equitation borrows some aspects of hunters and some of jumpers. In equitation, or "eq," the courses are like small jumper courses but are ridden as smoothly and fluidly as possible, showing off the skills of the rider. Judging is subjective and is based on the rider's position and effectiveness, not on the horse's performance.

Equitation classes are generally divided by age and are offered at different jump heights. They are highly popular with junior competitors (under age eighteen). The best young riders qualify for regional and national finals each year. Good equitation horses are expected to jump, jump, jump, in a flat reliable manner, and can log hundreds of miles over thousands of fences for a variety of young riders over their careers.

Hunters, jumpers, and equitation are overseen by the United States Equestrian Federation (USEF) and the United States Hunter Jumper Association.

Dressage

It's perhaps the most difficult equestrian sport to explain, yet dressage is the most basic of all the riding endeavors. It's the foundation on which almost everything you do with a horse is based.

Dressage is French for "training," although it traces its roots to Xenophon. The fundamental purpose of dressage is to develop, through standardized progressive training methods, the horse's natural athletic ability and will-ingness to perform, thereby maximizing his potential as a riding horse.[32] Dressage teaches the horse to move with straightness, suppleness, and acceptance of the bit. The horse should be relaxed and soft, moving with forward impulsion, and responsive to the rider's most subtle cues. At the higher levels of training, horses appear to dance, pirouetting and zigzagging across the arena, as light on their feet as ballerinas. Although dressage was born out of a practical need to train military horses to be highly responsive and agile during battle, it owes most of its history to the pursuit of riding as an art.

Dressage is practiced both as an art and as a sport, and purists view the two forms as being slightly different. Classical dressage seeks to adhere to the teachings of the equine masters, always striving for what is truly considered "correct." Competitive dressage, in theory, seeks the same goal, but may be influenced by the fashions and trends of the day and diverge from the truest form of dressage from time to time.

In dressage competition, horses show individually in a regulation-size arena and must perform a set pattern of movements at specific points in the arena, designated by letters. The pattern is called a dressage test. Several tests are offered at each level, and shows usually divide classes for each test by rider age and amateur/professional status. Tests are offered at nine levels in ascending difficulty.

At the more advanced levels, riders compete in musical freestyle classes, where they make up their own patterns of movements and set them to choreographed music. It typically can take a horse five to ten years to reach the highest, or Grand Prix, level of training, although few horses and riders ever reach that level. Many horse and rider combinations work their entire active lives together to achieve competence in mid-level movements. That said, basic dressage training can benefit virtually any horse, of any breed and age, because of its emphasis on achieving the ideal: harmony between horse and rider.

Dressage is governed by the USEF and the United States Dressage Federation.

Eventing

Also called combined training, eventing is the triathlon of the horse world. An event is one competition in three parts—dressage, cross-country jumping, and show jumping. Horse and rider pairs earn penalty marks in each phase, and the lowest cumulative score determines the winner.

The heart of these competitions is the cross-country test, a course of natural-looking, solid obstacles navigated at a gallop across varying terrain. Horses are expected to jump into and out of water, up and down banks, and over ditches.

Originally designed to test the mettle of military horses who were used in battle, the sport today tests the horse's versatility and resilience. An event horse must be focused and rideable in the dressage phase; brave and bold on cross-country; and poised, sound, and precise enough to navigate a tricky show-jumping course.

Each level of eventing asks progressively more of horse and rider. At the lowest level, it's a simple walk-trot-canter dressage test, a cross-country course of inviting obstacles taken at a forward canter, and a straightforward show-jumping course. At the uppermost level, the dressage test contains movements at the third level of competitive dressage, and the jump heights are just under four feet, with cross-country being ridden at a full gallop.

Eventing is the pursuit of versatility, developing a horse who is quite good at three different endeavors, rather than a horse who is excellent at only one.

The various eventing levels offer divisions separated by age (of the rider) and experience (of either horse or rider). The USEF and United States Eventing Association govern eventing.

Saddle Seat

A distinctly American invention, the saddle seat discipline came into being as a way to ride showy gaited horses comfortably for long hours around large Southern plantations. Today it encompasses a wide variety of breeds that show separately, unlike other English sports, where horses of any breed compete in classes together. American Saddlebreds, Tennessee Walking Horses, Arabians, Morgans, National Show Horses, and Freisans are among the breeds frequently shown in saddle seat classes. These classes take place at specialized breed shows and at open shows, which offer a wide variety of classes for different breeds and disciplines.

In saddle seat, the rider adopts a riding position more suited to the high head carriage and movement of the horse. The rider sits farther back, with legs slightly out in front of instead of directly below his hipbones but is still balanced over the horse's center of gravity. The rider also carries his hands higher, due to the horse's head carriage. Saddle seat uses a cut-back saddle, a flat saddle designed to be placed farther back on the horse's back and with a cutaway pommel to allow for the higher withers and neck set.

Horses are shown solely on the flat (without jumps) in group classes and generally are judged on their manners and way of going, although different classes vary in their requirements. Some divisions reward "bigger," flashier movement, while others are geared toward selecting an amiable pleasure mount. In some classes, special shoeing is allowed to alter or enhance the horse's gaits, while others allow only plain shoes. Certain breeds are required to show their specialty gaits, including the running walk for Tennessee Walkers, and the rack and slow-gait for five-gaited Saddlebreds. There are also equitation classes, which are judged primarily on the position and abilities of the rider.

Unlike some of the other classes you might see at English horse shows, saddle seat classes tend to be exciting and raucous, with exuberant applause from the crowd showered on the competitors throughout the class. The high-energy, high-stepping show horses thrive on the cheers and attention.

The USEF oversees most saddle seat classes, although individual breed organizations usually govern the classes at breed-specific shows.

A saddleseat rider appointed for the show ring in long coat and derby hat (her Freisan is equipped with a pelham curb bit and a crupper (a piece of tack that is looped around the horse's tail to keep the saddle securely positioned).

HOOFCARE AND LAMENESS

Going Gaited

Gaited horses and horsemanship are included here as a "discipline" primarily because their aficionados are drawn to the animals first and foremost for their gait rather than for other attributes that might make them suited for a specific activity. However, many specimens of the gaited breeds are extremely versatile and compete in other disciplines discussed in this chapter.

A gaited horse does not trot or pace but instead performs some version of a four-beat intermediate gait (the ground-covering gait between the walk and canter or lope). Most gaited breeds have a specific preferred gait, with other gaits considered undesirable or even penalized in the show ring. All gaited breeds perform some version of the walk, and some are also expected to canter or lope.

Discouraging the trot under saddle (where the smoothness of the four-beat gait is prized) can prevent gaited horses from competing in some open breed competitions that either require or strongly favor the trot. The majority of gaited horses compete in breed-specific shows that offer divisions for a variety of gaited breeds. Gaited horses can be ridden and shown under either Western or English tack, though some breeds have unique tack and attire rooted in the customs of their place of origin.

Only the Paso Fino Horse is recognized by and included as a breed division in the USEF, perhaps because the gaited breeds have developed their own rules, judging systems, and show circuits over time. (The Tennessee Walking Horse was included until the 1980s, when it was removed from the USEF, then known as the American Horse Show Association, or AHSA, rule book due to the breed's struggle with the problem of soring, discussed below).

While the gaits are bred into the gaited horse, some individuals perform them more easily and naturally than do others. A breed-gait expert may need to develop and refine a horse's correct gait (so the horse learns what is expected and does it willingly) and to assist the novice rider in perfecting and maintaining it, through patience, persistence, and long hours in the saddle. "Shortcuts" or gimmicks, such as weighted shoes, long toes, long-shanked bits, action devices, or pain-inducing techniques, should be rejected. Any gaited horse owner or prospective owner should ask questions about a potential trainer's methods, techniques, and aids. If they sound harsh, cruel, or illegal—stay away!

Soring

Soring is practiced on gaited horses to obtain a flashier, more extreme, and unnatural way of going—often rewarded in the show ring—than can be achieved by traditional, humane training methods. Irritating chemicals are applied to a horse's front pasterns to cause pain, or his front hooves are trimmed almost to the quick, then shod tightly in a procedure known as pressure shoeing. To avoid putting weight on his sore front feet, the horse snaps his front legs high off the ground and rocks back onto his hindquarters to produce an exaggerated, or "animated," gait.

In 1970 Congress passed the Horse Protection Act, which outlawed soring and mandated that the U.S. Department of Agriculture set up a process of inspections at Tennessee Walking Horse shows (where soring was originally seen) to detect it. As the practice spread to Racking Horses, Spotted Saddle Horses, and Missouri Fox Trotters, they, too, came under government scrutiny. These inspections continue today, but the level of compliance varies widely and soring remains a problem. Offenders have become adept at concealing soring or teach their horses not to respond to pain during an inspection (often using abusive tactics to do so).

The best way to enjoy your gaited horse to his fullest potential— without inhumane treatment or fear of violating federal law—is to choose a horse who moves as naturally as possible, without gimmicks or pain-inducing practices. Seek advice from owners and trainers who use only humane training practices. If you are bitten by the show "bug," research and choose those show venues where only the sound, natural horse is rewarded.

Competitive Trail Riding

For most of us, trail rides are leisurely affairs, for fun, to enjoy the scenery, or to take a break from work in the ring. But for endurance and competitive trail riders, the trail ride is the sport.

Competitive trail riding (or CTR) is based on the challenge of riding a planned course safely and without overly stressing the horse. The goal is to find the best horse-and-rider combination for trail riding. Horses and riders seek to complete the ride within a certain window of time, and horsemanship judges along the trail evaluate rider skills and safety by watching competitors navigate certain areas of the trail, or by asking them to complete a specific test (such as mounting from the ground or backing their horse). Veterinary judges also assess the horse's soundness and condition during several checks en route. After the ride, the judges determine the placings based on their on-course observations.

Competitive trail rides vary in length. The longest are about fifty or sixty miles and take place over two days. There are three levels (novice, competitive pleasure, and open), with the pace of rides increasing as one moves up the levels. Different weight classes may also be offered at each level.[33]

Endurance riding is competitive trail riding taken to the maximum and suited to elite athletes, both human and equine. It's a race to see which horse-and-rider pair can complete the course first. As in human marathons, only a few teams are generally in the event to win. Most simply want to meet the challenge and finish the race. In fact, the unofficial motto of endurance riding is "To finish is to win."

Veterinary checks are established along the route during which horses are evaluated to be sure they're fit to continue, and are meant to provide mandatory short rest periods. On longer rides, competitors generally have "pit crews" to assist them with caring for the horse and going through the veterinary checks.

A veterinary check is also conducted at the finish of a ride, and any horse who is unduly stressed is disqualified, even though he finished. In addition to an overall winner, a "best conditioned" award is given to the horse who was supremely prepared for the ride and finished in top shape.

Competitors in CTR and endurance can ride with either Western or English tack, although as one progresses up the levels, specialized endurance saddles (similar to a very minimalist Western saddle without a horn, very lightweight, and designed for comfort on long rides) are likely to be used.

Endurance rides are governed by the American Endurance Ride Conference, and CTR by the North American Trail Ride Conference.

Western Sports

The Western style of riding traces its roots to the Spanish conquistadors of the fifteenth and sixteenth centuries, who reintroduced horses to the Americas. Along with the horse, the Spanish brought cattle, and cattle ranching became the lifeblood of the American West. By necessity, Western riding evolved alongside—the deep seat of a Western saddle kept the rider secure while chasing after cattle; using just one hand for the reins left the other free for swinging a lariat, which could be tied around the saddle horn when a calf was roped.

Most people who ride Western today do so for recreation rather than for working cattle. These sports identify strongly with the cowboy persona, however; unlike the more formal English riding attire, the Western "uniform" is blue jeans, a cowboy hat, and cowboy boots.

Western riding also tends to more popular in the western and central portion of the United States, although there are Western riders all over the country. And although any breed of horse can be trained to go Western, the American Quarter Horse, who is almost synonymous with Western riding, overwhelmingly dominates these disciplines.

Reining

The sport of reining is somewhat similar to dressage, although the two pursuits couldn't be more different in outward appearance. Reiners, in their chaps and blue jeans, look nothing like dressage riders in their top hats and swallowtail coats, but both sports show off the skills of different types of horses in their purest form.

Reining competitions judge the abilities of ranch-type horses within the confines of an arena, replicating the talents required on the range or when herding cattle. Like dressage riders, reiners execute a set pattern of movements. There are ten different reining patterns, each containing the same maneuvers. A horse-and-rider pair starts with a score of seventy points, and points can be added or subtracted for each maneuver, depending on the quality of its performance.

The reining maneuvers are all executed at the lope, and include roll-backs (180-degree turns), "large fast" and "small slow" circles, spins (high-speed pivots on the hindquarters, also called turnarounds), lead changes, backing, and the crowd favorite, sliding stops. The performance should be smooth and precise, and the horse's attitude willing and without resistance. It should look easy and effortless, but the horse is completely attuned to the cues of the rider and is intently focused on his work. Unlike dressage horses, reining mounts are ridden mostly on a loose rein.

Reining competitions offer classes based on the horse or rider's age and experience (determined by how much money either has won in competition) as well as a rider's professional/nonprofessional status. Freestyle competition is also offered, where competitors choreograph their own patterns of maneuvers to music.

Reining is a relatively new as an organized sport—the National Reining Horse Association (NRHA), which sets the standards for competition worldwide, wasn't founded until 1966. The sport has experienced tremendous growth in the last decade, and the NRHA now counts more than fourteen thousand members in its ranks and sanctions about 660 competitions around the world.[34]

Reining is governed by the USEF and NRHA.

Cutting

In reining competitions, horses are asked to show off the skills that might make them good cattle horses. In cutting competitions, on the other hand, they have to prove it!

Cutting is the process of separating one cow from a group. Being a herd animal, the cow in question is likely to be rather uncomfortable with this state of affairs, and will do her best to return to the safe surroundings of her herd. It's the job of a cutting horse to prevent this, and a responsibility he handles on his own without assistance from his rider. The horse and cow stare each other down, feint, and whirl like professional basketball players, one trying to slip past, and the other trying to block whatever path is chosen.

A talented cutting horse has what's known as "cow sense"—the innate ability to outmaneuver and outthink his bovine charge in the same way that dogs of herding breeds instinctively know how to round up sheep. Although training fine-tunes the instinct, it's something a horse either has or doesn't have. It can't be learned if it's absent.

Good cutting horses were the prized members of the remudas (strings of ranch horses) that traversed the wide-open ranges whenever herds of cattle needed to be rounded up. Humans being the competitive folk they are, cowboys, of course, wanted to compare their prized cutting mounts to their rivals, and a sport was born.

Today, the best cutting horses strut their stuff in show arenas instead of on the open range. In competition, a rider is given two and a half minutes to allow the horse to demonstrate his cutting prowess. The horse and rider must cut at least two cows (of the rider's choosing) from the herd, including one from deep within the group. This involves the horse quietly and calmly snaking through the herd to the target cow, taking care not to upset or distress any of her herd-mates.

Once a cow has been cut from the herd, the rider must loosen the reins and give the horse his head. Until the rider decides to "quit" the cow, it's the horse's job to hold her away from the herd. The horse is awarded points for his skill, style, speed, and agility, and is penalized if he loses a cow and she returns to the herd.

Four other riders assist the contestant. Two are assigned to keep the main herd from interfering with the competing horse and rider; the other two prevent the cow who has been cut from running to the far end of the arena, away from the herd and the cutting horse.

As in reining, cutting classes are divided by age and experience. The National Cutting Horse Association sanctions competitions in the United States and Canada, and various breed shows and all-around Western shows also feature cutting.

Team Penning

Like cutting, team penning is a competition-ring replication of a situation encountered by actual working cattle horses. In this incarnation, teams of three riders work together to move three cows from a herd to a small pen at the opposite end of the competition arena.

The herd consists of thirty cows, each bearing a number from zero to nine. (Three cows in the group wear each number.) Before the timer starts, a number is called out, designating the cows the riders need to pen. They then have sixty seconds to find and move the designated cows; the team with the fastest time is the winner.

Like many other Western sports, team penning is popular at casual local get-togethers on summer evenings where folks bring their horses, share a bite to eat, and enjoy the camaraderie of some friendly competition. But this sport has become something of a national phenomenon; the United States Team Penning Association, founded in 1993 to provide some consistency and regulation for these scattered local events, now counts more than six thousand registered members and sanctions more than seventy-five pennings per year, attracting as many as a thousand teams at the largest shows.

A note about cutting and team penning: horse folk typically view these activities from the horse's point of view, that is, how skillful and well trained the horse must be to excel and how the horses seem to "take" to them in a way that seems fun for all participants. We do want to ask, however, that the cow's point of view in these events not be overlooked: the cattle deserve humane treatment, too. We urge anyone involved in cutting and team penning activities to make sure the cattle are well treated before, during, and after all practices and competitions.

Barrel Racing

In barrel racing, horses and riders negotiate a cloverleaf pattern around three barrels, and the team with the fastest "trip" wins. It sounds easy until you see it in action: the best barrel-racing horses are so fast that tenths of a second separate the placings.

The three barrels are set up in a triangle and placed a specified distance apart and from the start/finish line. Riders can start with the barrel on their left or the one on their right. The goal is to make the fastest time, without hitting a barrel (knocking a barrel over adds a five-second penalty to the rider's time). Competitions range from local get-togethers to national championships.

A barrel-racing duo on course.

Western Pleasure

This extremely popular discipline is a staple at any local show that offers Western classes and epitomizes what many consider the ideal horse for casual riding.

In Western pleasure, all contestants show as a group in the arena. They walk, jog, and lope on a loose rein in both directions, exhibiting smooth transitions in response to imperceptible cues from the riders. They must also rein-back and halt and are usually asked to show an extended jog as well. The horses are expected to be calm and unflappable, traveling at an easy pace with a low-set head and neck (the head about level with the withers) and exhibiting an alert and pleasant expression. These classes are evaluated subjectively, with the judge selecting the winner and other top placings.

You find Western pleasure classes at open and breed shows, most notably American Quarter Horse Association shows, as the Quarter Horse is considered the archetypal Western pleasure horse. Horse-and-rider pairs accumulate points by virtue of their placings at local shows, thereby qualifying for prestigious championship shows for their breeds.

For example, Quarter Horse riders qualify their mounts via AQHA-sanctioned shows, earning the right to compete at the AQHA World Championship Show, the world's largest and richest championship horse show, with more than $1.6 million offered in prizes and awards.[35]

Driving

As a modern-day sport, driving is dwarfed in size by the more popular disciplines, such as hunter/jumpers and reining, but it's a thriving part of equestrian culture that is gaining converts. While all the English riding sports maintain a strong sense of tradition, driving seems almost frozen in time. The carriages look as if they've just been driven out of the carriage house on a nineteenth-century English estate. The drivers might be decked out in top hats and swallowtail coats (for the gentlemen) or long skirts and hats with veils (for the ladies), with a lap robe tucked around them, harkening back to the sport's original trappings.

Driving can seem like something of a mystery to other equestrians. Since the sport is smaller in scope, it's not something with which many come in casual contact. It has its own set of equipment and terminology that can seem completely foreign, even to otherwise-experienced horse people. But there's also a level of intrigue—those of us who often have trouble managing to get one horse to do as we ask, even with all of the cues at a rider's disposal, are amazed at the feats a driver can coax from an entire team of horses.

In the show ring, classes generally fall into three categories: working (where the abilities of the horse are the primary focus); reinmanship (judged mostly on the skills of the driver); and turnout classes (where the quality and authenticity of the vehicle, harness, and dress are judged).

A lady competitor in a manicured show ring drives a pony put to a two-wheeled cart.

Many breed shows, especially those for ponies, offer driving classes. Open shows are run under the rules of the American Driving Society, but breed show classes may differ, depending on the sanctioning breed association.

Combined Driving

Imagine what eventing would be like with a horse and carriage instead of a horse and rider, and you've got a good sense of what's involved in the sport of combined driving.

Just like eventing, combined driving has three phases, and although the execution can differ from the ridden sport (horses hitched to carriages can't jump!), the aim of each phase is similar.

The dressage is exactly like its ridden counterpart, except that it is conducted in a larger arena, and the driver is allowed to use his voice as an aid. Horses show only at the walk and trot but demonstrate extended and collected gaits at the more advanced levels. Judges look for obedience, impulsion, and willingness as well as accuracy of the movements. The driver and horse (or horses) are also judged on their turnout and appearance.

The second phase is what's known as the marathon—it's an endurance test made up of either three or five sections, depending on the level of competition, where the last section is essentially a cross-country course with "hazards" instead of jumps. The hazards look like mazes and are made of natural materials, such as logs and brush, and incorporate water crossings and changes in terrain. Each hazard has a series of gates the carriage must pass through in a certain order, and the idea is to navigate the hazard as quickly as possible.

The other sections of the marathon, which precede the hazards portion of the phase, require the horse and driver to cover a certain distance within an optimal time and at a specified gait. Veterinary checks are conducted to be sure that horses are fit to continue to the next phase.

The final phase is the cones, which replicates the show-jumping portion on an event. Instead of a course of jumps, drivers must navigate between pairs of cones with balls sitting atop them. Knocking off a ball (or knocking over a cone itself) is the equivalent of knocking down a rail in show jumping.

Combined driving is offered at several levels—training, preliminary, intermediate, and advanced—and each level offers divisions for horses and ponies as well as for teams (singles, pairs, or higher multiples).

The sport is quite exciting to watch, especially the marathon phase, where carriages pulled by up to four horses blast through the hazards at high speed, making it look easy!

Combined driving is an international sport, with world championships offered every other year, and is part of the World Equestrian Games. At the national level, the sport is overseen by the American Driving Society.

A Final Word

Each equestrian discipline has its challenges, its traditions, and its advocates. None is inherently better, from the horse's perspective, than another. Each has its model horsemen, and each has its abusive followers. Which one you choose is not anywhere near as important as finding the right one for you. Work with instructors and ride a variety of horses. Find one who shows potential—or has experience—in the discipline(s) you want to pursue so your combined talents are well matched. Then, when you do bring a horse into your life, you will have the best chance of making him your partner and companion for life.

CHAPTER 7

Breeds

Breeds Versus Registries

FROM THE TINIEST SHETLAND TO THE MOST mammoth Percheron, all horses belong to the same species, *Equus caballus*. Within the species, however, the variation among breeds is tremendous: different sizes, shapes, colors, and conformation, and differences in aptitudes and talents to match. Within each breed there are significant variations (a registered Thoroughbred, for example, can be fourteen hands tall or seventeen hands tall, since size is not a distinguishing characteristic of this breed).

Before we look at common breeds, however, let's clarify the distinction between a breed and a registry. Breeds are basically an arbitrary assortment of desirable (from a human point of view) characteristics, including coat color (e.g., buckskin or palomino); size (consider the Shetland pony); and talents or conformation (such as the "inspected" Warmblood breeds, which are evaluated on their jumping ability, among other qualities). Registries are organizations that seek to perpetuate and improve a breed. In the United States, they are nongovernmental organizations. A registry may sponsor horse shows, maintain a record of registered animals, inspect possible candidates for inclusion in the registry, and charge fees for registering eligible animals.

Some breeds owe their existence to geography. Perhaps the horses lived on an island or were confined by rivers or mountain ranges—barriers that limited their gene pool as they evolved to best survive in their native habitats, leading to very distinctive breeds that came about naturally. Other breeds are primarily human constructs, the result of planned and selective breeding to produce a specific type of horse that excels at a particular job. In most cases, a combination of natural and artificial selection has produced the breeds we're familiar with today.

Every horse is an individual, of course. Some defy their breed's reputations, exhibiting a personality or ability that isn't the norm (for better or worse). But "breed" parlance is how many horses are advertised, categorized, and discussed in the horse world. It provides a good starting point in finding a horse of your own who has the temperament and skills you find attractive and avoiding those you find less desirable.

How Breeds Vary

Most of us can tell a Clydesdale (thanks to a famous brewery) from an Appaloosa, but can you discern a Standardbred from a Thoroughbred, or a breeding stock Paint from a Quarter Horse?

Sometimes the differences are quite minor and only visible to the very experienced eye. Many breeds of horses have ancestors in common,

The Belgian is a European draft breed.

as one breed might have been purposely infused with the blood of another to refine or improve it. For example, a specific Trakehner might count many Thoroughbreds among his ancestors and thus might look an awful lot like a Thoroughbred!

One of the more obvious ways in which breeds differ is size. On one end of the spectrum are miniature horses and the pony breeds; at the other, the heavy draft breeds; and in between lie the light riding horse breeds.

Many pony breeds originated in very harsh, inhospitable environments. Natural selection ensured that the native equines stayed small as they eked out an existence where larger horses likely wouldn't have been able to find enough food to survive. (This also explains why many modern-day ponies seem to stay fat on air alone.)

The influence of human hands is prevalent in pony breeds as well—ponies were in demand to work in coal mines, navigating low-ceilinged tunnels that would have been impossible for full-sized horses. And, as in present times, quality ponies have always been sought for children's mounts.

The draft breeds, on the other hand, were selectively bred to increase their size, enabling them to pull heavier loads and be more effective workhorses.

In addition to size, other physical attributes tend to differentiate the various breeds. Each breed has a "type," an ideal specimen that breeders seek to produce, depending on the horse's typical use. For example, breeds such as the Saddlebred and Morgan have a very upright head and neck carriage: this is a desired trait and is part of the ideal picture for that breed. Quarter Horses and Paints, on the other hand, are expected to have a low-set neck.

While size and type might be the most noticeable attributes of a breed, something else quickly becomes apparent as soon as you start working with a particular horse—temperament. The horse's attitude, demeanor, and trainability are often a function of breed. As horses are selectively bred for generations to fulfill a particular job, traits applicable to that job become a hallmark of the breed. These traits can be positive or negative, depending on the owner's expectations and the role the animal is expected to fill.

Thoroughbreds, for example, are often found to be "hotter" (more excitable) than Quarter Horses or draft breeds, which are known for their very docile, placid natures. Appaloosas are sometimes thought to be quite stubborn, while Morgans are frequently touted for their work ethic.

But what one owner might see as a detriment, another may find attractive. Thoroughbreds excel as event horses because of their boundless energy, and many Appaloosa owners say their horses' stubborn streaks are just a sign of their exceptional intelligence. Devotees of a breed often find their personality foibles as endearing as their strengths.

Finally, different breeds show marked variations in their movement. Compare the high-stepping, knee-snapping trot of the Saddlebred with the smooth jog of the Quarter Horse and the drive-from-behind move-ment of the Hanovarian. It's the same two-beat diagonal gait in all three horses, but it looks vastly different, depending on the breed. Some breeds also have specialized gaits of their own—the Tennessee Walker and Missouri Fox Trotter, for example, as discussed in chapter 6.

Overview of Common Breeds

Arabian

The oldest known breed of riding horse, the Arabian's roots can be traced back thirty-five hundred years to the deserts of the Middle East, where Bedouin nomads carefully protected and tended a breed of horse that was thought to have been a gift from Allah. Known for being fast, hardy, and intelligent, these treasured horses, bred carefully to keep the lines pure, were eventually imported to Europe and elsewhere to improve and refine other breeds. Today, just about every breed of light riding horse has been influenced by Arabian blood, primarily through the Thoroughbred.

Arabians are instantly recognizable by virtue of their delicate, dished faces and wide, expressive eyes. They have graceful, arched necks and long, flowing manes and tails that are never "pulled" (shortened by hand). Arabians are on the small side, usually between fourteen and sixteen hands, and they are unique among horses in that they have one fewer rib and three fewer vertebrae than other breeds.

Although they're prized for their beauty, they are also formidable athletes. Their toughness was established through centuries of survival in the harsh desert. The Arabian horse has found a devoted following among trail and endurance riders who want sure-footed mounts with the energy to go all day long.

In the show arena, you'll be hard-pressed to find a discipline in which the Arabian does *not* compete—pleasure, trail, dressage, hunter, costume, driving, saddle seat—versatility is the breed's middle name. Arabians are ridden both English and Western and compete in both Arabian-only and open shows.

The Arabian Horse Association, founded in 1908, is the official registry for the breed. It has forty-six thousand members, and currently counts about six hundred thousand full-blooded Arabians, four hundred thousand half-Arabians, and ten thousand Anglo-Arabians (Arabian/ Thoroughbred crosses) among its registrants.[36]

AMY KOLZOW

The AQHA registers Appendix Quarter Horses, horses with one registered Quarter Horse and one registered Thoroughbred as parents.

American Quarter Horse

The Quarter Horse is, by far, the most popular breed in the United States, with more than three million registered with the American Quarter Horse Association (AQHA).[37]

The Quarter Horse is considered the first modern breed native to this country, descending from the Arabians and Barbs brought to the New World by the Spanish conquistadors and imported English horses known as Galloways (the same stock from which the Thoroughbred later developed). These crosses produced a stout, muscular horse who proved very fast over short distances and came to be known as a "quarter-miler," or Quarter Horse. By the mid-1600s, Quarter Horse racing was a common and popular pursuit in the colonies.[38]

As pioneers pushed westward, the hard-working Quarter Horses came with them. The breed's speed and agility made these horses adept at working cattle; since Thoroughbreds and longer-distance races were beginning to eclipse the quarter-mile races in popularity, the ranch and open range gave the Quarter Horse a new opportunity to shine. Today, Quarter Horses are the breed of choice for ranch and cattle work.

Modern Quarter Horses are usually between fifteen and sixteen hands tall and are typically broad, chunky horses with very muscular hindquarters. They are extremely popular in all of the Western disciplines and continue to be raced today, generally against other Quarter Horses. Top racers can reach speeds of fifty-five miles per hour for short distances. Quarter Horses are perhaps most common as pleasure horses. They are known for their easygoing and well-mannered temperament and are easy keepers (able to maintain their weight on a minimum of feed), making them excellent family and children's horses.

Founded in 1940, the AQHA is the official registry of the Quarter Horse. The organization also registers what are known as Appendix Quarter Horses, those with one registered Quarter Horse and one Jockey Club-registered Thoroughbred for parents.[39]

American Saddlebred

In the days when horses were the primary mode of transportation, they had to fill many roles. They needed to be comfortable to ride over very long distances; strong and sturdy enough to pull a cart or buggy; and attractive and fancy enough to take a well-dressed rider or driver to church on Sundays. The American Saddlebred was developed to fit that bill.

His early predecessor was the Narragansett Pacer, an easy-riding horse developed from imported English Galloways and Irish Hobbies. The Narragansetts were eventually crossed with the early imported Thoroughbreds, leading to a breed that was simply known as the American Horse.

These horses had the Thoroughbred's size and good looks but retained the smooth gaits of the Narragansetts. They were equally at home being ridden, pulling a plow, or trotting smartly into town with a carriage and were known for being strong, willing, and even-tempered.

As settlers pushed west, these horses came along, and Kentucky became a breeding center, leading to the moniker Kentucky Saddler, and eventually, Saddlebred. They served with distinction in both armies during the Civil War and were the mount of choice for high-ranking officers. Robert E. Lee's Traveler, Ulysses S. Grant's Cincinnati, and William T. Sherman's Lexington were all Saddlebred-type horses.[40]

Typically, Saddlebreds stand between fifteen and sixteen hands high. Their most distinguishing characteristics are their high-set necks, which rise gracefully from prominent withers, giving the breed a regal air, and their lofty and animated gaits, performed with panache and aplomb. Saddlebreds are typically ridden and shown saddle-seat style, although they can also go Western, dressage, or hunt-seat style.

Saddlebreds perform two man-made gaits—the slow gait and the rack—in addition to the traditional walk, trot, and canter. The slow gait is like the walk in that both are four-beat, lateral gaits, and the sequence of footfalls is the same for both. But the slow gait is very collected and restrained, executed slowly and precisely.

The rack is also a lateral, four-beat gait, but is performed with high-stepping action and at great speed. It is smooth to ride and very animated and is typically performed to loud applause in the show ring.

Although the Saddlebred is best known as a gaited show horse, this talented breed can be seen in all disciplines. Saddlebreds are good jumpers, easy to drive, and can excel in dressage.

The official breed registry for Saddlebreds is the American Saddlebred Horse Association, founded in 1891.

The Gaited Breeds

A 2007 *Equus* magazine article listed twenty-six unique gaited breeds found in North and South America, and many more are found around the globe. Here are a few of the more popular North American breeds.

Tennessee Walking Horse

One of the best known and most ubiquitous of the gaited horses in North America, the Tennessee Walking Horse has also been exported for many years across Europe and as far away as the Middle East. The breed was founded in middle Tennessee as a cross of Narragansett and Canadian

Pacer, Standardbred, Thoroughbred, Morgan, and American Saddlebred stock. The Walker was developed for use on southern plantations, providing overseers with an extremely comfortable, hardy mount who could cover many miles without tiring himself or his rider. In his signature gait, the running walk (an extension of the flat walk in both stride and speed), the Walker can travel eight to twelve miles per hour and nods his neck and head in rhythm with his gait.

Several famous movie horses were Tennessee Walking Horses, including Roy Rogers' Trigger and Gene Autry's Champion. The breed is a popular mount of pack guides, park rangers, mounted police, and riding stable strings.

The Tennessee Walking Horse Breeders' and Exhibitors' Association is the breed registry, established in 1935. There are more than 430,000 registered Tennessee Walking Horses throughout the world, and it is the second-fastest-growing breed in the United States.

Other related breeds that have emerged include the Racking Horse, whose four-beat rack is often called a "single-foot" because only one foot strikes the ground at a time, and the Spotted Saddle Horse, which was developed by crossing Spanish-type pinto horses with gaited breeds (including the Walking Horse) to produce a colorful horse that is smooth-gaited.

Rocky Mountain Horse

According to the Rocky Mountain Horse Association (RMHA), around the turn of the twentieth century, a gaited stallion was brought from the Rocky Mountain region of the United States to the foothills of eastern Kentucky and was referred to by the locals as "the Rocky Mountain Horse." Although little is known of this foundation stallion's background, legend has it he was chocolate-colored with a flaxen mane and tail and had a superior gait, traits shared by many of the breed's specimens today.

The breed is characterized by a medium-size horse of gentle temperament, with an evenly timed, smooth four-beat gait similar to a rack: the Rocky Mountain Pleasure Gait. This gait, which made this breed popular on the farms and in the foothills of the Appalachian Mountains, is enjoyed today by trail riders and show ring exhibitors nationwide. In 1986 the RMHA established the breed registry and formed a panel of inspectors to examine all Rocky Mountain Horses before breeding for evidence of breed characteristics.

Missouri Fox Trotting Horse

The Missouri Fox Trotting Horse was developed in the nineteenth century in the Ozark foothills by pioneers who realized that a horse with a smooth four-beat gait would be ideal for the rocky, forested land. Farmers selectively bred for a gliding gait by blending American Saddlebred, Standardbred, and Tennessee Walker stock with that of Morgans, Thoroughbreds, and Arabians.

The horse appears to walk with his front legs and trot with his hind legs. But because the gait has a four-beat motion rather than a two-beat trot, it's easy to sit and can be maintained for long periods, reaching speeds of up to ten miles per hour. The "Fox Trotter" also performs the flat-foot walk and canter.

Recognized in 1958 the Missouri Fox Trotting Horse Breeders' Association (MFTHBA) claims more than fifty-two thousand registered horses in North America and Europe.

Paso Fino

The Paso Fino has a history in the Americas dating back five centuries. A blend of the Barb, Spanish Jennet, and Andalusian, the Paso Fino was bred by Spanish land owners in Puerto Rico and Colombia for use on their plantations, due to his endurance and comfortable gait. The Paso Fino began to be imported to the United States in the 1950s, and while the Puerto Rican and Columbian strains are still bred individually to retain their purity, they are also crossbred to capture the best of both.

The gait of the Paso Fino horse is a natural, evenly spaced, four-beat lateral gait in which each foot hits the ground independently, creating a rapid, consistent rhythm and exceptional comfort for the rider. It is performed at three speeds, the Classic Fino, Paso Corto, and Paso Largo, with varying degrees of collection, speed, and extension.

The Paso Fino Horse Association registers horses in the United States and serves as the breed's horse show-regulating body.

Peruvian (Paso) Horse

The Peruvian Horse can trace its origins to the horses brought to Peru by the Spanish conquistadors. The Peruvian was bred for gait, conformation, and temperament, resulting in a strong, hardy animal that enabled overseers to traverse their vast plantations.

In addition to its smooth gait, the Peruvian is best known for two unique breed characteristics—brilliant action combined with "termino," an outward rolling of the front legs and "brio," an attitude of arrogance, exuberance, and spirit. The signature gaits are the paso llano, a movement and footfall close to that of the rack, and the sobreandando, a faster, slightly more lateral gait.

The North American Peruvian Horse Association was formed in 2006, the result of a merger of the breed's two main U.S. registries.

Morgan

In 1789 a dark bay colt was born in West Springfield, Massachusetts. Over the next thirty-two years, this stout little horse was undefeated in races under saddle and in harness, as well as in pulling contests, and became a prolific and popular sire. The horse's name was Figure, but he was better known by the name of his owner, Justin Morgan.[41]

Although his origins are somewhat of a mystery, Figure became the foundation sire for the Morgan breed, stamping his get with his best qualities.

The human Justin Morgan was a Vermont schoolteacher who received Figure as a yearling as partial payment for a debt. The horse was small—no taller than fourteen hands—but muscular and strong and had impressive gaits. Figure was put to work clearing land in Vermont's rolling hills and became something of a local legend for his ability to pull out tree stumps and haul logs. He could outrun and outpull any other horse in the area.

Figure worked hard his entire life and was also used as a riding and driving horse. He was not only incredibly strong and blessed with great stamina, but he had a wonderful and gentle disposition as well. He was in high demand as a sire, and three of his famous sons—Bulrush, Sherman, and Woodbury—became influential sires within the breed.

Morgan horses became very popular in New England and northern New York. They worked on farms, pulled stagecoaches, and were used in the cavalry in the Civil War (primarily on the Union side) with great distinction. Morgans also had great influence on a number of other breeds, including the Saddlebred, Standardbred, and Tennessee Walker.

Today's Morgans generally stand between 14.1 and 15.2 hands tall. They have a high-set neck; a beautiful and distinctive head with small, wide-set ears and expressive eyes; a short, strong back; and muscular hindquarters. They are known for being very sound and easy keepers. They also sport long, thick manes and tails that are traditionally left untrimmed and unpulled.

Morgans are ridden saddle seat, English, and Western, and also driven, and can be seen competing in just about every discipline. The versatility that was Figure's hallmark is still a part of the breed today, as is his quiet, steady disposition.

The American Morgan Horse Association, founded in 1909, is the official registry of the breed, and currently counts about 108,000 registered Morgans.[42]

Thoroughbred

For more than three centuries, the Thoroughbred breed has been synonymous with horse racing. In the early 1700s, three Arabian stallions were brought to England, where racing was already a flourishing pastime, to cross with native stock in the hope of producing superior running horses. Those three foundation stallions were the Byerley Turk, the Darley Arabian, and the Godolphin Arabian.

BARBARA LIVINGSTON

The Thoroughbred Classics winner and stallion Hansel.

From those three sires descended a breed that was blessed with speed over long distances, strength, and endurance. The first Thoroughbred was imported to the United States in 1730, and by 1800, more than three hundred had crossed the Atlantic to be used for breeding and racing here.

The Thoroughbred breed is notable for the meticulous record-keeping that has accompanied its ascent. Today's Thoroughbreds trace their ancestry back through dozens of generations, all the way to the original three foundation sires. The official Thoroughbred registry in the United States is the Jockey Club, which was founded in 1894.[43]

Not only did Thoroughbreds revolutionize horse racing, they had tremendous impact on other breeds as well. The American Quarter Horse, Standardbred, Morgan, and American Saddlebred all derive in part from the Thoroughbred, and many of the European warmblood breeds have also benefited from an infusion of Thoroughbred blood.

Known for their tremendous heart and regal presence (often romantically called the "look of eagles"), Thoroughbreds are built to run. They

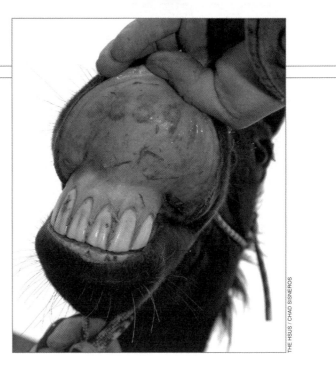

All registered Thoroughbreds who make their way to the racetrack are tattooed in order to document their identities.

sport powerful hindquarters that propel them at speeds of up to forty miles per hour. They are a light and lean breed, with long, slender legs and necks. The average Thoroughbred stands about sixteen hands tall.[44]

Thoroughbreds have also excelled as sport horses. The racing industry has little use for most Thoroughbreds after their racing careers are over, however, and racehorse trainers offer Thoroughbreds to local show horse trainers at low prices. Although a Thoroughbred with race training can be challenging for a novice to ride, many trainers have had success retraining former racehorses with good minds for intermediate riders and better. Thoroughbreds have dominated eventing for decades, thanks to their ground-covering gallop and bravery, and have also found success as show hunters, jumpers, dressage horses, polo ponies, fox hunters, steeplechasers, and even endurance horses. Many Thoroughbreds transition into sport horse careers if they aren't suited to racing, but some are bred specifically for sport and never set hoof on a racetrack.

The Jockey Club counts about thirty-four thousand foals born each year. Unlike most other registries, it only accepts horses who have been conceived via live cover (rather than through artificial insemination as well).

The Warmblood Breeds

When widespread use of the internal combustion engine began to make horses obsolete for work and transportation in the early part of the twentieth century, breeding began to take on a new focus—producing horses for recreation and sport. Nowhere was this transition more effective than in Europe, where horses have been carefully bred for centuries, often at royal or state-sponsored studs. These breeders began to adapt the riding, carriage, and cavalry horses they had previously developed to the new reality of the horse world.

The warmblood breeds are named for their countries or regions of origin. Some of the common warmblood breeds include the Dutch Warmblood (Holland), Hanoverian (from the Hanover region of Germany), Danish Warmblood (Denmark), Swedish Warmblood (Sweden), Selle Français (France), Trakehner (from the East Prussian town of Trakehnen), Polish Warmblood (Poland), Holsteiner (from the Schleswig-Holstein region of Germany), and Oldenburg (Germany).

The term "warmblood" was coined to reflect the fact that most of these breeds historically were mixtures of "hot-blooded" horses (Arabians and Thoroughbreds) and "cold bloods" (coach or carriage horses)—although it refers to temperament, not actual genetics. Most warmblood breeds have open studbooks: a horse of any breed can be introduced to the gene pool as long as he meets the strict criteria established for the breed. New blood is regularly infused into the breed to refine and improve it.

The warmblood registries all rely on a system of inspections to approve their breeding stock. The process differs from registry to registry, and many offer various levels of approvals. In general the process includes having judges inspect stallions and broodmares to see if they meet the ideal standard for the registry. Stallions are usually performance-tested as well, to ensure their abilities match their looks.

Due to decades of careful breeding to stringent standards, warmbloods have come to excel as sport horses and now dominate the upper levels of the three Olympic sports. Each warmblood breed has an American registry, usually affiliated with the registry in the horse's home country.

A Welsh Section B stallion being judged "on the line" (i.e., in the conformation class show ring).

Welsh Ponies and Cobs

Perhaps the best-known purebred ponies are the various types of Welsh ponies. Welsh ponies and cobs are divided into four types, corresponding with their respective sections of the Welsh Pony and Cob Studbook and their heights: section A, the Welsh Mountain Pony (not to exceed 12.2 hands in height); section B, the Welsh Pony (not to exceed 14.2 hands); section C, the Welsh Pony of Cob Type (not to exceed 13.2 hands); and section D, the Welsh Cob (13.2 hands and taller).

The Welsh Mountain Pony is considered the basis for all of the types. These tiny, hardy, beautiful ponies have roamed the harsh hillsides of Wales for centuries. The wild bands of ponies were influenced by the blood of other breeds, particularly the Arabian, which was brought to Wales by the Romans, and later, the Thoroughbred and the Hackney.

But the ponies remained of a distinctive type that is still evident today. Their hardiness is legendary, as is their beauty. Their heads show the Arabian influence, often having a slightly dished profile. They are natural jumpers and are also often used for driving. Known for their intelligence and excellent temperament, they have been a popular children's mount in the United Kingdom for generations.

Welsh ponies and cobs are very versatile and can be found competing in just about every discipline.

How Breed Factors into Buying

The breeds just described represent a sampling of the amazingly diverse array of breeds in this country and around the world. Some, like the Quarter Horse, number in the millions; others may be represented by just a handful of horses in a remote corner of the world.

Breed should not usually be the deciding factor in a horse purchase. Unless your goal is to participate in a breed-specific discipline, a certain breed is not usually necessary. Nor is it required that a horse be of *any* breed—there are plenty of grade horses (those of undetermined or nonspecific origin) who are wonderful mounts. But a horse's breed can give you some insight into who he is, where he came from, and where he might be going.

The Past and the Future

Buying a horse of known breeding (i.e., that the *pedigree* is known, not just the breed) may be a little like having a crystal ball that allows you to see into both the horse's past and his future. The picture is fuzzy, but you'll sometimes be able to get some useful hints.

Meticulous record-keeping is the mainstay of any breed registry. It's what allows a sire or dam's progeny, as well as all of their competitive accomplishments, to be tracked and recorded. Breed registries keep lists of leading sires, as determined by points or prize money earned in competition, to determine which horses are fathering the next generation of winners. Even if a horse has never jumped a jump or run a race, looking at his pedigree can tell you a bit about what he's capable of, if the odds are in your favor.

An example of the vagaries of breed popularity, the Gypsy Vanner (so named for the gypsies who typically use the stocky piebald animals to pull their vans, or wagons), being shown here in dressage, is highly prized in the United States despite his remarkable similarity to the colored, draft-type "tinkers' cobs" available for a song in Great Britain.

Horses are more than the sum of their accomplishments, however. A particular mare may be reputed to have an extraordinarily kind temperament or a stallion may be known for producing sons and daughters of remarkable soundness. That information can sometimes be discerned from a pedigree as well. (To reaffirm: many horses of unknown breeding have made wonderful partners and companions as well.)

Suitability for a Discipline

Every breed has an ideal type, the theoretical "perfect horse." The type differs from breed to breed. Small variances in conformation can have a great effect on how a horse moves, how fast he runs, how high he jumps, and how sound he stays throughout his lifetime.

Even within a breed, there can be variations in the ideal type. A Quarter Horse intended for racing looks quite different from one bred for Western pleasure riding, for example.

Most breeds are built to do a certain job, designed over hundreds of years of selective breeding. This can work either for you or against you as someone looking for a new horse. You're stacking the deck in your favor if you choose a horse who was designed to do the kind of job you want her to do. If you purchase a Thoroughbred as an event prospect, you already know the horse is bred to have an efficient gallop and high endurance, qualities that will serve you well when traveling cross-country. If you want to show a gaited horse, you know that a Paso Fino or an Icelandic horse has the gaits to fit the bill.

While some individual horses can excel in disciplines unusual for their breed, they are the exception rather than the rule. That Morgan you love *might* be able to jump well enough to be a show hunter, but the odds aren't in your favor, and you might be setting both yourself and the horse up for a lot of frustration by asking him to do something he wasn't designed to do.

The Importance of the Individual

"A good horse is never a bad breed." The message of this old horseman's saying is that, if the horse standing in front of you is perfect for what you want to do, she *is* the right horse, regardless of breed.

Do you like her personality? Does her temperament match the demands of her intended career? Is the price right? Is she physically suited for the discipline you want to pursue? Is she healthy and sound? If so, it shouldn't matter if she's a different breed from the one you had in mind, or a strange combination of several breeds. Don't let preconceived notions or ignorance about a breed (called breed prejudice) close your mind to a great match.

Breed designation is not the be-all and end-all, and it offers no guarantees. There is wide variation within any breed, genetics being what they are. Even though most grandchildren of the great

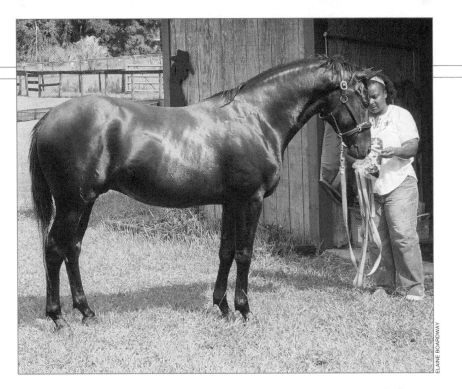

Not all breeders walk in lockstep with a specific registry or strive to meet a show ring standard. P. Wynn Norman (above), breeder of Theodore O'Connor (page 251), has an unconventional approach to breeding an athletic, competitive horse. Kevlar is "Teddy's" full brother: both are one-eighth Arabian, one-eighth Shetland Pony, and seven-eighths Thoroughbred. Although not conformationally perfect, Kevlar proves that Teddy was not an "accident" but part of a well thought out plan.

Thoroughbred racehorse Secretariat are accomplished athletes, a few might be pony-size and unable to outrun the hay delivery man.

And while we often speak of a breed's common traits in a positive light, there are plentiful breed prejudices as well. All Arabians are "crazy"; Thoroughbreds are hot and spooky; warmbloods are "dumbbloods"; Saddlebreds "can't do dressage." There's often a kernel of truth in those biases, but it's unfair and unrealistic to condemn an entire breed. Horses are individuals: for every breed prejudice, there are many, many individuals who prove them wrong. An educated rider is able to look beyond what a breed is "supposed" to be, and instead see the horse who is actually there.

Papers and Registries

One segment of the horse-oriented human population believes there's a cachet to having a horse "with papers." In some locales, highly organized breed associations offer large, frequent, and well-run shows that are "the best game in town" for show competitors, particularly for young riders. For such folks, breed-registry papers are virtually required for their horses to compete locally, since these shows are open only to their registered horses. However, if you don't plan to breed your horse or participate in these breed shows, your horse's pedigree and registration papers may not be terribly important to you. Most sports don't have any breed restrictions or require that horses be registered with a breed organization.

Most breeds have one official registry that has been in existence for decades, even a century or more. Examples include the American Quarter Horse Association and the Jockey Club. Such organizations generally accept registrations for any foals from two registered parents.

Other registries accept horses of different breeds, but most of have extremely stringent selection criteria. Unfortunately, anyone can "invent" a breed, create a registry, and hand out registration papers (for a fee, of course) to anyone who meets certain criteria. The fact that a horse has papers or a registration certificate from an organization doesn't mean the documents are worth much more than they're printed on—whether or not being "registered" is anything to be proud of depends on the registry in question.

CHAPTER **8**

Housing

HAVE YOU EVER HAD THE MISFORTUNE OF enduring a truly awful living situation? Perhaps you lived in a tiny, windowless basement apartment with a cockroach problem. Or maybe you had a horrible roommate who made any time spent at home miserable. Now imagine you had no way to extricate yourself from that living arrangement and you were stuck there twenty-four hours a day, seven days a week, 365 days a year. That would be your horse's predicament if he is kept at a sub-par facility.

Horses thrive out in a field and in good company.

Where and how your horse lives affects not only his physical health, but his mental health as well, and is perhaps the single biggest influence on his day-to-day life. The importance of where you keep your horse cannot be underestimated.

At the same time, however, it's important to remember that what a horse truly *needs* is minimal. Most horses are perfectly happy and healthy out in a field with good grass; clear, cool water; and a run-in shed. But most horse owners have other considerations as well—cost of board, amenities, distance from home or work, the cost of purchasing property, and so on.

The trick is to find a balance between what will keep the horse healthy and happy and what suits the owner's wants and needs. Although everyone's circumstances are slightly different, the basic requirements are pretty universal. Your horse needs housing, whether a run-in shed or a stall; he needs turnout; he needs friends, equine or otherwise; he needs adequate, good-quality food; and fresh water. You need a place to ride him.

Shelter

Horses are designed to live outside. Mother Nature has equipped them well, giving them thick furry coats in wintertime and long tails to whisk flies away in the summertime.

If a horse is in good health and is acclimated to the local weather, he doesn't *need* to be kept in a stall, and many horses actually prefer not to be. A run-in shed gives him the opportunity to get out of the bitter wind, driving rain, or brutal heat—although you're likely to find him out in the elements a good portion of the time anyway.

Most horses are perfectly happy with that living arrangement, but there are some who might not thrive in such a situation. A horse who has just recently been moved from a warm climate to a cold one likely won't fare well if pasture-kept his first winter, for example—he won't have had a chance to adapt to his new surroundings and won't grow a thick enough winter coat to keep warm. Special care must be taken with older horses as well because they can become chilled or over-heated more easily than their younger counterparts. Even horses used to living outside can become more susceptible to the elements as they age. Keep a close eye on any elderly residents of your pastures, especially in the event of a cold rain or biting wind.

Pasture dynamics also play a role. Although a given run-in shed might be large enough to accommodate several horses, if you have one particularly dominant horse in the group, you're likely to find him in the run-in and the other horses standing dejectedly outside.

A run-in should be large enough to allow all the horses in a group to stand inside comfortably, without feeling crowded and should also allow them to "escape" from it easily if a fight breaks out. Most are built as three-sided enclosures that face south to take advantage of warming

Lightweight blankets, or sheets, can keep a horse cleaner, making grooming less of a chore.
The fit and weather-appropriate weight of the blanket should be checked daily.

sunshine in the colder months. The open construction allows horses to enter and leave easily, thus minimizing disagreements, and provides for plenty of air circulation to keep the inside cool in summertime. In very hot climates, simple shelters that consist of only a roof might be used, just to provide shade.

One method of helping horses keep warm and dry in inclement weather is to blanket them. Although a normal, healthy horse who is acclimated to his surroundings and grows a sufficiently thick coat doesn't usually *need* to be blanketed, some owners do choose to blanket their charges. It helps keep them cleaner, making grooming less of a chore in the muddy months. A blanketed horse also grows less of a coat, which is helpful if the horse stays in work during the winter—he won't get so sweaty and won't take so long to cool down properly after a ride (but he will need to be kept blanketed throughout the winter). Blanketing is a necessity if an owner chooses to clip the horse's winter coat, as the animal will need a replacement for his own natural insulation.

If you do need to blanket your horse, make sure you have an assortment of clothing in varying weights—a light sheet for chilly days and a heavy blanket for bitterly cold ones. Think of the variety of coats and jackets in your own closet; if your climate is such that you need an array of outerwear, your horse does, too.

Any blanket that your horse wears outside must be waterproof. A soaking wet blanket is actually *worse* than no blanket at all. Remember also that a horse's coat keeps him warm because it's fluffy and traps an insulating layer of air within the thick fur. A blanket will make the coat lie flat and will inhibit the natural function of the coat, so be sure the blanket itself is thick enough to keep the horse warm.

Blankets should fit well, being neither too loose nor too tight. A blanket that's too big might slide too far to one side, allowing the horse to step on it or get tangled up in it. This will not only destroy the blanket but may also cause the horse to panic and lead to an injury. A blanket that is too small can bind in certain spots and cause rubs—bare spots that can actually be rubbed raw. Most blanket manufacturers provide instructions for how to measure your horse for a blanket and select an appropriate size, or you can ask someone at your local tack shop to help you.

Although horses are quite happy living outside, their caretakers sometimes prefer to keep them in stalls, at least part of the time. It makes individual feeding regimens possible, provides a secure environment for a foaling or ailing animal, and offers more protection from extremes of elements and insects. Barns also can be more comfortable, secure, and convenient for the humans who are working with the horses.

A pretty barn does not necessarily equal a *good* barn. Although everyone likes fresh paint and new construction, it matters little to the horses. More important for their sake is that the barn is safe, sturdy, and well kept. Stalls should be large enough for a horse to turn around comfortably (ten feet by twelve feet or twelve feet by twelve feet is considered standard), safely constructed (no protruding nails or loose boards on which a horse could injure himself), and well bedded with good drainage, so the horse isn't standing on wet bedding. Doorways should be wide enough for a horse

A shed-row-style barn has all stalls facing toward the outside rather than toward an aisle, as with a center-aisle design. Water runs off the roof, making the immediate area below muddy, and a minimal roof overhang provides no protection from the elements other than the stall for routine and other care.

A six stall center-aisle barn is a popular design nationwide. It may have a tack room or office in place of one stall. It provides good ventilation via doors and windows and the added benefit of a covered center aisleway in which the horse can be tacked up, shod, or examined by a veterinarian.

Although horse barns are traditionally center-aisle or shed-row style, structures originally designed for other species or of a unique style can be modified for horse use.

The doorway into this stall is too narrow and the ceiling height too low for this big Belgian draft horse, who could easily pull the galvanized metal roof off the enclosure and injure himself.

Barn conversions should incorporate window materials (never use glass, as here), dimensions, and placement that are safe for housing horses. What might be adequate for another species can be downright dangerous for horses.

to pass through comfortably (four feet wide is common) and safely with room to spare. Ceilings should be high enough to allow plenty of clearance for a big, bronky two-year-old to stand on his hind legs without hitting his head (ten to eleven feet is safe/standard), and aisles should be free of clutter. Doors should have heavy-duty, secure hinges and latches to keep stalled horses from making mischief in the aisles or escaping completely.

Even a roomy, sturdy stall can cause problems if you don't bed it appropriately, however. There are numerous bedding products from which to choose, although you'll likely be limited to what is offered in your local area or at your favorite feed/horse supplies dealer.

Bedding should be soft and absorbent, cushioning the horse when he lies down and absorbing urine in a manner that makes bedding easy to remove from the stall. The most common bedding by far in recreational barns is wood shavings or sawdust. This product is relatively inexpensive, readily available, and makes a stall easy to clean. The shavings soak up the urine, so that wet spots are easy to remove, and manure can be sifted from usable bedding with a pitchfork. Shavings and sawdust can be purchased in individual bags or delivered in bulk. You can also often find a local sawmill that provides sawdust by-product at very low cost. Sawdust is dustier than shavings, however, and if you go with this option, you must be certain that the sawmill in question *never* cuts wood from black walnut trees. Standing on black walnut shavings will cause laminitis in horses. You also want to be sure the sawdust by-product is free of nails or other debris.

Straw (usually wheat straw) is readily available and inexpensive. Most racetrack barns use straw, and it's also used as bedding for foaling mares. A stall bedded with straw is bright and appealing, and usually less dusty than one bedded with shavings. Straw does not absorb urine quite so readily as shavings, however, and it's more difficult to muck a straw-bedded stall (although with practice, most horse folk can master

A well-appointed stall in a center-aisle barn. Note the sawdust bedding; two plastic water buckets safely affixed to the stall wall; plastic feed bucket; and hay fed on the stall floor, rather than in hay racks or nets, to allow the horse to eat in a more natural posture. The wood walls are in good repair; the stall bars allow a mischievous occupant to see all the barn doings while preventing him from poking his head into the aisle to harass passing horses and/or barn workers.

Clean, bright straw makes excellent bedding, but it is not a food-stuff— and should never be confused with hay (pictured on page 182).

THE HSUS / KEITH DANE

it). An added benefit is that used straw bedding is very easy to compost and is often used by mushroom farmers. If you can find a farmer willing to haul your manure pile away, you'll save the cost of removal and recycle your bedding at the same time.

Manure management is important not only for aesthetic and hygienic reasons, but also for fly control. Manure and wet stall bedding provide ideal places for flies to breed, so removing manure from the premises as frequently as possible is integral to controlling these harassing insects. Stalls should be cleaned at least daily and pastures as frequently as possible, with the waste collected away from the barns and grazing areas and removed regularly.

At this horse trial venue, used stall bedding is trucked away as fast as the wheelbarrows are emptied on the pile; you can also compost, spread, or give away manure-filled bedding.

HOOFCARE AND LAMENESS

A fly mask provides protection from biting insects while allowing the horse to see clearly. (It should be removed at night.)

Even the most diligent manure management can't completely eliminate flies around a barn, however, so you need a second (and perhaps third and fourth) line of defense. Open any equine-supply catalog, and you'll find scores of options—fly-deterring sprays, wipes, roll-ons, and ointments, all of which are supposed to make your horse less "palatable" to the biting insects; fly traps; fly masks, which keep bugs out of horses' eyes and ears; feed-through fly control, an edible supplement that kills fly larvae in horse manure; fly predators, which are harmless, stingless wasps that also kill fly larvae in manure; fly spray systems, which operate on timers and mist the entire interior of a barn with fly spray at regular intervals; and dozens more. The particular methods you choose depend on your own situation. For example, feed-through fly control is only effective if every horse on the property receives it, so it makes little sense to administer it to your own horse if none of the other horses where you board receives it.

Although stalling a horse in a barn part time has some benefits, it has its drawbacks as well. Barns can be very dusty places, especially in wintertime, when they're sealed up against the cold (for the humans' sakes more than the horses'). The lack of fresh air can cause horses to develop respiratory issues. Hay stored in a loft above the stalls also contributes to respiratory problems. A well-constructed barn should allow for lots of ventilation, even in cold weather.

A barn—*any* barn, even the fanciest and best-kept—is also rife with fire hazards. Hay, shavings, and wooden construction can all go up in flames in an instant from an electrical malfunction, a lightning strike, or a stray spark, and horses trapped in their stalls have no way to escape.

Turnout

Horses are roamers. They spend their days moving around slowly, eating grass, and watching the world go by. They stand around with their buddies, scratching each other's withers and engaging in mutual fly-swishing. Every once in a while, a cool breeze comes up and they get a little frisky, tear around at warp speed for a few minutes, and then go back to moseying and eating grass. They roll in the dirt and even snooze stretched flat out, enjoying a spring sunbath.

This is what horses do and what is natural for them. Unfortunately for the horse, horse-keeping the way it is practiced in some parts of the country doesn't provide that freedom. In California, land is so expensive that one hundred horses may be kept in small pipe corrals on acreage that accommodates four or five horses "back east." Turnout space is too limited, if it's available at all, and what space does exist might not have much (if any) grass. Whether land is available or not, many people are reluctant to turn their horses out in groups for fear of injury. To the horses' ultimate disservice, many owners of valuable show or sport horses don't turn them out at all as a result.

When you consider the way horses spend their days when left to their own devices, it's obvious that standing in a box all day, every day, can hardly be considered humane except when necessary for the horse's

An uncapped metal T-post (left), used here to anchor woven wire fencing, can cause eye and other facial injuries—as well as serve as a potentially dangerous scratching post. Vinyl or PVC fencing (right) is attractive, but the boards can become dislodged or sag due to pressure from horses for whom the grass is greener on the fence's other side.

health. Some horses may develop stable vices like stall walking or cribbing to alleviate the boredom. Others may be able to tolerate confinement if they get lots of exercise under saddle. A horse kept alone does better if field kept, and his welfare and needs must be considered.

Every horse should have at least some time out of a stall each day to just "be a horse"—wander, roll, sniff the fresh air, snooze in the sun. The amount of turnout any particular horse requires varies with the individual.

Turnout options vary widely, depending on where you live. In very densely populated areas where land is at a premium, there may only be space for a small paddock where horses are rotated for an hour or two (or less) throughout the day. (It is hard to make the case that this is a good option for long-term horse happiness and health, however.) Some facilities offer only individual "runs" attached to each stall, so horses can come and go as they please, but can't gallop or experience real freedom. Perhaps there is one twenty-acre field where a dozen horses go out together. In the arid west, you only find grass where pastures are irrigated. Even a lush pasture in the Kentucky bluegrass can turn into a dry lot if it's overgrazed, providing little actual grazing to the horses kept there.

Whatever options your location and budget allow, safety should be a turnout priority. Pastures should be checked occasionally for groundhog holes, toxic plants, and other dangers. They should be free of junk or debris—including stored or rusting machinery, trash piles, and falling-down farm buildings. Water should always be available in buckets, automatic waterers, or troughs that are kept clean.

Fencing should be highly visible and strong, and should minimize the risk of injury should a horse break through it or become caught up on it. Even the best fencing can become unsafe if it falls into disrepair, so regular maintenance is a must. Wood fencing should be checked regularly for loose boards or protruding nails, and fencing with wire mesh should be checked for bent or broken wire, or areas where a horse could put a hoof through the mesh. PVC fence boards can become loose and easily dislodged over time, so they must be maintained to be effective, and high-tensile wire must be tightened periodically.

Although electrified fencing may sound draconian, when used properly, it's quite effective. It prevents horses from chewing wood fencing or fighting across fences with their equine neighbors, and thus helps the fencing stay in good repair. Horses learn very quickly to leave electrified fencing alone, but the shock won't hurt them. It feels like getting pegged in the arm with a baseball: it stings like the devil for a moment, but does no permanent harm. (Anyone who has kept a horse at a facility with electric fencing has had an "oops" and touched the wire...and lived to tell the tale.)

Many horse owners have concluded that single-wire electric fence is not a suitable perimeter fencing on its own, however, as it's not very visible, and a panicked horse might try to run through it. It can be shorted out by fast-growing weeds or disabled when power is cut off, something savvy horses seem to sense as soon as the charge is lost, and they will take that as an opportunity to escape. When used in conjunction with wood, vinyl, or mesh fencing, or to cross-fence or

Barbed wire is cheap but totally unsuitable for confining horses, even in conjunction with woven wire (as here) or board fencing.

otherwise cordon off a small section of a larger, fenced enclosure, it works quite well. Multistrand electric tape also has its proponents.

One type of fencing that is *never* appropriate for use with horses is barbed wire, despite the fact that it is relatively inexpensive and seemingly ubiquitous in some parts of the country. The sharp points of twisted wire can injure a horse even when the fence is well maintained, and they can tear a horse's leg to shreds if the horse gets caught up in downed or sagging sections of wire.

Riding Facilities

For many of us, most of the fun of having a horse is riding him, and exercise is not only an integral part of your horse's care but also, for most people, an important way to bond. The facilities available for riding will likely play a large part in where you decide to keep your horse. Keep in mind that riding arenas, jumps, lighting, and other amenities are also expensive, and facilities offering them are likely to charge more for board than do those that offer basic horse care alone.

Will you often be riding before or after work in the wintertime, when daylight hours are limited and artificial lighting is a must? Do you want to ride regardless of the weather? Are you comfortable riding in an open field, or do you have a green or spooky horse who needs an enclosed area for safety's sake? Such issues will have an impact on your decision as well.

Many boarding facilities offer indoor or covered riding arenas. These are wonderful in the northern states—you can ride inside when the ground outside is frozen solid or snow-covered. Covered arenas are also widely used in the southern and western states, providing a shaded area during the sun-baked part of the day. If you're not a die-hard who needs to ride every day all year round, or if you live in a more temperate part of the country, an outdoor ring is probably perfectly sufficient.

Whether outdoor or indoor, dedicated riding rings should have good, consistent footing—a well-maintained and -drained surface, free of holes. The surface may be made of sand, dirt, bluestone, or a branded mixture of synthetic and natural materials. Good footing, which should be installed by a professional, can be expensive, since it typically involves excavating existing material, grading, and removing trees, rocks, and/or dirt. It does require maintenance: periodic dragging (using a tractor-drawn harrow to loosen and turn over compacted footing material) and, sometimes, watering to reduce dust. But the benefit is that you'll have a constant, all-weather surface on which to ride, and the footing will slightly cushion the concussion on your horse's legs.

A dedicated riding arena is not a necessity, however. For many riders, any large, flat area in a pasture works just fine. The drawbacks are that grass footing can become muddy and slippery in wet weather or rock-hard when baked in the summer heat (meaning your horse's legs will take more of a pounding), and you may wear "paths" around the perimeter from use. But if the weather cooperates, and you take care to keep the footing in good repair, such natural areas can be as good as any riding ring.

If you need to ride after dark, you're likely to want a facility that either has an indoor lighted arena or one that has installed lights around an outdoor arena or riding area. We have known creative and dedicated riders who work their horses in a safe, known area by full moonlight, in the light of their car's headlights, or with a helmet-mounted miner's light, so anything is possible!

You might not need an arena at all if you plan mostly to trail ride, in which case you want to be sure the facility has easy access to good riding trails. If you'll need to cross or ride along roads, make sure they won't be too busy at the time of day you're likely to be riding, and, of course, make sure your horse is traffic-safe. If you need to hack across private property to reach the trails, be sure the property owners have granted permission to do so to the barn's boarders and other customers. Always take care not to damage private property. Don't ride anywhere but an established trail or service road when it's excessively wet; never cross planted crop fields or harass farm animals; always leave gates— open or closed—as you found them; and return to pick up manure if necessary. It takes only one thoughtless guest or trespasser to end riders' access to a private property, perhaps permanently.

Companionship

If you keep your horse at a large boarding facility, you won't have to worry about him being lonely. But many owners who plan to keep horses at home might not realize the importance of equine companionship. A horse kept alone is usually unhappy, and many are downright frantic. Horses are herd animals and are used to being in groups. They're happiest when they've got a buddy or two, preferably where they can be in physical contact, either turned out together or able to sniff noses across a fence line.

A single horse might be content if other horses are within sight, say, on neighboring properties. If not, consider getting another horse to keep your horse company—a miniature horse won't add much more work or expense, and is likely to make your horse much calmer and happier.

Or you might see if you can find a boarder, if you don't want financial responsibility for another horse of your own. Failing everything else, horses sometimes find goats to be good companions.

Boarding Versus Horses at Home

It's probably become very obvious that you have a significant choice to make when deciding where to keep your horse, at home or away. The right choice for you will vary, depending on your own situation. If you're not an experienced horseperson, boarding at a facility with a knowledgeable staff is likely to let you sleep more easily and keep your horse healthier and safer. But if you've already ridden around the block a few times, you might be more than capable of caring for your own horses, if you have the right facility.

Boarding

Boarding facilities can range from a private barn that takes in one or two extra horses to help cover its expenses, to equestrian metropolises with multiple barns, multiple arenas, resident trainers, and dozens of horses. What they have in common is that the staff, not the owners, is responsible for the horses' basic care—feeding, watering, stall cleaning, and turnout— as well as for keeping an eye on the horses' general well-being and alerting the owner to an emergency. This is usually referred to as full-care board. The horse owner is responsible for riding, grooming, and other nonemergency care, and for paying all the bills.

The main attractions of boarding for most amateur horsemen are convenience and access to facilities that are beyond their financial resources alone. You can get up in the morning, go to work, then go to the barn to ride later if you feel like it. You don't have to feed the horses and muck stalls in the wee hours of the morning before you go to work. You don't *have* to go to the barn every single day. You can be away from home for more than twelve hours at a time without worrying that the horse is fretting for his dinner. You can go away on vacation for a week without having to arrange for someone to care for your horse.

Most boarding facilities are run by experienced equine professionals—barn managers and owners who make their living in the industry by buying or selling horses, teaching lessons, or training young horses. If you're a little light on experience yourself, it can be very reassuring to know that more expert eyes are keeping watch over your horse. These individuals know when the veterinarian needs to be called and what good-quality feed looks like. They might put all boarders on a standard shoeing and vaccination schedule, saving you the trouble of making the appointments and keeping track of vaccinations yourself.

Boarding also saves the horse owner from having to order and store feed and bedding and maintain a facility—including pastures, barns, manure pile, fencing, and arenas. All the horse owner has to worry about is taking care of and enjoying her own horse.

Boarding amenities may be as modest as a simple riding ring or as lavish as an indoor arena, miles of private trails, and a heated lounge or tack room. Many boarding facilities have in-house instructors for those riders who want regular training. (Some barns require that you take lessons with the resident trainer to board there.) Very intensive programs might have the rider in lessons three or four times a week, with the trainer riding the horse on non-lesson days. In a more laid-back atmosphere, it might only be one or two lessons a week, but you always have the trainer on-site if you need assistance or have questions.

One often overlooked advantage to boarding is the opportunity to be part of a group. If you're in training, you'll ride with the same group of fellow students every day, perhaps going to shows or other competitions together. You won't necessarily need your own horse trailer, since you can ride along with others. Even in a non-training situation, you can enjoy the camaraderie and safety of having other people around while you're grooming, tacking up, and riding—fellow horse folk to cheer you on or join on long trail rides. Watching other riders and trainers deal with a variety of horses, day in and day out, can provide an invaluable opportunity to learn which techniques and approaches work and which don't. By carefully observing, and asking questions of, those who are more experienced, you can incorporate the good into your own horse care regimen and reject the inhumane, the dangerous, or the ineffective.

The main drawback of boarding is expense. You're paying a portion of the salaries for the barn staff, large or small—stall muckers, grooms, maintenance staff, and barn manager. The facilities at boarding barns— the arenas, the barns, and fields—are a major financial investment, and the barn owner typically recoups those costs through boarding fees.

When you board your horse, you're putting the bulk of your horse's care into someone else's hands. This is a wonderful convenience when the care is good and your horse is handled well. But what if a stable employee is unnecessarily rough with the horses? What if the person who feeds in the mornings doesn't always show up, or the stall mucker does a lousy job whenever the barn owner isn't around? What if the barn owner decides to save money by substituting poorer-quality hay or less grain?

Most horse owners are only at the barn for a couple of hours a day a few days a week and may not witness any problems in person. They might, however, notice that their horses are losing weight or suddenly becoming head-shy. Many barn owners are reluctant to raise boarding rates in the face of rising costs and may cut the quality of feed or hay or the amount of bedding in the hope that their customers won't notice the change. Sudden changes in your horse's condition or behavior should not be shrugged off but addressed first through a cordial discussion with the barn owner or manager.

Boarding a horse is an act of trust. You are entrusting to others the responsibility of taking care of your treasured friend and are paying them for this service. If someone is new to horses and not yet very knowledgeable, the signs that something is wrong might be missed.

What to Look For

Boarding a horse is supposed to be a convenience, but if you are in a constant state of worry, wondering whether your horse has been fed or turned out or has had his stall cleaned, you have pretty much negated the convenience factor. The goal should be to find a facility that *eases* your burden, rather than adds to it.

So how to find such facilities? It can be difficult, because the bad facilities advertise just like the good ones do. It helps to be educated and observant and to seek out opinions from everyone else you know in the local horse community. The horse world is a small one, and if a facility is known for providing substandard care, people will know.

You should visit any barn where you're considering boarding. Call first, introduce yourself, and ask if it has any openings for new boarders (even if it's full, it's worth going by in case you can get on a waiting list).

You want to meet as many people on the barn staff as you can. Ask about their experience and credentials, their areas of interest and expertise. The knowledge of a good horseman is not bound by discipline, but if you're looking to take lessons, you want to find someone who has experience with your chosen sport.

Tour the facility. Look at the turnout paddocks and note how many horses are in them and how the grass is doing. Are the paddocks over-grazed and bare? Do the horses have hay to eat if there's no grass?

Pay close attention as you walk through the barn. Are the aisles clear, with equipment not currently in use stored out of harm's way, or are buckets, bridles, and hoses strewn everywhere? Peek in several of the stalls. Are they light and airy, or dark and dungeon-like? Are they well bedded with straw, wood shavings, or other absorbent product? Do they look—and smell—basically clean, or is there a strong urine odor? Do stalled horses have water buckets that are clean and at least half-full of water? What kind of hay and grain is furnished? Is a feeding schedule posted, indicating an individualized feeding regimen? Do stalled horses have at least a bit of fresh hay to munch on? Good barn owners take pride in good housekeeping because they know it reflects good overall management.

Post-and-board fencing is the choice of many longtime horsemen; it can be expensive to install and maintain but provides a good sturdy visual barrier and enhances property values.

BIGSTOCKPHOTO / JESSICA CORNETT

What is your general impression of the facility from the horse's point of view? Forget whether the barns are pretty or freshly painted—are they in good repair? Is the facility neat and workmanlike? Is the fencing well maintained and sturdy? Look for evidence that safety is a priority: fire extinguishers should be in obvious places, and emergency phone numbers and "No Smoking" signs should be posted conspicuously.

Look at the horses themselves. Are they in good weight? Is there a bloom to their coats? Are their feet trimmed and cared for or chipped and broken off? They're the ones who can speak volumes about the quality of care at any given facility without ever saying a word, even if you don't know alfalfa hay from orchard grass.

Only when you've formed your impression of the management should you let yourself focus on the amenities and assess whether they suit your needs. Ask how crowded the arenas are at the times when you'll be riding,

Good barn management dictates that baled hay and bagged feed be raised on wood pallets, away from moisture; lids on containers securely snapped in place; and bedding in waterproof bags. (Pitchforks and other dangerous equipment should be stored prongs down, however.)

and what the rules are for using them. Are the boarders pleasure riders, competition-bound, dressage, or Western, or a mix of all disciplines? You're likely to spend considerable time with these folks so determining generally if you will be a good fit is a good idea.

Unfortunately, in many parts of the country, potential boarders may have limited choices in facilities when they factor in boarding fees, commuting distance, standards of horse care, and rider amenities. It is always best to place horse care at the top of the list.

Horses at Home

If you find yourself quaking in your boots over the prospect of turning your horse's care over to someone else who might not feed him, clean his stall, or turn him out for days at a time, you're not alone. It seems that the more you know about horses, the more you can find wrong with various boarding facilities. For many horsemen, the dream is no longer just to have a horse, but to have the horse in the backyard, where they can see him through the kitchen window.

Boarding a horse cannot compare to having him at home. When he lives in your backyard, you're the one he nickers to for his breakfast. You can bring him in early out of an icy rain or put him out early before the summer flies are active. You can bed his stall as deeply as you like, since you're the one cleaning it and paying for the bedding.

Since, technically, your labor is free, you're likely to find that keeping a horse at home is less expensive than boarding as well. You don't have to pay someone else to order the hay and the grain or clean the stalls. You aren't paying for improvements to someone else's property. What you invest in barns, fencing, and other amenities will increase your own property's value.

You also don't have to worry about dodging other riders or lesson kids in a crowded arena, nor will you need to lock your tack trunk, lest some brushes or saddle pads "grow legs and walk off." You can keep everything in the tack or feed room in its prescribed place—at least until you realize how much effort it takes to do so!

In addition to being able to micromanage your horse's care, you have the opportunity to get to know your horse much better. You'll learn what time of day he takes his nap and where he drops his manure. You'll learn how quickly he finishes his hay and how much water he typically drinks in a day. You can run a hand down his legs morning and night and get a feel for his bumps and swellings, and how they might change when he's been turned out all day, or if he's been stuck inside because of bad weather.

In short, you'll get to know absolutely everything there is to know about your horse, much more so than even the most dedicated boarder can discern. There's simply no substitute for time spent in your horse's company, observing him from your house's second-story window or standing at the fence line drinking a cup of coffee as he swats flies under a tree half a pasture away.

If you're not an experienced horseman already, you'll find your knowledge increases exponentially when you're the one in charge. You have to learn a good bale of hay from a bad one and how to wrap a leg so the bandage stays in place overnight, because no one else will be around to do it for you. Eventually, you see your horse take an "ouchy" step and immediately begin to tick off the possible causes: Hoof abscess? Loose shoe? Laminitis? You will notice that your horse hasn't finished her feed and think: Impaction colic? Bad batch of feed? You're on your way to being a first-rate horseman.

Before you can even consider backyard horse-keeping as a possibility, you must own property with a rather large "backyard." This is not an insignificant investment, especially in densely populated parts of the country, where land values are high. Most towns have zoning restrictions that dictate the size property you'll need, assessing a certain per-horse acreage minimum.

You also need to invest in a barn or run-in shed (with or without electricity and running water), fencing, and perhaps a horse trailer. You need a place to store hay and bedding and a way to dispose of manure. You need extra liability insurance. And you need all of the "stuff" that goes along with keeping horses—buckets, wheelbarrows, pitchforks, hoses, troughs, maybe even a tractor and a harrow.

In the long run, keeping a horse at home is likely going to be less expensive, but the initial outlay in purchasing a horse property or getting a non-horse property set up for horses can be substantial.

One of the benefits of keeping a horse at home is that you handle all the care. The downside to this is…you handle all the care. *All of it.* Even if it is fifteen below zero and you've got the Martian death flu, someone still has to feed the horses and clean the stalls. A vacation in Paris? Great, but can you find a "farm sitter" or friend to cover horse-keeping while you are gone? What if a horse is sick or injured and needs constant care throughout the day? That can pose big problems if you work outside your home or don't have family or horsey friends as a backup. Will your boss understand if you need to take an unscheduled personal day to cold-hose your horse's suddenly swollen knee? Who is going to put ointment in the filly's eye four times a day for the next ten days? Feed stores, local newspapers, equine professionals (veterinarians and farriers), and horsey neighbors can be a source of horsemen willing to undertake some short-term tasks, but the costs can add up.

Horses like routine. They want to be fed at the same time every day and come in and go out at the same time every day. If your job often requires you to stay at the office later than you'd planned, you might come home to angry (or, even worse, colicky) horses who expected their dinner hours ago. There are many ways you can make things easier on yourself—like having your horses live out most of the time, rather than keeping them in stalls—but you are very much tied to their needs and schedule.

You need to take care of your property: mow and seed the pastures, fix the broken fence boards, paint the barn, and drag the arena. You might find that taking care of the horses and the property leaves you little time or energy to ride (sadly ironic, since riding is probably why you have a horse in the first place).

In a one- or two-horse operation, you might find it difficult to get appointments with farriers or veterinarians, because you don't have as much business to offer them as a big boarding facility does. It might also be difficult to arrange delivery of hay, feed, or bedding when you're buying in small quantities, five bags of grain or a hundred bales of hay at a time, unless you are willing to purchase minimum quantities or pay additional delivery fees. If you want to take lessons, you either need to find a trainer who is willing to come to you, or you have to put your horse on a trailer and haul to her location.

Keeping a horse at home can also be a very solitary experience. Many horse owners enjoy the time alone with their horses, but others find they miss the camaraderie of having other horsey people around. Unless you live in a horsey neighborhood, you need to have your own transportation or pay for someone to haul you and your horse to a show or clinic. You won't have a trainer or barn manager to talk to if you have questions or problems. If you're not comfortable being totally self-sufficient or investing time in building a horsey-neighbor support system, home horse-keeping is probably not for you.

Living in the backyard can also be somewhat lonely for your horse, if he's used to being in a large and bustling barn. If kept alone, he may pace the fence line for hours at a time or seem to withdraw into inactivity. Even two horses on the property can become "herd-bound"—so attached to their friend that they will not leave the barn without him (although acclimation may make the partings less stressful).

At a boarding facility, there's almost always someone else on the property—other boarders, barn staff, the barn owner, a trainer. If Old Paint spooks, shies, bucks, or otherwise causes you two to part company, chances are good that the sight of your riderless horse galloping around the property will bring someone running. But what if you're riding in your own secluded field, or you fall on an icy patch outside the barn door, and no one else will be home for hours? A cell phone can summon help if you are conscious (and the phone hasn't been damaged in the fall), but serious accidents can happen around horses at any time.

One possible solution to many of these problems is to take on a boarder yourself, perhaps a friend or someone else in the neighborhood who rides. Then you'll have company while working around the barn and someone to ride with, as well as someone who's familiar with your farm and horses if you need a caretaker. If you only have one horse, a boarder gives him a pal without your having to take on the financial responsibility for another horse of your own. Your little horse facility can generate a small income to alleviate some of your costs (although liability insurance and other expenses may have to be factored into the equation).

Self-care and Co-ops

If you're not happy with the full-care board options in your area but aren't quite ready to be your horse's sole caretaker, there is a compromise. You can board at a self-care facility, where you basically rent a stall but do all of the care yourself, or you can try to find (or organize) a co-op barn, where several boarders share the responsibility of caring for their own and the others' horses.

The self-care option usually is not offered at large boarding facilities, since it is easier—and more cost effective—to have all the horses on the same schedule. You're more likely to see it at private barns, where the property owner has an empty stall or two (or even an entire empty barn) and wants to make a little bit of extra money by renting the stalls out.

Self-care arrangements vary. Be sure to have each party's responsibilities spelled out in a signed contract. The property owner might simply rent out the facility as is and leave all care and upkeep to the boarder(s) or provide maintenance—fixing broken fence boards, keeping the arena dragged—but leave all daily chores to the renters.

As a self-care boarder, you are usually responsible for all aspects of the horse's care, including feeding, cleaning stalls, and turnout. You'll pay significantly less than you would for full-care board, since you're assuming all of these responsibilities instead of paying someone else to do them. Your workload will be similar to what it would be if you had the horse on your own property, but you won't have to purchase the property and build or maintain the structures.

Self-care board is an appealing option if you want more control over your horse's care (such as feed choices) and have the time to do so, but aren't quite ready or able to buy a farmette of your own. If there are other horses and riders at the barn, you'll be able to enjoy their company and won't always have to ride alone, but most self-care facilities are much less busy than a big, full-care barn.

You are the sole caregiver/decision maker for your horse. You need to find someone else to care for him if you're sick or have to go out of town—even at the last minute. You also have the added burden of traveling to the barn twice a day to feed, turn out, bring in, and so on, or arrange a schedule with other self-care folks to cover those tasks. For most people, self-care is only feasible if the barn is very close by.

On paper co-op boarding situations seem to be the best of both worlds. A group of like-minded horse people get together and rent out a barn themselves or organize around one member who has her own barn and property. All of the horse chores are divvied up into shifts throughout the week, typically mornings and evenings, depending on the schedules of all boarders. It might suit one person to handle all morning tasks and another all evenings, or both shifts on specific days, leaving others chore-free. (Such duties as dragging the ring or mowing pastures might also be divided up, or you might organize group chores, such as painting a barn or building jumps.)

In this arrangement you are doing more work in each shift, since you're caring for several horses instead of just your own. You have the flexibility to trade shifts with your fellow boarders for vacations or late night plans, and you still have a great deal of control over your own horse's care.

The success of a co-op depends on its members. If one person in a group doesn't do a good job mucking stalls or is late for feeding, all of the horses suffer. It's paramount that all the members share similar horse-keeping philosophies and get along well on a personal level, as you'll rely heavily on each other. Organization is also key: someone needs to be responsible for ordering feed and hay and coordinating farrier and veterinarian visits, and the schedule of daily chores must be established and adhered to religiously.

Co-ops work best in areas with lots of horse people and lots of small barns for rent. The facility should be close to all of the participants, and you need people with time flexibility in the case of an emergency. If you show up to feed one morning before work and discover that another person's horse is colicking, who is responsible for staying with the horse and waiting for the veterinarian—you or the owner? Without a barn staff whose job it is to care for the horses first and foremost, owners have to be willing and able to drop everything in an emergency to be able to care for their horses.

If you have a good group of like-minded people with flexible schedules and are lucky enough to find a nice facility with a pleasant landlord, co-ops can be very effective and a lot of fun. Sometimes you can find people advertising to fill an open co-op spot on tack shop bulletin boards or in local horsey publications. Or you can always start one yourself, if you can recruit friends to join you in the adventure.

Feeding

WHEN YOU SPEND TIME AROUND HORSES AND realize just how many bizarre ways they can find to injure themselves, you understand why basic safety is so important. A horse scratching his head will find the one protruding nail in a stall and try to rip his eyelid off with it; another one drinking from a trough will get his foot tangled in the hose coiled around the adjacent hydrant and pull hose, hydrant, and hide up and off trying to extricate himself.

What might not be quite so readily apparent are the many pitfalls of the equine digestive system. Two of the most dangerous maladies that can afflict horses—colic and laminitis (also known as founder)—are often directly related to what the horse eats and the equine digestive tract.

A nutritious and balanced diet is just as important for horses as it is for humans. A horse who is fed well (meaning quality, not just quantity) will seem to glow from the inside underneath his blindingly shiny and dappled coat. Not only will he look good, but he will also approach his work with energy and enthusiasm, filling his devoted human partner with well-deserved pride.

Entire books have been written on feeding the horse, and we're not going to try to explain everything there is to know here. We do give you enough of an overview in the hope that it will motivate you to delve into one of those books later on—or at least call your county agriculture extension office for some free pamphlets on the subject.

The Rules of Feeding

The very first time you went near a horse, you probably started hearing The Rules. Don't walk behind a horse—and don't run anywhere, ever. Always feed treats on your flat palm with fingers outstretched. When riding, the Rules include Heels down! Eyes up! Then there are the Rules that don't serve much purpose but are followed anyway, such as leading and mounting a horse from the left side.

The rules of feeding are the big ones, the iron-clad tenets of the horse world, taught to little Pony Clubbers and 4-Hers who aren't even big enough to lift a bale of hay. You don't need to memorize every twist and turn of the horse's hundred-foot-long digestive tract, you just need to remember the simple rules, and you'll have a good foundation upon which to build.

Rule #1: Grain: Feed Little and Often

In chapter 3 we discussed the fact that the horse is a grazing animal, and his digestive system is designed for a near-constant intake of low-calorie food throughout the day. Horses who spend much of their time in stalls aren't doing much grazing, but their natural feeding patterns can be replicated by keeping hay in front of them for a good portion of the day. They can nibble at it for a while, take a break and snooze for a while, and then come back to it. This not only gives horses something to do, preventing them from becoming bored and developing stable vices if stalled for extended periods, but it also keeps some roughage constantly moving through their systems.

If grain is fed, it should be given in multiple smaller meals rather than one large one. Most horses are grained twice a day for the convenience of human caretakers, but if a large quantity must be fed for whatever reason, an additional lunchtime feeding might be in order, to avoid feeding too much grain at once and to provide stalled horses with a nice mid-day activity.

Small, frequent meals not only are more natural for the horse, but they also allow the horse to better digest and use his food. When too much food is fed at once, it's rushed through the system and not digested as effectively as when it moves through at its customary slow pace.

Rule #2: Feed Plenty of Roughage

A corollary to the above, this rule emphasizes the importance of roughage—grass and/or hay—over grain. Roughage is what the horse is meant to eat, and his digestive system is geared toward using the nutrition in those grassy stalks. A horse should eat 1.5 to 2 percent of his body weight in roughage every day. (The one exception is the founder-prone horse, for whom fresh grass and rich hay varieties can be a problem.)

Many horse owners tend to focus much more intently on the grain portion of the diet. Grain is sold by brand-name and is often supported by national ad campaigns; it comes in a spiffy bag with a picture of a beautiful, well-fed horse on the front and a long list of ingredients on the back. Hay, by comparison, is just...hay. It comes in bales from the farmer down the road. No slogans or marketing promises—just cured grass.

But in reality, good old hay should be the mainstay of the diet. Many pleasure and trail horses don't even *need* grain: good-quality hay and/or pasture is plenty. If hay isn't enough, grain can be added, but the bulk of a horse's calories should always come from roughage.

Rule #3: Feed According to the Horse's Needs

Each horse is an individual and has different needs, in the same way that two people of the same size can have vastly different caloric needs.

A starting point for deciding how much any given horse should be fed is his size; a twelve-hand pony obviously does not need to consume as many calories as an eighteen-hand draft horse. The other major factor is the amount of work a horse does—a horse who works hard requires more calories than does a pasture puff.

In keeping with the "feed lots of roughage" rule, you should begin designing your ration around the amount of hay or pasture your horse gets. Horses who are grazing on good pasture the majority of the day don't need much hay, if any, since they've already got bellies full of grass. Horses who don't get much turnout or are not on good pasture will need more hay, whether they are inside or out. If a horse finishes all the hay you give him and looks for more, you can add another flake or two, as long as he doesn't get too pudgy. If the horse is trampling his leftover hay (or, to add insult to injury, using it as his toilet) or if he's getting fat, you can cut his ration back. (You know you've hit the ideal balance when the trim horse is cleaning up his hay at every meal but not obsessively looking for more. If you have concerns, a weight tape will help you estimate your horse's weight from week to week.)

Most horses who are in work get at least some grain, and some horses who are "hard keepers" (i.e., on the skinny side) need grain regardless of their work program, just to keep their weight at a healthy level. Less is always more when it comes to grain, so start with the minimum (either the ration he was on before coming to your barn, if you know what that was, or what a veterinarian or competent barn manager recommends) and adjust it upward if necessary. (The quantity guidelines printed on bags of horse feed are based on protein content and "average"-size horses. They don't apply to individuals and can be hard for nutrition newbies to figure out without guidance.)

With a little bit of tweaking, you'll find the right balance of pasture, hay, and grain for your particular horse's needs. But you're not done—your horse's ration should always be considered a work in progress, not a finished masterpiece. It should change anytime your horse's workload or the quality of your feed changes.

For example, in many parts of the country, pasture is poor to nonexistent in wintertime or during months of drought, so supplementing pasture with hay is in order. In the spring, the grass comes in thick and lush, and hay rations can be cut back or eliminated completely, depending on how much pasture is available. Whenever good-quality hay is left uneaten (by one horse or the whole herd) from one feeding to the next, quantities can be reduced slowly.

If a horse in hard work (five to six days a week of strenuous riding, driving, or training) develops a hoof abscess and needs a few days of stall rest while it drains, you should cut his grain back temporarily, because he won't need those extra calories.

Rule #4: Change Feed and Feed Schedules Gradually

Whenever you make a change to your horse's ration, whether it's increasing or decreasing the amount or changing to a new kind of feed, you should make the change incrementally. Sudden differences in the amount or type of feed can lead to colic or founder.

If you're changing the amount of feed, increase or decrease each meal a little at a time, over several weeks, if possible, until you reach the desired amount. (Even a starving horse can metabolize feed only so efficiently and, if confronted with a sudden, large influx of calories, can be made ill, or worse.) One method for changing a ration (or *type* of feed, as opposed to the *amount* of feed) is to replace 25 percent of the ration with the new ration every two days so that it takes six days before the horse is eating 100 percent of the new ration[45].

Rule #5: Measure Feed Accurately and Feed Consistently

Ask someone how much feed his horse receives, and you usually get an answer measured in flakes of hay and scoops of grain. While this is a convenient way to measure feed in the barn, it's best to start off knowing what your horse's baseline nutritional needs are, based on weight.

When you first acquire your horse, the previous owner will tell you what feed she's been eating, and how much. He may tell you she gets two cups, two quarts, two scoops—but scoops and other measuring vessels are not all the same. You should start off by measuring your horse's feed by weight. You can buy a simple kitchen or postal scale, or you can weigh your horse's portion on the scale at your local feed store. Once you figure out how much your horse's typical ration weighs, you can measure that portion at feeding time using a scoop, coffee can, or whatever suits your needs.

If you later decide to switch to a different kind of grain that has more or less volume per pound, but with the same nutritional content, you'll know approximately how much you need to feed *by weight* to get the same amount you were feeding with the old grain.

The average thousand-pound horse who relies on hay for all his forage (say, in winter, when pastures are dormant) typically eats fifteen to twenty pounds of hay per day. Most of us dispense hay in flakes; however, the amount of hay in a flake can vary greatly, depending on the size of the flake and the kind of hay. If you don't know how much the bales of hay you are feeding weigh, you can use a bathroom scale to check, then feed that portion of a bale that your horse needs, every day. The goal is to feed your horse enough hay to keep him at his ideal weight and provide him forage throughout the day without waste. If he's looking (or sounding) ravenous at feeding time or is using uneaten hay as his toilet, adjust his hay ration accordingly.

Rule #6: Don't Feed Immediately Before or After Exercise

Think about tucking in for a hearty meal, and when you're finished, pushing back from the table and going straight out for a three-mile jog. How well would that sit with *your* digestive system? Alternatively, think about how you feel immediately after strenuous exercise. Are you interested in eating right away, before you've even stopped gasping for breath? No? Well, it's no different for your horse.

Ideally, you should wait an hour or so after your horse has finished a meal before riding him. If you're going to do something really strenuous, it should be closer to three hours. (Most event horses, for example, do not get fed any breakfast before they run cross-country.)

Having the digestive system full of food gives the horse's lungs less room to work, and makes strenuous exercise harder on him. In addition, blood flow is diverted away from the digestive organs during periods of exertion, so gut movement slows and colic may be a real danger.

If you must work your horse around mealtime, feed perhaps a third of his usual portion beforehand (you can save the rest for after your ride), particularly if all the other horses in the barn are tucking into their meals, and don't work him very hard.

You also need to exercise caution when feeding a horse after work. Let the horse cool down completely—his breathing rate should be back to normal, and his skin should not feel hot or sweaty.

Conventional horsey wisdom used to dictate that a horse should not be allowed to drink large quantities of water after hard exercise. Small sips of water were allowed, but allowing a hot and thirsty horse to drain a bucket was a *big* no-no. However, considerable research was done on cooling horses out after exercise in preparation for the 1996 Olympic Games in hot and humid Atlanta. Studies showed that a horse's thirst reflex is highest just after exercise—allowing him to drink his fill of cool (not ice-cold) water helps speed the cooling process, rehydrates the horse, and has no adverse effects[46].

Rule #7: Routine, Routine, Routine

Horses thrive on routine, and their amazingly accurate internal clocks make them much better timekeepers than their human caretakers. Many a horse owner has been distracted by work around the barn only to be reminded by her stalled charges rattling their buckets because dinner is five minutes late!

Horses should be kept on a consistent feeding schedule, with meals arriving at the same time each day (ideally, within an hour). Most horses aren't harmed by an abrupt change in schedule, although stalled horses, in particular, will certainly be very annoyed. But for horses who are prone to colic, a sudden change in routine can be more than an annoyance and might be enough to trigger a colic episode.

Assessing a Horse's Needs

There's no magic formula to assist you in deciding how much to feed, although you or your barn manager can take a guess to start with, based on what you know about the horse or on what horses of similar size and workload need to maintain their condition in your management program. It's basically a system of trial and error, with adjustments based on the horse's actual condition and energy level.

To be able to assess what changes should be made in a horse's diet, you need to be able to assess the horse himself to determine if he needs more or fewer calories.

In 1983 veterinarian Donald Henneke developed an equine body scoring system to be able to better quantify what is, in essence, a subjective judgment: is a horse too fat or too thin? The system divides the horse's body into six parts: the neck, withers, shoulder area, ribs, loins, and tail head area. Each of these parts are scored on a scale from one to nine, according to certain specified criteria, then the scores are averaged for an overall body condition score. A horse who scores a one is emaciated, while one who scores a nine is considered obese.

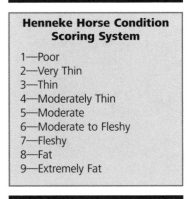

Henneke Horse Condition Scoring System

1—Poor
2—Very Thin
3—Thin
4—Moderately Thin
5—Moderate
6—Moderate to Fleshy
7—Fleshy
8—Fat
9—Extremely Fat

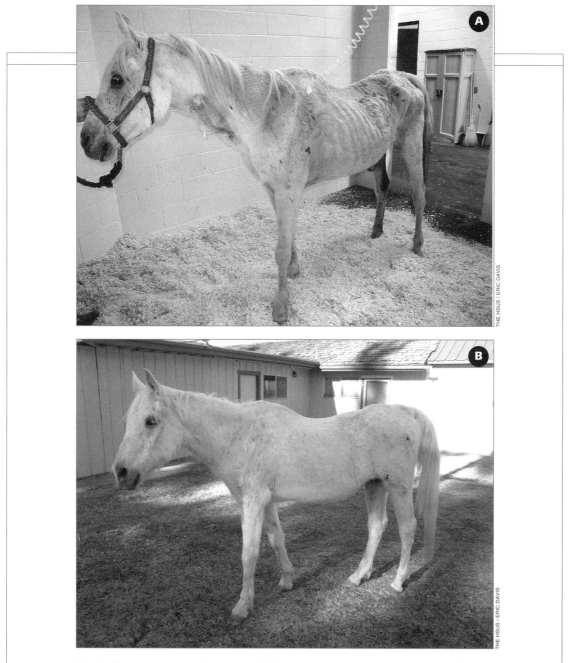

This Arabian came as a starvation case to a California humane organization: the horse's condition was rated a 1 (emaciated/poor) (Photo A); after recovery months later, the horse was rated a 6 (Photo B).

FEEDING

The Henneke system is now widely used by law enforcement agencies to determine more easily when horses are not being cared for properly, but it's a useful tool for the average horse owner as well. Using it teaches you to assess small changes in your horse's condition more objectively and to look at the overall picture, rather than just the size of your horse's belly.

Although a five on the Henneke scale is ideal, a range of body conditions is considered normal. Like humans, horses are all built differently—some are very slight and naturally tend to be thin, while others are of a more stout construction.

A horse's "ideal" weight also depends on his job. A Thoroughbred who is racing fit is expected to be on the lean side, with a pronounced "tucked up" look, like a greyhound. In contrast, a show hunter or western pleasure horse is expected to be almost a bit plump, with a well-fed, rounded appearance.

Individual horses can vary widely in their ability to put on and maintain weight. An "easy keeper" usually tends to be on the fleshy side, and his owner is constantly fighting to keep his weight in check. These horses easily maintain their weight on hay and pasture, and might even need to have their access to pasture restricted when the grass is very lush.

A "hard keeper," on the other hand, loses weight very easily and has a difficult time putting it back on. He may be a finicky eater, easily distracted from finishing his meal, or without much of an appetite at all. Any kind of stress—a trailer trip, a slight illness, or a cold winter—might cause him to lose weight. Such a horse can go from being just a bit thin to dangerously underweight. Hard keepers often need grain, since grain is a much more highly concentrated source of calories than is hay. Their owners must be especially vigilant, keeping an eye out for the slightest drop in weight so the trend can be reversed quickly.

Many older horses become hard keepers, even if they had no problem maintaining weight in their youth. Their teeth may have worn down considerably as they've aged, making it more difficult to chew food, or their bodies are no longer as efficient at using the food they *do* eat. These horses might do better on pelleted feeds that can be wetted down for feeding,

Roughage—grass or hay (here being loaded into a loft via a hay elevator)—is key to a horse's diet.

making an easy-to-chew mash. There are also special feeds formulated just for senior horses that may help older equines stay at a good weight.

It's important to assess your horse's weight regularly. Small, incremental changes over time might go unnoticed, so be cognizant of telltale signs, like needing to tighten or loosen the saddle girth. Many pastured horses lose weight over a cold winter, since they use calories to stay warm. Weight loss can be hidden under a heavy hair coat and revealed only after the shedding season arrives with warm weather. It's much easier to correct the problem if you catch it early.

Hay

Hay is the portion of the diet that most horse owners know the least about. At boarding facilities usually only one type of hay is offered, and the owner's only input is how much of it the horse receives. If you don't stable your horse at home and have never purchased hay yourself, your knowledge is probably minimal. Even if you don't buy your own hay, you should be aware of what your horse is eating, what constitutes good hay, and what the basic hay varieties are.

There are two main varieties of hay, grasses and legumes. Grass hays include timothy, coastal Bermuda, brome, and orchard grass. Different varieties grow better in different parts of the country, so "grass hay" in Pennsylvania might mean timothy, while in Texas it might mean coastal Bermuda grass. Grass hays are high in fiber and relatively low in nutrient content, which makes them very safe to feed free-choice. The primary legume hay fed to horses is alfalfa, which has a higher protein content than grass hay and less fiber, making it a much richer hay. It's also highly palatable, and most horses enjoy it immensely. But because it's so much richer than grass hay, it must be fed in smaller quantities. It is possible to overfeed alfalfa hay; unlike grass, it is not usually fed free-choice. Clover, another legume, is often found mixed with orchard grass or timothy and is also highly palatable.

You can often purchase a grass/alfalfa mixed hay, which has some of both. (The two different kinds of hay are planted as a mixture in the same field and harvested together.) Mixed hay has the benefit of extra nutrition from the alfalfa but contains enough grass that it can be fed in larger quantities.

Making hay is as much art as it is science. The goal is to cut it at just the right time, maximizing the nutritional content, which rises as the grass grows and then starts to drop off at a certain point. Cut hay dries (or "cures") in the field for several days and is then baled. A hayfield is cut several times in the course of a growing season; each harvest is referred to as a cutting.

Hay is greatly affected by the weather, both as it grows and after it is cut. In drought conditions hay doesn't grow so well, and the final product is very stemmy with a low nutritional content. Once hay has been cut and is drying in the field, weather can wreak havoc with the process. Cut hay that has been rained on takes longer to dry completely. If the hay's moisture content is too high when it is baled, it can develop mold or can ferment and produce enough heat to cause spontaneous combustion.

Most of the intricacies of making hay are beyond the realm of knowledge of the average horse owner, so having a good, knowledgeable hay dealer is critically important. Reputable hay growers produce a consistently good product that they stand behind, and you can count on them

Although the square bales seen on page 179 are more common, round bales of grass or timothy hay are a good solution for horses on acreage with insufficient pasture. Typically more hay is wasted in a round bale than in a square bale, even when bales are placed in bale holders, because horses pull hay out from the inside of the bale as they eat.

to provide quality hay year after year. Unfortunately, though, everyone is subject to the vagaries of the weather. In drought years, even the best hay growers struggle to produce good hay.

Some hay brokers may try to sell an inferior product. Every horse owner should be educated in what differentiates a good bale of hay from a bad one, to be able to assess hay before buying it, and to be able to tell when bales in your own hayloft have become unsafe to feed.

A good hay *looks* appealing. It's green; soft, not stemmy, to the touch; and contains a high proportion of leaves and plant heads. It smells fresh, not musty. There's no evidence of bugs, debris, or mold. When you break a bale open and pull it apart, there should be minimal or no dust. In contrast, poor hay looks dried out and dull—more brown than green. It feels coarse in your hands, with lots of sharp stems, and it does not smell fragrant and appealing.

Brown, stemmy hay won't hurt your horse (although he might decline to eat it, leading to waste), but it is very low in nutritional value. Dusty hay, however, can cause respiratory problems in horses and should not be fed;

FEEDING

A good, fresh grass hay (left) has plant heads without stemmy weeds, field debris, or bugs.

Moldy hay (right) contains patchy gray "turned" areas and has an unappealing odor.

if you have no choice but to feed hay that's dustier than you would like, you can soak it in clean water before feeding it to prevent your horse from inhaling the dust. Soaked hay must be fed immediately, though, because it can mold if allowed to sit.

The quality of hay can vary bale to bale, especially if certain bales are exposed to the weather when hay is stored, if it is stacked outside and kept under a tarp, for instance. The weathered bales are not of as high a quality as those inside the stack and probably should be discarded. Any bale that is discovered to have mold in it should be thrown out immediately in its entirety. Moldy hay should never be offered as feed, used as bedding, or placed on a manure pile where horses might attempt to consume it, as mold can cause severe illness in horses. It's wise to develop a habit of quickly evaluating every newly opened bale of hay to be sure it's of good quality, as a bad bale can pop up in even the best loads. Contact your hay dealer if you find bad bales, since some, particularly local suppliers, offer credit for any bad bales they may have produced despite their best efforts at quality control.

Hay can also be fed in pelleted or cube form, available from commercial mills through your feed supplier.

A portable feed bunk provides a trough for feed and offers hay at nose level (although ground feeding hay more closely approximates the horse's natural feeding posture and lessens the possibility of eye injuries caused by hay stalks at eye level).

AMY KOLZOW

Grain

Many recreational horses do not need grain; their energy requirements are low, and as long as they're easy keepers, they usually do just fine on hay and pasture. Horses who are in hard work, however, need the extra calorie boost that comes from grain, as do horses who are hard keepers and have trouble maintaining their weight.

According to a 2005 study by the U.S. Department of Agriculture, more than 90 percent of equine operations feed grain.[47]

Grain is available from most feed dealers in two forms—whole grains (oats, corn, etc.) bought by the pound and bagged, processed, branded varieties from commercial mills (sweet feed, pellets, etc.). If your horse is at a boarding barn, the barn manager most likely offers one or two choices (although many are willing to feed something else if you provide it), which makes your decision easier. But if you're purchasing grain on your own, where do you begin?

Let's start with two of the most common kinds of prepared feeds, textured (or "sweet") feeds and pelleted feeds.

Sweet feed is so called because molasses has been added to make the grain more palatable and to bind mixtures of grains together. Sweet feed

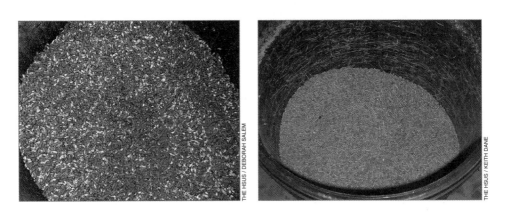

A commercial sweet feed (left) may include corn, oats, molasses, and pelleted feed and typically is available in a variety of protein content formulations for horses of different ages and activity levels. Pelleted feeds (right) (stored here in a clean, rodent-proof container) are a mixture of food stuffs processed into uniform pellets.

usually consists of a mixture of various grains (oats, corn, and barley are common); molasses; and added vitamins, minerals, and protein (usually in the form of pellets). You can easily see the various whole or crushed grains in a handful of sweet feed.

Sweet feed is an excellent choice for picky eaters and for owners who need to mix less-palatable medication or nutritional supplements into their horses' grain. The slightly sticky texture of sweet feed prevents powdered additives from sifting through the grain, and its sweet taste masks medicinal odors. Sweet feeds offer consistent quality, since they are produced to adhere to certain nutritional standards, and they're widely available in bagged form from any feed dealer. Molasses (which can cause excess edginess in horses prone to hyperactivity) can cause sweet feed to spoil easily in hot, humid weather, so it's best to purchase this feed in a quantity that can be used relatively quickly or to store it in a climate-controlled environment.[48]

Pelleted feeds are a mixture of grains, vitamins, minerals, and protein finely ground and processed into uniform pellets. (A different variation of this process produces extruded feeds, which consist of larger, less-dense pellets.) Pelleted feeds have a low moisture content, so they can be stored for a relatively long time. They can also be soaked in water to make an easy-to-eat mash for horses who are prone to choke or for older horses with poor teeth.

Like sweet feed, pellets are commercially available in bags. Most horses eat pellets well, but some finicky eaters may not like them as well as sweet feeds. Any powdered supplements added to pellets often end up left at the bottom of the bucket. This problem can be solved by adding a spoonful or two of bottled molasses, as needed.

Some varieties of pellets are marketed as "complete feeds." They contain a high percentage of fiber and can serve as the horse's entire diet; no hay is required. They're useful for older horses whose teeth might be in poor condition and who have trouble chewing hay or grass and can even be fed as a soaked mush if necessary. They're also often fed to horses with respiratory ailments that are exacerbated by the dust in hay. In locales where hay is scarce or where it varies widely in cost or quality, complete feeds may be a good option.

Both pellets and sweet feeds are carefully balanced to include all the vitamins and trace minerals horses require, so unless your horse has special needs, you can be reasonably sure all of his nutritional needs are met. Both have nutritional labels that tell you the ingredients and the percentages of various nutrients, usually as a maximum or minimum percentage. The ingredient list is not as detailed as it is on human food because the contents may vary slightly from batch to batch, and because many feed manufacturers want to keep their exact formulations secret from competitors.

Many horse owners feed unadulterated grains, like whole or crimped oats and cracked or rolled corn, either on their own or in conjunction with other feeds. These may be milled locally. The quality of these grains can vary more widely than among prepared feeds, and they do not contain

FEEDING

185

Beet pulp, a by-product of the sugar beet industry, can be purchased in sweetened or plain varieties and is a popular horse feed.

added vitamins or minerals to ensure a balanced diet, so you may have to supplement these on your own.

Selecting a feed for your horse depends on many factors, including the amount of work your horse receives, his age, and any specific nutritive requirements. Specific guidance on determining the feed that's right for you is beyond the scope of this book. Your veterinarian can give you some general guidance, however, and feed companies have nutritionists on staff who can help you determine which of *their* feeds is best suited for your horse. (Of course, in addition to providing customer service, they have a vested interest in convincing you that their feeds are better than the others on the market.)

In general, you want to select feed that meets or slightly exceeds all of your horse's requirements and that your particular horse finds palatable. You want to choose a feed from a reputable company—national or local—that uses high-quality ingredients and processes feed in an environment where it can't be contaminated, and you want to purchase the feed you use from a dealer who has a constant fresh supply (feed loses nutrition as it ages), carefully stored where it won't be subjected to excessive heat or moisture or exposed to rodents.

In addition to reading the label, you should visually inspect the grain product (although this is more productive with unprocessed grains and sweet feed than it is with pellets). Are the kernels plump and mature? Does there seem to be an excess of unidentifiable "filler"? Do whole grains like oats or corn seem stale and dusty? Once you've decided on a feed type or brand, check the quality of any new bag you open and dump into your feed bin. If old or improperly stored, grain can be infested with insects or become moldy. Immediately discard/return any bag of feed you open that is "buggy" with weevils, moldy, or smells "off."

One age-old horseman's practice is feeding bran mashes, either as occasional treats or for digestive health. Wheat bran is not nutrient-dense, so the small amounts usually fed to horses do not add much nutritional content, but feeding mashes is thought to increase gut motility (activity), although there's disagreement over how much value, if any, bran mashes have in that regard. Wheat bran is also very high in phosphorus, and because the ratio of calcium to phosphorus must be kept around 2:1, you might need to add additional calcium to your horse's diet if you feed him bran. Bran mashes are probably not a necessary part of a horse's diet, but they are a nice occasional treat on cold winter mornings, or a good method of providing hydration to a horse who might not be drinking enough water on his own.

Rice bran has a very high fat content and is often fed as a supplement for hard keepers, or as an alternative to grains for horses who can't tolerate high levels of starch. If you choose to feed rice bran, be sure to purchase only the stabilized variety—unstabilized rice bran becomes rancid very quickly.

While grass hay (not legume hay) can usually be fed to horses in large quantities without any adverse effects (other than the horse getting too fat), feeding too much grain *can* be detrimental. An overgrained horse may be hyperactive because of all those excess calories. Extremely high grain intake—usually the result of a horse getting into the feed room's grain bin and gorging himself—can be extremely dangerous because it can lead to bouts of colic or laminitis (see chapter 10).

Grain should always be stored in horse-proof containers, preferably behind a closed and locked door in a feed room or spare stall. Grain should also be protected from rodents or hungry wildlife (like raccoons), for sanitary reasons and to prevent your barn from becoming attractive to disease-carrying or otherwise undesirable critters.

Pasture

Chapter 8 discussed the importance of turnout for a horse's well-being. Unfortunately, however, turnout time doesn't always equal grazing time.

In densely populated areas near major cities, turnout might only be available in small paddocks or pastures that are quickly overgrazed. In other parts of the country, lush grass simply doesn't grow, and turnout is primarily for exercise, not grazing.

When it's available, though, pasture grazing is exactly how Nature intended horses to eat—fresh, green grass, nibbled at throughout the day as the horse ambles around. It's a perfect food source for horses, when properly managed and maintained. It doesn't require delivery or storage, and other than the cost of periodic seeding and fertilizing, it's free!

If your horse is fortunate enough to be able to consume a significant portion of his diet in fresh forage, your pastures aren't "just grass": they're an important part of your feeding program and should be treated as such. A well-maintained pasture should be soil-tested every few years to determine what nutrients are lacking or overabundant. Good pasture requires periodic seeding, fertilizing, and weed control. Your local cooperative extension agent can provide valuable information on managing pastures in your particular location, including seeding and fertilizing recommendations.

Much of pasture management isn't made up of soil testing or expert advice, however—just care. Most important is to avoid overgrazing. If pastures don't have enough grass to accommodate your herd grazing 24/7, the horses should only be turned out on them for part of the day and should have their diets supplemented with hay. If you have ample pasture land, you can rotate horses throughout various pastures, letting them graze one while another is resting (allowing the grass to grow and the manure to dry out and be absorbed into the soil). You can also divide one large pasture into sections with temporary electric fencing, and rotate horses through the sections, since horses graze small areas more effectively than large ones.

Although grass is a horse's natural diet, too much of a good thing can cause problems. A horse unaccustomed to eating grass can easily founder if allowed too much time on lush pasture (see chapter 10). As with all dietary changes, introduction to pasture should be done gradually. Allow a horse to start with limited turnout—as little as fifteen minutes a day if the grass is especially lush. Make incremental increases until the horse has acclimated and can be on a regular turnout schedule. Note any signs of inflammation in the feet (ask your equine practitioner to show you how to use hoof testers to check for tenderness).

Any horse can founder, but ponies are especially prone to foundering on grass, and overweight animals are also at greater risk. A horse that has foundered once is at increased risk of foundering again, so extreme care should be taken when allowing these horses out on grass. You might want to limit pasture turnout to a few hours a day or put a grazing muzzle on a horse, which restricts the amount of grass he can eat. Some horses have medical issues, such as insulin resistance or Cushing's syndrome, that make them very sensitive to the sugars in grass.

Most pastures grow more than grass, including trees, weeds (such as ragweed and thistle), and invasive plants as well. Many varieties of plants are poisonous to horses, and if you manage your own pasture, you need to become familiar with the ones common to your area so you can eradicate them. Your local cooperative extension office should be able to provide some information specific to your locale, but you can also find plenty of books and websites with detailed photographs and descriptions.

If grass is adequate, most horses leave harmful plants alone, but when pastures are overgrazed and horses are looking for anything green to eat, they're much more likely to consume something dangerous.

A Last Word

While concentrates (grains) can make up for digestible caloric deficiencies in low-quality roughage (hay), they cannot make up for the digestive and psychological benefits of roughage. There is a growing body of evidence to show that colic, including the more severe types of displacements, is less common in horses whose main caloric intake comes from natural pasture or good, long-stemmed hay. Roughage also benefits horses' dental health. While processed feeds (pellets and grain mixes) can be more convenient for the owner, they do not mimic normal feeding behavior, in which horses spend a significant amount of their time eating followed by rest or exercise, then more eating. When horses are deprived of normal feeding behavior, they are more likely to develop disorders such as cribbing, wood chewing, stall walking, and sand eating. These obsessive/compulsive behaviors are not good for the horse's health and are a common reason for horses becoming "unwanted." Mimicking natural feeding behavior by having horses on pasture or feeding at least three times a day is a good idea.

CHAPTER 10

Veterinary Care

WITH ANY LUCK, YOU'LL BE ONE OF THOSE fortunate owners who only sees the veterinarian twice a year for vaccinations. Your horse will never get sick, never take a lame step, never have an accident.

But, if you're like most of us, sooner or later in your horse-owning career, your veterinarian will be on your phone's speed dial. Horses can be complicated, fragile, accident-prone creatures who seem to make a hobby out of finding new methods of hurting themselves or new ways of stumping your veterinarian.

The relationship you have with your veterinarian is an important one. You want to find an equine practitioner whose judgment you trust, who is educated and keeps current on new findings, and whose horse care philosophy matches your own. For new horse owners, it's especially important to find a veterinarian who is happy to answer your questions and further your own education—someone who lets you stick your hand in the horse's mouth to feel the sharp points on his teeth for yourself, or shows you how to find the digital pulses on his feet. Most veterinarians want educated horse owners for clients and are happy to answer your questions.

Many horse owners, as they gain confidence and experience, handle minor issues on their own—it's both economical and practical to deal with a small cut or scrape yourself. But educated horse owners are cognizant of the limits of their own knowledge, know enough to call the veterinarian when their methods aren't working, and know there are certain situations where a veterinarian is required immediately.

Although it's easy to focus on the scary emergency situations, it's also important to cover all the bases when it comes to preventive care. Vaccinations, dental care, and deworming play a huge part in keeping your horse healthy and happy. But most likely you'll also be faced with injuries and accidents, so you need to be prepared for those as well.

Vaccinations

When you consider the huge assortment of vaccines that are recommended for horses, the saying "healthy as a horse" might seem to be a misnomer. But horses are unique among companion animals in that they frequently travel to shows, trail rides, and lesson barns, where they come into contact with other, strange horses. This creates an atmosphere where diseases are easily transmitted.

Even the most robust vaccination schedule doesn't protect a horse against everything, but there are many diseases for which extremely effective vaccines exist, and widespread use has dramatically improved overall equine health.

There's no one-size-fits-all vaccine protocol for horses. Pregnant mares and breeding stallions receive vaccines that your typical riding horse does not. Horses who live in a closed herd—retirees who live in an owner's back field year-round—have less opportunity for exposure to some diseases and might receive fewer vaccines than horses who are kept at large barns with lots of traffic in and out, or those who travel frequently to shows.

Different parts of the country have different recommended vaccination regimens, depending on the local weather and the diseases that are endemic in that particular area. For example, the vaccines for mosquito-borne illnesses are generally administered just before mosquito season begins, which varies, depending on where you live. In the parts of the country where mosquitoes are present year-round, these vaccines might be given twice a year instead of just once.

Your veterinarian is your best resource for determining what vaccinations your horse needs. He knows which ailments are common in your area, what vaccination schedule works best, and your horse's lifestyle, including management system (box stall versus dry pasture versus irrigated pasture), and the diseases to which he might be exposed. Your veterinarian is also up to date on the latest research into vaccine protocols and the efficacy of new vaccines that have just come on the market.

This is a good time to mention the importance of obtaining a veterinary history on your horse when you first obtain her, if at all possible, and keeping that history, including vaccination records, current throughout her life.

Here is an overview of the most common diseases for which vaccines are available. Consult your veterinarian for more information on any of them.

Tetanus

Tetanus is a highly fatal disease caused by anaerobic bacteria commonly found in the soil and fecal material. If the bacteria get into the body via a puncture or other wound and begin to grow, they produce an extremely potent toxin. That toxin effects the nerve signals that tell muscles to relax, causing what used to be known as "lockjaw"—the horse exhibits a sawhorse stance and seeming paralysis of the facial muscles, including the jaw. He eventually goes down, stiff-legged, and dies shortly thereafter.

Because horses are very susceptible to tetanus and live in an environment where it's quite prevalent, this vaccination is a standard in every equine health protocol. It's an extremely safe, extremely effective vaccine, generally administered once a year. (It's usually part of common combination vaccines.)[49]

Rabies

Rabies is a fatal disease that can affect any mammal; about fifty horses die of rabies in the United States every year.

The virus is present in an infected animal's saliva and is usually transmitted by a bite, although it can also be transmitted if infected saliva comes in contact with an open wound or mucous membranes. The virus spreads through the central nervous system, eventually reaching the brain. Symptoms vary widely, but behavioral changes are considered one of the most common signs. Other symptoms might include depression, a mild fever, excessive salivation, difficulty swallowing, convulsions, and a lack of appetite. Symptoms progress very quickly, and an infected horse generally dies within five to seven days.[50]

Rabies is seen in raccoons, skunks, foxes, coyotes, and bats, with all of whom horses may come in contact in their barns or pastures. The disease is endemic in every state but Hawaii, although some parts of the country see a much higher frequency of rabies than do others.

Eastern, Western, and Venezuelan Encephalomyelitis

Eastern equine encephalomyelitis (EEE), Western equine encephalomyelitis (WEE), and Venezuelan equine encephalomyelitis (VEE) are sometimes referred to as "sleeping sickness." EEE and WEE are a concern in the United States; VEE is generally a concern only in South America, but occasional cases have been reported in Mexico and southern Texas.

EEE, WEE, and VEE are viruses transmitted from birds and rodents, which are reservoirs for the disease, to horses by mosquitoes. (All three can also infect humans.) EEE is the most deadly of the three, with a fatality rate of 75 to 90 percent. The fatality rate for VEE is 40 to 80 percent, and for WEE, 20 to 50 percent.[51] All affect the horse's nervous system and produce neurological signs. Horses who survive infection frequently suffer permanent neurological damage.

Vaccines exist for all three diseases, although only WEE and EEE are commonly vaccinated against in the majority of U.S. states. The vaccines are extremely effective and are often given combined in one injection.

West Nile Virus

West Nile virus (WNV) is another mosquito-borne disease, very similar to EEE, WEE, and VEE. A relative newcomer in the United States, it was first diagnosed in New York in 1999, but has now spread across the entire country. The virus infects the central nervous system, causing neurological symptoms. The fatality rate is about 30 percent.[52]

Fortunately, a vaccine was quickly developed that has proven very safe and effective, leading to a marked downturn in the number of cases, even as the disease spread over a larger area of the country. There were more than fifteen thousand equine cases of WNV in 2002; that number dropped to less than five thousand in 2003 and to just over thirteen hundred in 2004.

Equine Herpesvirus

For most of the ailments we've discussed so far, vaccinations provide near-immunity. Unfortunately, not all vaccines are quite so effective. One disease for which this is the case is rhinopneumonitis, which is caused by the equine herpesvirus (EHV). There are several varieties of the virus, but the ones that cause serious illness are EHV-1 and EHV-4.

EHV is unique in that horses can be infected with the virus, but show no symptoms. It's estimated that about half the equine population are latent carriers of the virus. If a latently infected horse is stressed, however, he can begin to shed the virus, subsequently infecting other horses. The virus is spread very easily from horse to horse and can even be carried from one barn to another on the clothes, shoes, or hands of humans. (Humans cannot be infected with the virus, however.)

EHV typically causes respiratory infection, and affected horses exhibit a snotty nose, cough, and fever. Infection with the virus can also lead to abortion in pregnant mares.

A mutant strain of EHV-1 causes neurological symptoms—lack of coordination, hind end weakness, and eventual paralysis. The fatality rate of the neurologic form is about 40 percent, and several high-profile outbreaks have been seen in recent years at show facilities, veterinary hospitals, and racetracks.[53]

Unfortunately, the vaccination for EHV cannot protect against the neurologic form, only the form that causes respiratory illness and abortion. Vaccination does seem to lessen the severity of symptoms, however, if a vaccinated horse contracts the neurologic form of the virus.

Equine Influenza

Just like humans, horses are subject to infection from the influenza virus. It's not the same virus seen in humans, but the effects are similar: a respiratory infection that is only rarely fatal, but is highly contagious and makes victims feel completely miserable. Symptoms include fever, runny nose, cough, and loss of appetite, and it can take months for infected horses to recover, although most do recover fully.

The equine influenza vaccine offers good protection, although not full immunity. Vaccinated horses who do become infected generally experience milder symptoms.

Strangles

A bacterial infection caused by *Streptococcus equi*, strangles is a very common disease that has afflicted horses for centuries. It's highly contagious, although not usually fatal. The bacteria cause a respiratory infection (usually accompanied by mucus in the nose) that leads to swelling of the lymph nodes in the head and neck.

The strangles vaccination does not offer full immunity, but it may lessen the symptoms if a horse does manage to become infected. It's available both as an intramuscular injection and an intranasal vaccine.

Potomac Horse Fever

First documented near the Potomac River in Maryland in 1979, but now found throughout the United States, Potomac horse fever (PHF) is caused by bacteria (*Neorickettsia risticii*) that are usually found in streams. Infection causes inflammation of the horse's intestinal tract and is usually accompanied by fever, diarrhea, and a generally depressed demeanor. The disease has a fatality rate of about 30 percent, but can be treated successfully with antibiotics.

The PHF vaccine does not offer full immunity, as it's only effective against one strain of the bacteria, and horses can be infected with different strains in different parts of the country. Vaccination does lessen the severity of symptoms.[54]

Deworming

As long as there have been horses, parasites have preyed on them. The term "parasite" is broad and encompasses a number of different creatures that take up residence in or on the horse's body as uninvited guests.

Parasites wreak havoc in numerous ways. They can physically damage tissue within the body by migrating through it, obstruct arteries, suck blood, and usurp the nutrition from food the horse consumes. A horse infested with parasites looks unthrifty, with a dull, scruffy coat and a potbelly. He is likely to be underweight and have a difficult time putting weight back on. The existence and extent of parasite infestation can be confirmed with a fecal sample that is examined for parasite eggs. The higher the number of eggs, the worse the infection.

Deworming drugs, known as anthelmintics, first became available in the 1960s, finally providing horses some protection against parasites. Deworming programs have become quite robust since then and are credited with significantly increasing the life expectancy of the average horse. Although parasites are still ever-present, and horses always pick them up from their environment, a strict deworming program prevents them from ever building up to a significant level in the horse and causing real damage.

The primary parasites that affect adult horses are large and small strongyles, tapeworms, pinworms, and bots.

The Deworming Program

Horses pick up most parasites as larvae. Once inside the body, these larvae mature into adults and lay eggs, which are passed out with the horse's manure. The eggs hatch into larvae, which the horse ingests, starting the life cycle all over again.

The goal of a deworming program is to break this life cycle, usually by killing the adult worms before they can lay eggs. Deworming programs have evolved considerably in the last forty years. Today, there are two primary weapons in a deworming program, periodic and continuous dewormers.

Periodic dewormers are typically oral paste medications dispensed with a syringe, but they're also available as pelleted or powdered feed additives. Continuous dewormers are pelleted feed additives that are given in very small doses every day.

Most horse owners choose a periodic deworming program that relies on paste medications. Paste dewormers are readily available over the counter and are easy for the horse owner to administer. Most are "broad spectrum," meaning they kill a wide variety of parasites.

A periodic deworming program essentially purges the horse of any parasites picked up since the last treatment. The idea is that the periodic purges prevent the worm load from ever becoming so substantial that it causes harm to the horse.

A horse owner's other option is a continuous deworming program, in which a small amount of dewormer is fed to the horse daily, along with his grain. The goal here is to kill any larvae the horse has ingested on a daily basis, before they can mature. Because the active ingredient in daily dewormers is not effective against bots, manufacturers recommend that horses on these programs be paste wormed every six months with a medication effective against that particular parasite.

There are significant differences among deworming protocols, based on geographic area. Your equine practitioner should be involved in any deworming decisions you are considering.

Drugs and Resistance

When anthelmintics first became available, they were generally effective against only one kind of parasite (or maybe two), so veterinarians recommended rotating among the different classes of drugs to provide full protection. The thinking was that if your dewormer didn't kill tapeworms, for example, this time around, you'd get them eight weeks later when you used a different dewormer.

Today, most dewormers are broad spectrum and are effective against several different kinds of parasites, but not all dewormers are effective against *every* kind of parasite. In addition, certain drugs can have more of an impact if they're given when they have the greatest effectiveness. Because local environmental factors greatly affect when certain parasites are most prevalent, your veterinarian is the best source of help when designing a rotational worming program.

Rotation is also considered important to help prevent the emergence of parasites that are resistant to common drugs. Every dewormer lists its main active ingredient on the box; there are typically several different brand names that all use the same active ingredient. If you plan to rotate dewormers, don't just change brand names; make sure you are using a different drug each time.

Other Methods

Any deworming program typically focuses on the various anthelmintics used, but there are other aspects to parasite control as well. First and foremost is manure management. If manure is removed from stalls and paddocks frequently, there's less opportunity for horses to become infected with the parasite larvae that hatch from that manure.

Horses are naturally inclined to defecate in certain portions of a pasture but graze in others, thereby naturally doing some manure management of their own. This only works if pastures are large and not overcrowded, however; if pastures are overgrazed and grass is rare, horses ignore their instincts in favor of getting some grass to eat.

Although manure is an excellent fertilizer and is commonly used on pastures, it should only be spread after it has been composted (which means it's been left to sit for a long period). The intense heat of that process kills any emerging parasite larvae. If *fresh* manure is spread on pastures, you're coating your pastures with parasite eggs and larvae as well as fertilizer.

Dental Care

You might consider the horse's mouth—and specifically his teeth—to be like a finely tuned grass/hay consumption machine. But like any machine, your horse's teeth need periodic maintenance to keep them operating as they should.

Horses' teeth continue growing throughout their lifetime, so their mouths are in a constant state of slow change. The teeth on their lower and upper jaws don't meet exactly—the upper jaw is slightly wider. The grinding action that a horse uses wears down the surface of his teeth but can also leave sharp "points" or "hooks" on the outer edge of the upper teeth and the inner edge of the lower teeth, because those edges don't come in contact with their opposing teeth.

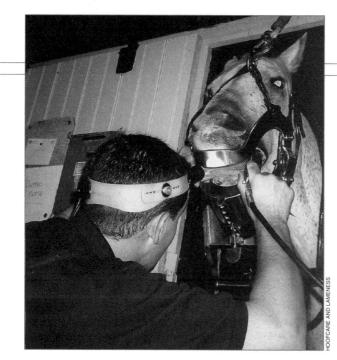

Floating a horse's teeth can be done by a veterinarian or an equine dentist.

HOOFCARE AND LAMENESS

If those points and hooks are not attended to, they can become quite sharp and cause serious discomfort for the horse. A horse whose teeth need attention might seem to have difficulty chewing—dropping partially chewed pieces of hay or grass, or mouthfuls of grain—and has trouble maintaining his weight. He can become aversive to the bit while being ridden, perhaps flipping his head with discomfort or objecting to being haltered or bridled.

To prevent the hooks and points that occur naturally from becoming a problem, a horse's teeth should be checked routinely, either by a veterinarian who does dental work or a specialized equine dentist. In a process known as "floating," the sharp parts of the tooth are filed down, usually with a motorized float, but sometimes by hand with a metal file.

Most horses only need to be floated once a year, but horses who crib or have conformation defects in their mouths—like a parrot mouth (overbite) or undershot jaw (underbite)—might need more frequent dental attention. It's a good habit to have your veterinarian check your horse's teeth twice a year, when he is administering spring and fall vaccinations.

Coggins Test

One final and simple, yet important, piece of your health maintenance plan should be a Coggins test. This simple blood test, which has been in use since the 1970s, screens for antibodies to equine infectious anemia (EIA), or swamp fever, a viral disease transmitted by mosquitoes. Horses can be EIA carriers and show no symptoms, so the Coggins test is important to prevent such horses from spreading the disease. About three hundred horses are discovered to be EIA-positive in the United States every year.

Drawing a Coggins every spring is a ritual for horse owners, as this paperwork is required to transport a horse out of state or to go to just about any kind of competition. Most boarding barns require a negative Coggins as well before they'll let your horse set foot on the property.

But even if your horse rarely leaves the farm, it's a good idea to make this inexpensive test an annual ritual. A Coggins can also be used as proof of ownership, since it includes your horse's identifying marks.

Becoming Familiar with "Normal"

As important as a veterinarian is to any horse's health and well-being, an educated owner is equally important. It's the observant owner who can notice that something's "not quite right," perhaps well before things become serious. It's the owner who can give a veterinarian the valuable information about a horse's daily habits, diet, and idiosyncrasies that can help make a diagnosis.

To detect subtle changes in your horse's habits and demeanor and to assist your veterinarian by providing that all-important information, you need to be intimately familiar with what constitutes "normal" for your horse, both his physical and his mental state. While small changes in your horse's usual behavior or subtle physical changes are not automatically cause for worry, they should be noticed and filed away. Often, subtle changes can point to a much larger problem, and you're the one who notices and is able to connect the dots to address the problem most quickly.

Vital Signs

Whenever a veterinarian is assessing a horse who might be ill, the first thing she does is look at the horse's vital signs. As your horse's caretaker, you, too, should have this skill—first, to establish what your horse's normal vital signs are, and, second, to be able to check them in an emergency or when you suspect something is wrong.

To take your horse's vitals, you should be armed with a digital watch or one with a second hand. You want your horse to be relaxed and standing still, so the easiest place to do this might be in the crossties in the barn aisle or at a tie-ring in his stall. You don't want your horse to be eating or otherwise preoccupied. Ideally, he should be bored, half-asleep.

Let's start with the horse's temperature. You need a thermometer (either a glass one intended for use with horses, or a regular digital thermometer from the drugstore) and a jar of petroleum jelly, either brand-new, or one you have specially dedicated for this purpose. If you're using a glass thermometer, it should have a string tied to the end that you can hold onto. (You can also attach the string to a hair clip, and then clip it to the horse's tail.)

After washing your hands, dip a finger into the petroleum jelly and use a glob of it to lubricate the thermometer. With your watch at the ready and your horse either tied or being held, stand to the side of your horse's rump, facing his tail. Use one hand to lift the tail and move it to the side, and the other to slide the thermometer carefully and gently into the horse's anus. (Make sure that you're standing off to the side, but close to your horse, so he can't kick you.) If you're using a mercury thermometer, check your watch, or, if you're using a digital, hit the button. Hold both tail and thermometer, and when the appropriate amount of time has passed (per the thermometer's instructions: for glass, three minutes), gently remove the thermometer.[55] It is helpful at first to watch closely as your veterinarian performs a temperature check, then repeat the procedure yourself under his watchful eye.

The normal temperature for a horse is considered to be 100.5 degrees, but as in humans, some variance above and below is to be expected. It's usually not cause for worry unless the temperature is over 102 or below 98. Your horse's temperature is also affected by the outside temperature and is slightly elevated after he's been ridden. To get a really accurate estimate of your horse's normal temperature, try taking it at different times of the day for several days.

An elevated temperature is the first warning sign of the onset of many illnesses, so if you are ever "on alert" for a possible outbreak of disease, you should make a habit of checking your horse's temperature twice daily. This way, you'll notice immediately any change and can take action.

Any horse owner easily notices if a horse's rate of respiration is extremely elevated, such as after strenuous exercise—the heaving flanks are hard to miss. But it's also important to be able to check a resting respiration rate. To do this your horse should be quiet, relaxed, and standing still. Have your watch ready and stand at your horse's shoulder, facing his flanks. You can also try putting a hand lightly on the flank, so you can feel your horse take a breath as well as see it.

Watch or feel for the inhale and exhale, and the rise and fall of your horse's flanks, for several breaths to become attuned to your horse's rhythm, then check your watch. If your horse will stand still long enough, you can count for a full sixty seconds to get the most accurate measurement. If not, try to count for as long as you think the horse will stand still—fifteen, twenty, or thirty seconds—and then multiply the number you get to determine the breaths per minute.

A normal respiration rate is considered to be between eight and sixteen breaths per minute. An elevated respiration rate, or one that does not quickly return to normal after exercise, is generally a sign of distress.

If you have trouble detecting your horse's breaths by watching or feeling his flanks, you can also try putting your hand in front of his nostrils, where you can feel him blow out. The problem with this method is that horses usually try to sniff your hand instead of breathing normally. He's paying attention to *you* and might not stand still for very long. But if you leave your hand there for a few seconds while encouraging your horse to stand still (and ideally go back to sleep), you should eventually be able to get an accurate count.

To take your horse's pulse, stand to his side by his head. Put one hand on his nose or halter to hold his head still, and put the index and middle finger of your other hand along the bottom of his jaw, right near where his curved cheekbone begins and his lower jaw ends. (Don't use your thumb; your own pulse makes it impossible to feel your horse's.) Keep the pressure of your fingers relatively light and feel around for the gentle throbbing sensation of a pulse. It takes some practice to find. If you're unable to do it, have someone experienced help you find the spot.

Once you've found the pulse, keep your horse still and check your watch. Count for fifteen seconds, then multiply by four to get your horse's heartbeats per minute. Normal resting heart rate is about thirty to forty beats per minute. An elevated pulse in a horse at rest usually means he's in pain or distress.

Being able to take your horse's pulse is also handy if you're working on improving his fitness. You can jump off after finishing a trot or gallop set and take a quick pulse: as a horse gets fitter, his heart rate after exercise decreases.

Other Indicators of Distress

Whenever your horse seems slightly "off," these checks will help confirm or alleviate your fears and give you some more information to pass on to your veterinarian.

Capillary refill time (CRT) is a test of the horse's circulation. To check capillary refill, pull up your horse's upper lip and press on his gums, right above his upper teeth, with your thumb. Press down firmly for two seconds, then lift your thumb: you should see a white mark where your thumb was, and it should disappear in one to two seconds as blood returns to the capillaries. If the white mark remains for longer than two seconds, it can indicate that the horse is going into shock.

Observing the color of the horse's mucous membranes (his gums and the linings of his nostrils and eyelids) can provide another indicator of distress. In a healthy horse, mucous membranes should be a pale pink. If the mucous membranes are much paler than normal, much redder than normal, grayish-blue, or yellow, call your veterinarian.

A quick listen to your horse's gut sounds helps to assess if there might be digestive trouble going on. Put your ear up against the lower half of his barrel near his flank (or use a stethoscope). Check both sides: if you hear gurgling and grumbling, all is well. If you don't hear anything, that's cause for concern.

Finally, there's a very simple test for dehydration that every horseman should know. With your thumb and index finger, pinch a "tent" of skin in the middle of your horse's neck. Let it go, and watch how quickly it snaps back into place. If the skin stays "tented" for more than one second, the horse is dehydrated. The longer the skin pinch remains, the more dehydrated the horse is.

Practice taking your horse's vitals and doing all of these quick tests. During your veterinarian's next routine visit, ask the expert to watch your technique. You not only will have added to your horsemanship skill set but you also will have valuable tools available with which to assess your horse's normal state.

Legs

With age and use, all horses start to accumulate what horse people call "jewelry"—little bumps, lumps, and swellings on their legs. The presence or lack of these little imperfections isn't as important as whether any of them has changed. A *new* bump or swelling might indicate a strain or other injury brewing. It's important to know every inch of your horse's legs and to check them daily for any changes.

You're probably already familiar with most of your horse's lumps and bumps, but make a point of really going over his legs and memorizing their topography. Do it both before and after the horse is ridden, and when the horse first walks out of the stall, since many horses stock up (accumulate fluid in the legs) when they have not been moving around. (If you don't know whether your horse is one of those, this is a good opportunity to find out!)

Look at both front legs in comparison to each other, and both hind legs. Are there any differences? Is one knee or hock larger than the other? Is there a windpuff (a small swelling on the fetlock) on one leg, but not on its opposite?

After doing a visual inspection, run your hands all over your horse's legs. Feel the joints and take note of any swelling, or "filling." (Don't forget the stifle joints, which you can feel best by standing directly behind the horse, if it's safe to do so.) Ideally, the knees, hocks, stifles, and fetlocks should all feel flat and firm, not "squishy."

Check the splint bones, which are on the sides of each leg, and take note of the location of any splints. Old splints are hard and cold; new ones are warm and painful. Horses can get splints on their hind legs, but they're most often found on the front ones, and generally on the inside, as opposed to the outside, of the leg.

Also run your hands down the back of your horse's legs to feel his tendons and ligaments. Familiarize yourself with any normal soft spots and swellings. For example, blood vessels right under the knee can sometimes be mistaken for a swelling along the tendon. Any injury to a tendon or ligament will be accompanied by heat and swelling, but it can be very slight if an injury is just starting to brew. By checking your horse's legs regularly, and especially if you ever feel like he's "not quite right," you might be able to detect a very small injury before it becomes a major one.

It's also a good idea to know how your horse normally moves. Watch him on the longe line or work him in a round pen occasionally so you're familiar with his normal way of going and can spot any changes.

Habits

In addition to all of the physical indicators, your horse's demeanor will tell you when something's not right. If he doesn't feel normal, he's not going to act normal. Train yourself to notice little things. If your horse doesn't greet you at the pasture gate as usual, but instead remains standing in the field with his head hanging low, check for other indicators that might show you something is wrong—an obvious wound, a damaged gate or other problem in the horse's environment, or an untouched meal in the feed tub. Calling to your horse might start him limping toward you, a clear indication of where the problem lies, or worse, disclose an unwillingness or inability to move.

It might be that your horse is in the middle of a nap; if so, you'll realize quickly that nothing is out of the ordinary. But the more attention you pay to small changes in behavior, the better you're able to notice when something goes wrong and spare yourself the reproach of not taking action sooner.

Note your horse's eating and drinking habits. Does he tend to leave some of his hay and go back to it later, or does he eat it all in one sitting? Does he just take occasional sips of water from the bucket in his stall, preferring to wait and guzzle from the trough once he's put out? Does he occasionally leave some of his grain uneaten, or is he a bucket-licker who gets every last kernel?

Be cognizant of your horse's stall habits. Some horses leave all their manure in one pile in a particular corner of the stall, while others defecate whenever the mood strikes, turning their stall into a manure pit. If your horse's normally neat and tidy stall is a mess in the morning, it should set off alarm bells instantly. He might have been in discomfort and pacing half the night. If there is no manure in the stall, an impaction colic may be brewing. This is a serious situation (see page 209).

Pasture behavior can tell you a lot, too. Does your horse immediately head for his favorite dirt spot and roll when you turn him out? If he suddenly stops that behavior, it could be an indicator that he's sore somewhere. Does he like to lie down during his daily nap? After the heart-stopping experience of glimpsing your horse lying pancake flat and motionless, you will learn that this sleep pattern is normal for many horses.

If you keep your horse at home and handle his care yourself, familiarizing yourself with his routine is pretty effortless, but it's a little more work if you're at a boarding barn. If you have a responsible barn manager, he will taking note of these things and should be able to alert you if there are any major changes. But you should learn your horse's routine yourself: go to the barn at different times of the day, make a point of being there during a farrier's visit, and ask questions of the barn staff when your path crosses theirs. That way you'll know what's "normal" for your guy if you ever take him off the property.

Major Medical Issues

Colic

Colic is a generic term for any sort of equine abdominal pain. It can be something very mild and almost unnoticeable that passes on its own or with minimal human intervention. It can also be a serious, life-threatening issue that requires risky and expensive surgery. And sometimes it can be fatal.

Every horse is susceptible to colic. Your feed and management choices can greatly reduce, but never eliminate, your horse's risk. It's important to be familiar with this ailment and learn the signs of trouble, especially since rapid veterinary intervention can prevent a mild colic from becoming much worse, and can greatly improve a horse's chances of survival when the case is serious.

Horses who are colicking generally act depressed and usually, although not always, will be off their feed. They may have slightly or significantly elevated vital signs, slow capillary refill time, and abnormal color in the mucous membranes. They also show several telltale signs that are typical of abdominal discomfort—kicking or biting at their bellies or turning to look at them; repeatedly lying down and getting up in an effort to alleviate their discomfort; pawing; stretching as if to urinate; and rolling, sometimes violently.

If you think your horse might be colicking, remove the feed and water from his stall. Call your veterinarian and relay all the symptoms, your horse's general demeanor and vital signs, and any other important information. Don't administer any medication unless your veterinarian tells you to do so. While waiting for your veterinarian to arrive, hand-walking your horse might help the colic resolve itself and will keep your horse from rolling. It used to be thought that rolling could contribute to a twisted intestine, and while that's no longer the conventional thinking, you probably want to try to minimize rolling if you can do so safely, just so your horse doesn't injure himself by thrashing around.

There are many different types of colic, but the most common are impaction colic and gas colic.

Impaction colic is the result of a blockage somewhere in the horse's digestive tract, usually from partially digested food that is not moving through the system as it should. It can occur in either the small or large intestine, but most often happens in areas of the large intestine where the tract narrows and then widens again. The horse experiences pain when the muscles in the walls of the intestine contract strongly to attempt to move the impaction along.

Because food material moves through the digestive system rather slowly, impaction colic can take some time to make itself evident. Signs may be very subtle at first but become much more obvious as the horse's condition deteriorates and pain increases.

A horse suffering from an impaction colic shows signs of depression and abdominal pain, although her vital signs may still be within normal limits at first and gut sounds likely still evident (and may even be louder than usual). The horse may stop passing manure or produce abnormal manure that's very dry or coated in mucus.

Treatment often includes giving the horse intravenous fluids, not only to keep her hydrated but also to encourage increased secretion of water into the intestines, helping to soften and break up the blockage. Your veterinarian is likely to administer pain-relieving medications that relax the smooth muscles of the intestines, also to help the impaction pass.[56]

Gas colic occurs when a buildup of gas causes distention of a portion of the intestine. It can be caused by ingesting a large amount of rich food, like spring grass, which then ferments in the digestive tract, or by a sudden feed change. The horse shows the typical signs of colic, and his flanks may look slightly bloated, but usually gas colic is diagnosed because of an absence of indicators of the other types of colic, rather than an affirmative diagnosis.

Fortunately, gas colic can usually be resolved relatively easily. Your veterinarian will likely administer some pain medication, but otherwise, the treatment of choice is often simply walking the horse to encourage increased gut motility so the gas passes.

Most of the time, impaction and gas colics can be treated successfully on the farm. But some colic cases are extremely grave and require emergency surgery if the horse is to have any chance to survive.

The horse's intestines are not firmly anchored in his abdominal cavity and can sometimes move out of their normal positions. When this happens, it's possible for a portion of the intestine to twist, and if the twist is tight enough, blood flow to parts of the intestine is cut off, and the tissue starts to die. When the intestines are damaged, they leak toxins, making the horse gravely ill. Emergency surgery is required to resolve the twist—also known as a torsion—and perhaps remove damaged sections of the intestine.[57] Advances in surgery, anesthesia, and after care make surgery a reasonable option for many life-threatening types of colic.

Laminitis

Like avoiding colic, avoiding laminitis is often cited as the reason for following many "rules" of horse management. Laminitis is a disease that is still not well understood, is difficult to treat, and often does not have a very successful outcome. The Thoroughbred Barbaro, the 2006 Kentucky Derby winner who shattered his hind leg in the Preakness Stakes, recovered from his broken bones; however, the painful and incurable laminitis he developed months after the initial injury led to his being euthanized.

Laminitis is a disease of the sensitive laminae of the hoof. The laminae are living tissue that form a sort of suspension system in the hoof, attaching the bones of the foot to the wall of the hoof. When a horse has laminitis, the laminae begin to break down and may fail altogether. When the breakdown is severe, the bones of the foot can rotate and even pierce the sole of the hoof. This drastic occurrence is technically called "foundering," a result of the laminitis so linked in the minds of most horsemen that founder and laminitis are often used interchangeably.[58]

The disease exists in two forms, acute and chronic. Chronic laminitis is less severe and is usually seen in overweight ponies or stocky breeds of horses. Whenever such an animal gets too fat or has eaten too much rich grass, he has a bout of laminitis. These cases are usually milder, and the damage done inside the foot is not usually as severe as with acute laminitis, but the damage from repeated bouts can be cumulative. Horses with chronic laminitis may show rings or ridges on the walls of their hooves as the hooves grow, each ring revealing a different episode. Acute laminitis comes on very suddenly, can be extremely painful, and is much more serious.

Laminitis has many different causes. It can be traced to toxins released from the digestive tract during a bout of colic, or the result of a horse getting loose and gorging himself at the grain bin. It can be mechanical, caused by the excessive pounding of riding a horse on very hard ground (known as road founder) or an overweighting of one limb, such as when a horse is favoring the opposite leg due to an injury. Horses with insulin resistance or Cushing's disease are much more prone to laminitis.

The exact nature of what happens within the foot during an episode of laminitis is, like much of the disease, not fully explained. But it's believed that blood is routed away from the laminae, which then suffer tissue damage. Inflammation and increased blood flow occurs, which causes extreme pain because the foot is bound by the solid structure of the hoof wall.

The classic founder stance, in which the horse is rocked backward to take his weight off his front feet.

Laminitis most often affects the front feet, but can be seen in all four feet as well. In the case of a horse compensating for an injury on the opposite limb, just one hoof may be affected.

A horse that is suffering from laminitis displays a typical "founder stance": he rocks back onto his hindquarters, in an attempt to get weight off his aching front feet. His hooves are hot to the touch, and you may be able to feel a pounding pulse in the fetlock (known as the digital pulse). Laminitis is an emergency situation, and your veterinarian should be called immediately, since it's thought that most of the damage occurs very quickly after the onset of symptoms.

The primary concern with laminitis is whether the supportive structure of the laminae stays intact. When the attachment provided by the laminae is weakened, the coffin bone, which is at the bottom of the bony column of the horse's leg, is not held firmly in place. The tendons that attach to the coffin bone exert rotational forces on the bone, and the coffin bone can start to rotate within the hoof. Coffin bone rotation can be seen on radiographs. In very severe cases, the bone may rotate far enough that the point of the coffin bone pierces the sole of the horse's hoof.

VETERINARY CARE

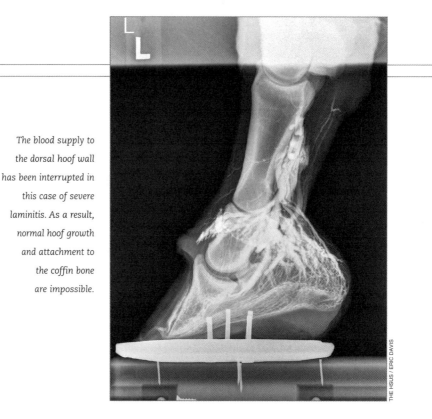

The blood supply to the dorsal hoof wall has been interrupted in this case of severe laminitis. As a result, normal hoof growth and attachment to the coffin bone are impossible.

THE HSUS / ERIC DAVIS

Even more severe than coffin bone rotation is "sinking": if the laminae fail completely, there's nothing holding the horse's hoof wall to the bones of the foot, and the entire bony column of the leg sinks. This typically is a life-threatening condition for which euthanasia is recommended.

Treatment for laminitis generally involves anti-inflammatories, and your veterinarian may recommend soaking your horse's feet in cold water. Your farrier plays an important role in your horse's treatment as well, as horses who have suffered laminitis, especially if there has been any rotation of the coffin bone, need corrective trimming and/or therapeutic shoes and pads. Cryotherapy (cold therapy), heat therapy, loading variation, vasodilatory drugs (which increase blood flow in the foot), anti-inflammatory medications, and diet/weight management are possible treatments.[59]

Any horse who has foundered is at increased risk for doing so again and must be managed very carefully. Close attention must be paid to his diet, his weight, and especially to his access to lush grass.

Lamenesses

Just like humans, horses can have aches and pains, especially as they get older. In the case of equine athletes, they're putting a lot of stress on their bodies and are always at risk for acute injury or developing a chronic condition.

Exploring all of the myriad lamenesses horses can suffer in detail is beyond the scope of this book, but we do think it's important to understand some of the common causes of lameness and to recognize when your horse is lame, so you can consult with your veterinarian to obtain a diagnosis and a course of treatment.

The term "lameness" generally encompasses any injury that causes pain to the degree that it affects a horse's gait. Included are soft tissue injuries, such as a strain to a tendon or ligament, and permanent arthritic changes in the bones of a joint, such as the hock or the fetlock. Horses can even sustain small hairline fractures. The possibilities, unfortunately, are nearly endless.

Any horse in hard work is at increased risk for developing lamenesses, especially as he ages and accrues more mileage, but you also find lamenesses in horses who have led relatively easy lives as pleasure horses or pets. Often, what sets a sound horse apart from one with chronic lameness issues is a mystery.

One of the most important contributing factors to a horse's soundness (or lack thereof) is his conformation. The horse supports his half-ton of weight on his legs virtually his whole life. If his legs are not put together correctly, certain areas are stressed and are then at risk for injury.

For example, a horse with very straight pasterns tends to have a more jarring and concussive gait than a horse with sloping pasterns, which can lead to lamenesses such as navicular (a degenerative condition of one of the bones in the foot). A horse with overly sloping pasterns exerts more force on the tendons that support that leg, making him more likely to suffer a bowed tendon.

The way in which the horse is ridden contributes greatly to his soundness. It's wise to think of a horse as having a finite number of jumps, barrels, spins, or pirouettes in his future. Unfortunately, we don't know exactly what that number is, but it's a reminder to use a horse gently. There's no reason to jump the same fence or run through the barrels a dozen times. You're only putting more "miles" on the horse and ushering him more quickly toward the end of his serviceable life span. It is often the case that a rider needs much more practice mastering a skill than does his horse—in such circumstances, rides on other horses can be his horse's best ally against injury caused by excessive use.

Footing also plays a great role in soundness. Very hard footing leads to more concussion on the feet and limbs; extremely soft and deep footing leads to more stress on the tendons and ligaments. A good rule of thumb is to avoid excessive hard work in footing that is either too deep or too hard.

And, finally, it's important to recognize the relationship between soundness and fitness. A stressed or tired horse is at much greater risk of injury than is a horse who operates well within his physical limits. An unfit horse needs to be brought back into work gradually, with slow increases in what you ask of him. Pulling a horse out of the pasture for the first time in three months and going for a trail ride with lots of hills and galloping is a surefire way to bring on an injury. But with an appropriate return to fitness, the same trail ride won't cause an issue.

Unfortunately, even horses with stellar conformation and the best of care can develop lamenesses. Recognizing lameness, both visually and by feel, is a skill that takes some time to develop. If you don't have much experience with lameness yourself, see if you can ride along with your veterinarian on a few calls one day or ask your trainer or barn manager to help you learn to see and feel the signs the next time the manager has a lame horse under her care. Recognizing a slight lameness early on will help to prevent further damage and give your horse a greater chance for full recovery.

Many lamenesses are accompanied by heat and swelling in the affected area. Here is where knowing the topography of your horse's legs is put to good use. If you suspect a lameness, run your hands along your horse's legs, especially the joints and the tendons and ligaments that run down the back of each leg, comparing each leg to its counterpart on the opposite side. A warm or swollen spot that isn't usually there and doesn't exist on the opposite leg is a good indicator of an injury.

Watching the horse move is one of the best ways to assess lameness. A horse who is in pain attempts to relieve pressure on the affected limb by altering his gait. His length of stride with that leg is shorter, leading to an unevenness that can be very slight or quite pronounced. If you watch where each horse's foot falls as he walks or trots, you can sometimes see that he's stepping shorter with one leg—not reaching up under himself or forward as far with that leg as he is with the other.

You might also notice a slight bob of his head, one telltale sign of lameness. The horse jerks his head *up* slightly when the lame foot touches the ground because it causes pain. The "bob" you see is the horse relaxing back to his usual head position when the sound foot touches the ground. A head-bob might be noticeable at the walk but is usually more pronounced at the trot.

Watching a horse on the longe line is often the best way to detect lameness, because the small size of the circle forces the horse to bear more weight on his inside limbs. If he's lame on the right front leg, for example, he looks much more "off" being longed to the right than to the left.

As a rider, you're most likely to first notice a lameness by feel. You may swing up into the saddle and instantly notice something is wrong. During the course of a ride, you might have a nagging feeling that something seems "off." Or you may just have fleeting moments where it feels as if your horse takes an uneven step.

If you're getting that "something's not quite right" feeling, try trotting your horse in a small circle in both directions. When there's a marked difference in the way the horse moves and feels in one direction, it's a good indication of lameness.

It's best to err on the side of caution. If you're riding and something *seems* off, but you're not sure, you're better off quitting for the day, performing a leg and hoof examination, and checking your tack. If the horse is not sound the following day, or if any visible signs of injury or trauma emerge, it's time to call your veterinarian for an expert opinion.

Recognizing an Emergency

As you observe your veterinarian treat your horse for minor problems, you become pretty good at following his instructions on your own when similar problems present themselves. You learn to evaluate a cut, scrape, or minor swelling, monitor it for signs of trouble or healing, and become confident enough in your own basic knowledge that you can try a few things on your own for minor injuries, with the ever-present caveat that you'll be on the phone to the veterinarian posthaste if things get worse, or if there's no improvement in a day or two.

Certain situations have CALL THE VET NOW written all over them. Time is often of the essence; some minor dithering and amateur doctoring on

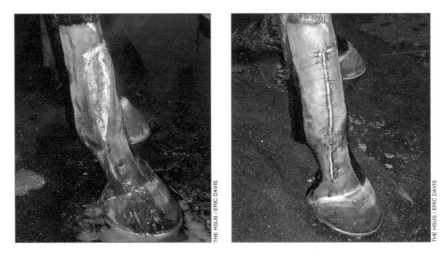

A bloody laceration like this one, at left (caused by a sharp edge on a broken partition of a horse trailer), requires veterinary attention; in this case, to remove damaged skin and stitch the wound. (The wound healed without significant scarring.)

your part can delay the treatment your horse *really* needs and might cost him his life (see page 229).

Every horseman sooner or later walks into the barn or pasture only to see a horse with a bloody laceration. Many times such wounds look much worse than they are, but all should be treated with an abundance of caution. In dealing with these injuries, the location is critical. The particular danger zones for lacerations/puncture wounds in the horse are:

- over any joint;
- on the back (palmar or plantar surface) of a leg—an injury to a flexor tendon is much more serious than to an extensor tendon;
- on the coronet (or coronary band) of the hoof; and
- on the middle third of the bearing surface of the hoof.

Large puncture wounds to the thorax and abdomen (such as those resulting from a metal T post) can enter these body cavities and be life

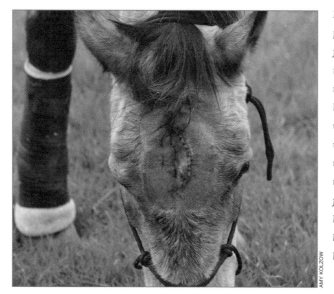

Recovery is possible, even from a devastating injury. After this mare fractured her skull, her veterinarian was able to put the pieces back together in time for her to celebrate her thirtieth birthday fully healed.

AMY KOLZOW

VETERINARY CARE

threatening. Wounds on the large muscle masses of the chest, rump, and neck can look horrible, but they heal quite easily and don't compromise survival or soundness. Though large amounts of blood can be lost with such injuries, horses have a lot of blood.

Assess whether the wound is still bleeding. If the wound is bleeding heavily or spurting blood, use anything you have handy that's clean—a towel, a big wad of first-aid cotton, a T-shirt—and put pressure on the wound to stop the bleeding with one hand while you call the veterinarian on your cell phone with the other. (Well-padded bandages stop nearly any bleeding. Tourniquets should not be used, however.) If the wound isn't bleeding anymore, but it looks as if the horse has lost lots of blood, call the veterinarian ASAP.

If the wound isn't actively bleeding, take quick stock of the horse's condition. You don't need to do a full run-through of his vital signs; just do a thirty-second version. Take a glance at his flanks and see if his breathing is heavy or shallow, slide a finger under his jaw to see if his pulse feels very fast or very slow, and flip up his lip and quickly check his capillary refill time and the color of his gums. If things seem relatively normal, you can take a bit more time to assess the situation; but if the horse seems to be in distress or going into shock, call the veterinarian before you go any further.

Assuming the horse is stable and calm, use a hose to gently wash away the dried blood and take a good look. A wound that's very deep, or one that has created a flap of skin that's hanging loose, requires stitches. Time is of the essence in these cases. Ideally a wound should be stitched within the first six hours after injury. If you're unsure whether the wound needs stitches, call your veterinarian and describe the cut, and let him decide.

Any wound that involves a joint or a tendon sheath should be seen by a veterinarian, regardless of other factors. Infection in either is very dangerous, so you want your veterinarian involved right away.

The most basic common emergency (for non-race horses) may be one of the most preventable: an injury caused by improper fencing or stabling.

Infected fetlock joints, severed flexor tendons, infected hocks, and fractured legs all can cause the horse severe pain and cost thousands of dollars in care, whether the horse is in the richest county or the poorest.

The other major heart-stopper for horse owners is colic. It can be very acute and very painful, with the horse thrashing around and in obvious pain, or it can be very silent and insidious, with the horse standing mostly quiet but in distress.

As we've indicated, some colics are quite minor and resolve quite easily with minimal intervention, but it's still best to place a call to your veterinarian once you are convinced something is wrong. Even if you're relatively sure the colic is just a mild tummy ache, and you don't want to "bother" the veterinarian with a false alarm, a brief phone consultation will alert you to what the veterinarian wants you to monitor. Don't wait until you're *sure* it's an emergency to discover your veterinarian is out of town or not immediately reachable.

Report what symptoms you noticed when and under what conditions, whether your horse is sweaty and agitated, or calm but in slight discomfort. Take his vitals, listen for gut sounds on both sides, and check his CRT and mucous membranes. Take note of the condition of his stall: is it messy, as if he's been walking around in circles? Does he have shavings in his tail, indicating that he's been down? Is there less manure than usual in the stall? Has he finished his last meal?

Pass all of these observations along to your veterinarian, who will use this information to assess the severity of the situation. If the colic seems very mild and the veterinarian is comfortable with your ability to manage it, she may give you some basic instructions and have you call back in an hour or two with a progress report. But if the veterinarian thinks it sounds worrisome, or the horse is particularly fragile (an elderly horse, for instance, or one who has had previous colic episodes), she may want to see the horse sooner rather than later.

Any colic, regardless of severity, warrants a call to the veterinarian, even if it's just a "heads up" that you might need help later. Colic is one of the leading killers of horses, and even a mild bout should be taken very, very seriously.

In addition to the big two—serious wounds and colic—there are other instances that merit an immediate veterinary call (see page 229).

Any veterinarian will tell you it's better to call when it isn't really necessary, than *not* to a call until it's too late. Your veterinarian knows you don't want to spend the money on an emergency call if it's not necessary, but you should at least make initial contact, describe the situation, and listen to your veterinarian's counsel.

Make sure that you have all of your veterinarian's phone numbers conspicuously posted at your barn, as well as the numbers of a few backup practitioners, in the event that your primary veterinarian is already out on an emergency call or is otherwise unavailable. Program the numbers into your cell phone as well.

Being Prepared

To be prepared for minor injuries, every horse owner should have on hand a fully stocked first-aid kit with all the essentials (see page 223). Put everything in one spot, such as in a clear plastic bin, clearly labeled "First Aid," so others can find it in your absence. It's also helpful if the box is portable, so you can take it with you whenever you travel with your horse.

Check your kit periodically to see if it needs restocking, or if any of your medications has expired. If possible, keep the kit somewhere climate-controlled, so it isn't exposed to extreme heat or cold.

The longer you have horses, the more injuries you'll come across, and you'll soon amass a collection of your favorite products for all the minor cuts and scrapes your horse presents to you. Make sure that you always have whatever products and materials you prefer on hand and easily accessible so you're prepared for an emergency.

Disaster Planning

Most horse owners are good about preparing for everyday emergencies, since most horses can make minor emergencies seem like an almost-

Your First-Aid Kit

Your first aid kit should include

- an antiseptic (Chlorohexidine or Betadine solution)
- triple antibiotic ophthalmic (Neosporin) ointment
- a box of sterile rolled cotton or sleeves of sterile gauze pads (3 x 3 or 4 x 4) (to ensure that you always have something clean on hand with which to clean a wound)
- prepackaged EZ scrubs or an antiseptic soap (Chlorohexidine or Betadine)
- non-stick gauze pads
- bandaging materials (VetRap or elastic bandages, and a supply of sheet cotton)
- bandage scissors (blunt-ended and angled, making it easy to cut off a bandage that's already been applied)
- thermometer
- stethoscope
- commonly prescribed medications—Bute (the horsey equivalent of Tylenol or Advil), Banamine, etc. (to be used only under instructions from your veterinarian)
- needles, needle syringes, oral dosing syringes (to be used only with instructions from your veterinarian)
- military compress bandage (or "war bandage")—designed to stop significant bleeding and containing a large sterile bandage pad and two rolls of sterile gauze bandage
- flashlight (or headlamp)
- wire cutters
- clean towels
- duct tape
- examination or surgeon's gloves
- hydrogen peroxide (to remove blood from hair)

everyday event. While it's important to be prepared for the run-of-the-mill injuries, you also need to think about the unthinkable—hurricanes, wildfires, blizzards, terrorist attacks. Disasters, which can happen anywhere, include barn fires, hazardous-materials spills, propane line explosions, and train derailments, all of which may require evacuation. You should be prepared to move your horses to a safe area.

The risks you face will vary widely depending on where you live, but you can think about disasters as falling into one of two categories—situations where you need to evacuate, and situations where you're stuck on the farm with limited resources and need to get by.

If you are unprepared or wait until the last minute to evacuate, emergency personnel could tell you to leave your horses behind. Your horses could be unattended for days, without food or water.

In the event that you must evacuate, you will need transportation for your horses. If you have your own truck and trailer, keep them in good running order, to be used at a moment's notice. If you don't have your own rig, or if your rig can't take all of your horses in one trip, try to make arrangements with a friend who has extra spots in his trailer ahead of time, so you're not calling around frantically at the last minute.

Make sure your horses know how to load and load *well*. During an emergency, when everyone is rushed and frantic, the *last* thing you want to do is to try to calmly cajole an unwilling loader. If your horse hasn't learned how to load yet, make it a priority to teach him right away—don't put it off.

Take the time to put together a list of the things you'll need if you ever have to leave in a hurry (buckets, portable water jugs, halters with name tags, lead ropes, extra feed, medications, a first aid kit, cat carriers for the barn cats). Think about how you could easily and quickly collect these things, and then make sure you're prepared to do so. Keep a portable container handy that holds four or five days' worth of your horse's grain. You can fill the container quickly and won't have to drag along a whole fifty-pound bag.

Make copies of your horse's Coggins test, vaccination records, bill of sale, and other important paperwork, and keep them in a waterproof envelope in your tack room or towing vehicle. Include photographs that you can use for identification or to prove ownership, if necessary. These should be shots taken from both sides of the horse and of his head, showing any identifying markings.

Finally, think about where you could go, if necessary. If you live in a hurricane-prone area, state or local authorities may have predesignated facilities inland (fairgrounds or racetracks with lots of stalls available) as evacuation destinations. (Your local animal care and control agency, agricultural extension agent, or local emergency management authorities can provide this information.) Make a list of these facilities, plot out several evacuation routes you can use to reach them, and keep those written directions and a good map in your towing vehicle. Alternatively, make arrangements with friends or family who have horse property at a safe distance from home to put you and your creatures up for a few days. Give yourself several options, so you can choose the best one for the situation at the time. Inform friends and neighbors of your evacuation plans. Post detailed instructions in several places (the barn office, horse trailer, barn entrances) to ensure they are accessible to emergency workers in case you are away from home and unable to evacuate your horses yourself.

There are times when evacuating is more dangerous than staying, or you may simply not have any advance warning. A tornado might knock out electricity, or a blizzard may leave you and your horses snowed in. For these scenarios, you need to be prepared to be self-sufficient for a few days, until help and resources can reach you, or until the situation resolves itself.

A primary concern for horse facilities during power outages is providing water for the horses. Keep large, clean containers that are specifically designated for emergency water reserves—plastic garbage cans or extra water troughs, for instance—and if you have any warning that a storm is approaching, fill up every spare container you own before it arrives. Consider buying a water storage tank that you can keep full just for this purpose for the disasters that come without warning. Consider investing in a generator that can run your well pump if the power is out for any length of time.

Think about your property and whether horses would be safer inside or out in a storm. If your barn is old and not particularly sturdy, your horses might be better off in a pasture—you don't want them trapped if the barn collapses. If you're in a flood-prone area, you definitely *do not* want to leave horses locked in their stalls. Their natural instincts will help them find high ground in the event of a flood, but they'll drown in their stalls if locked inside.

If you do plan to leave your horses outdoors in certain situations, make sure you have spray paint and livestock markers, as well as break-away halters with indelible name tags, on hand. The tag should include your name and phone number, your horse's name, and the number for a friend or family member who lives outside the area. Since horses can lose their halters in a storm, physically paint a phone number on your horse's side with spray paint or a livestock marker.

Make sure you always have plenty of hay, grain, medication, and bedding—don't allow your supplies to run low. In the event of an unexpected emergency, you may have to make do with what you have for several days.

If you keep your horse at a boarding barn, these emergencies are mostly out of your control, but talk with your barn manager and ask about any emergency plan. If the manager doesn't have one, help him come up with one.

Emergencies are so varied and so unpredictable, it's almost impossible to imagine every scenario you might face. But if you take the time to think about the situations you might encounter, where you could go, and what your horse would need, then plan around those possibilities, you'll be in much better shape than if you leave everything up to chance.

"Disaster Preparedness for Horses" (available from The HSUS, 2100 L Street, NW, Washington, DC 20037) is a brochure that can be helpful in your planning process; the American Red Cross's website features "Barnyard Animal Rescue Plan," from the Animal Rescue Council; the American Association of Equine Practitioners posts relevant links on its site; and the Maryland Horse Industry (*www.marylandhorseindustry.org*) offers some good information as well.

Patience Is a Virtue

If you are fortunate, you will never have to deal with a Category 5 hurricane or a wildfire roaring down a canyon during your horse-owning career. You *will*, however, face numerous instances in which your nursing skills are put to the test after the veterinarian has packed up his bag and left you and your horse alone. The veterinarian's post-visit instructions may mean days—even weeks—of soaking a foot, wrapping a leg, salving an eye, or irrigating a wound.

Your best ally will be your patience as you learn how to wrap, soak, salve, irrigate, inject, dose, hand walk, and/or mix medications. That patience will be put to the test if your horse's fear or pain causes him

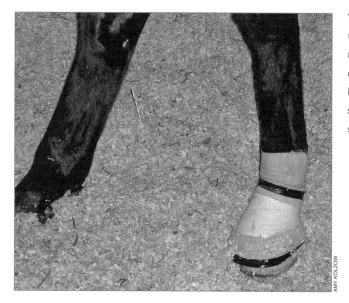

The horse owner will need to monitor this taped and bandaged heel cast to make sure the tape stays in place.

AMY KOLZOW

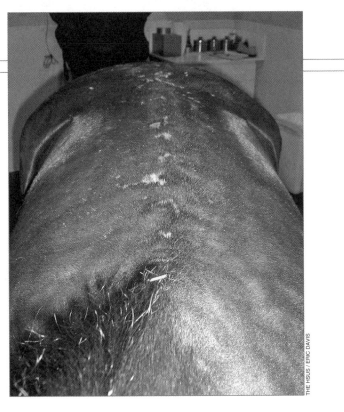

A case of "rain rot" (caused by a bacteria getting into skin damaged by constantly being wet) responds to simple treatments, including coal tar shampoo or vinegar.

THE HSUS / ERIC DAVIS

to fight your nursing care, or if his initial cooperation turns to outright resistance to repeated unpleasant procedures.

A second set of hands is always helpful. If a helper isn't available, plan each treatment carefully to avoid an unproductive or dangerous battle with your patient. Remove all extraneous equipment from the treatment area and make sure extra towels, an adequate lighting source, and all medications are close at hand. Experiment with safe restraint methods—some horses are more comfortable in a stall than on crossties; others may respond best if you hold the lead rope in one hand and administer care with the other rather than tie them to a fixed object. Try to remain reassuring, methodical, and calm during the treatment. Be philosophical about collateral damage: a soaking bucket will overturn; bottled medication will spill or stain your clothing; VetRap will be wasted as you rewrap. Practice makes perfect eventually, and you will reap the added benefit of seeing your horse return to health with his trust in you intact.

Ten Symptoms Requiring Immediate Veterinary Attention

These situations indicate nonspecific but potentially serious problems. A list of possible causes of these symptoms is not included, because owners should call an experienced veterinarian when they are observed. These are emergency situations and are not a time for inexperienced diagnosis.

1. Horse unable to stand.

Like other prey species, horses normally stand when approached. Horses feel safest when they are in a position to escape if necessary. A horse who is unable or unwilling to do this may be injured, colicky, or suffering from neurological disease.

2. Horse unwilling to eat.

The digestive tract of the horse is designed to have feed passing through it more or less continuously. Horses may ignore palatable feed if distracted or frightened, but only for a short period. They are designed to eat continuously. Failure to take interest in food may indicate gastrointestinal discomfort, pain, or other serious conditions. (On the other hand, horses drink infrequently and only for a short period.)

3. Horse unable to bear weight on one leg.

Horses should stand with "a leg on each corner." Complete unwillingness to use one or more legs for support may indicate a fracture, severe tendon or ligament injury, or an infected joint. A simple sole abscess may cause a horse to be "non-weight bearing," but the alternatives are serious enough that a diagnosis should be made as soon as possible.

4. Horse exhibiting acute lethargy.

If a horse suddenly becomes uninterested in his surroundings and does not respond to stimuli normally, he is likely suffering from a painful, metabolic, inflammatory, or neurologic abnormality. A gentle horse, sleeping in the sun, can certainly look lethargic. However, a voice command, hand contact, or haltering should arouse his interest in his surroundings. (Obviously, this response is governed by the horse's normal personality.)

5. Horse exhibiting open mouth breathing.

Horses are "obligate nasal breathers." Even with extreme exercise, horses rarely breathe through their mouth unless they are in distress.

6. Evidence of sweating without exercise.

On a hot day, horses sweat moderately on their chest and shoulders. However, a horse that is "wringing wet" without a history of exercise should be examined for other signs of pain or colic.

7. Horse exhibiting flared nostrils and rapid respiration without exercise.

Horses flare (or widely open) their nostrils and breathe more rapidly than normal when exercising or when frightened. In the absence of these conditions, these responses are reason for alarm.

8. A laceration or other wound on joint or back surface of a leg.

Wounds over joints may have entered the joint capsule and contaminated the joint space. The success of treating joint infections is directly related to how soon therapy is started following the injury. Similarly, the flexor tendons on the back (palmar or plantar) surface of the front and rear limbs are encased in synovial sheaths, which are much like joint capsules. Injury to these areas also constitutes an emergency. (On the other hand, a very large cut into the muscles of the chest or rump, though nasty looking, is much less likely to have serious consequences.)

9. Horse rolling repeatedly.

Horses naturally roll and will lie down for short periods of time. This behavior should not be of concern. However, when a horse rolls, gets up, goes down and rolls again, and repeats this process several times, you should be concerned about abdominal pain.

10. Horse squinting.

Horse eyes are fragile and prone to serious injuries and disease, such as uveitis. While these conditions are not life threatening, evidence of eye pain should be taken seriously. Failure to do so can result in loss of vision.

N.B. Any acute lameness or joint swelling in a foal. Foals in the first few weeks of life are prone to severe bacterial infections, referred to as septicemia. As the bacteria that cause this condition usually localize in the foal's joints, the first symptom is often acute lameness. Unfortunately, owners frequently assume that this lameness is just "a sprain" or that "the mare stepped on the foal." In fact a mare very rarely injures her foal in any way. An acutely lame foal should be assumed to have an infection until proven otherwise. The cost of waiting is often the foal's life.

CHAPTER 11

Farriery

EVERY DISCUSSION OF THE IMPORTANCE OF farriery invariably starts with the old adage, "No hoof, no horse." Those four words put into perspective what many horse owners have learned through months or years of frustration, and what many educated farriers have tried to impress upon the horse community via books, lectures, and magazine articles. It doesn't matter how talented your horse is or how wonderful he is to ride: if he doesn't have a foot to stand on, so to speak, you won't be able to enjoy those other qualities.

Unfortunately, it's easy to overlook the humble hoof. It's not soulful, like your horse's soft eye, or beautiful to the touch, like her gleaming coat. No one ever gasps when a horse is led by and exclaims, "Look at those feet!" Even the best hoof doesn't really help a horse's performance, although bad ones certainly can hinder it. Good hooves provide comfort, stability, and shock-absorbing capability for the horse's whole body.

In many horsemen's circles, whether a horse has good feet is an afterthought—it's nice if he does, but not a deal-breaker if he doesn't. This rather blasé attitude has found its way into the breeding shed as well. Horses are bred because they've performed well, not because they have the desirable thick soles and well-balanced hooves.

In our infinite wisdom, we human beings have populated the world with lots of horses who might have ended up as lion food in the wild. (You can't run away from a lion if your feet hurt, after all.) To be fair, there are also lots of horses with decent feet, and lots more whose hooves are downright stellar. If you have an average horse, chances are good that his feet are okay, but might need a little help here and there.

This is where your friend the farrier (a hoof-care professional, as opposed to a blacksmith, who forges iron) enters the picture. While no farrier should be expected to work miracles and turn terrible feet into wonderful ones, a skilled farrier can help manage any small problems and prevent them from turning into big issues. Unfortunately, a less-than-stellar farrier can turn good feet bad in rather short order, one of the reasons why farriery is an art and a skill that takes years to master.

As the owner, your role is to learn as much as you can—about shoeing in general and your horse's particular needs—and to be an advocate for your horse's feet. This means keeping him on a consistent schedule with your farrier, doing your part to maintain his hoof health between appointments, and educating yourself enough to differentiate between a foot that's shod or trimmed well and one that isn't.

Like your own fingernails, the horse's hoof grows continually and must be trimmed periodically to prevent it from getting too long and or out of shape. The rate of growth is affected by the weather (the hoof grows more slowly in cold weather), whether the horse is getting adequate nutrition, and the amount of exercise a horse gets (growth is slower in horses who are idle than in those who are worked).

An unshod horse who travels five miles a day on a good dry surface wears his feet down naturally, making trimming potentially unnecessary. A horse who does not wear shoes and does little to no work may need trimming every six or seven weeks. Shod horses need reshoeing every five to eight weeks.

Waiting too long between farrier visits can lead to lost shoes or cracks and chips in the hoof wall, which can become severe and cause lameness if not corrected. Hooves that are overdue for trimming or shoeing can become unbalanced—asymmetrical and not uniform in shape. An unbalanced hoof does not bear the horse's weight evenly, leading to increased stress in parts of the hoof or leg, and can cause lameness.

A horse's hooves are the foundation of everything he does, so you want to make sure they're well cared for and as strong as they can be.

Extreme neglect of the hoof can have disastrous results, including cracks and damage to the outside layer.

FARRIERY

To Shoe or Not to Shoe?

There's one important difference between the equine hoof and the human fingernail. Since you do not walk on your fingers, the growth of your nails is unimpeded. Horses, however, spend some twenty-plus hours a day standing, walking, and running on their hooves, often on rough or rocky ground. Their hooves wear down over time, at about the same rate as they grow. This was nature's way of keeping a hoof in balance before farriers were invented.

In domestication, however, horses' hooves sometimes wear down more quickly than they grow, depending on the strength of the hooves and the way in which the horse is kept. The art of horseshoeing is thought to date perhaps as far as back as 500 BCE, and had likely become commonplace by the Middle Ages.[60] Shoes protected the hoof not only from wear, but also from extreme footing that might be found in mountainous terrain or on the battlefield.

In modern times, protection from wear and rocky footing are still primary uses for shoes, but they're also used for performance reasons. A shoe with permanent caulks or temporary screw-in studs (both similar to cleats on athletic shoes) can give a polo pony or show jumper much better traction, allowing for quick stops and tight turns on slippery grass. Reining horses are shod with special "sliding plates" on their hind hooves that allow them to perform their trademark sliding stops, and police horses might wear rubberized shoes to keep them from slipping on pavement.

Shoes also have a number of therapeutic uses. An egg-bar shoe (one that is a closed circle, rather than the usual horseshoe shape) can help horses with under-run heels grow a more normal hoof. Horses who have suffered a bout of laminitis with rotation of the coffin bone can be shod with pads to help realign the bones of the lower leg.

Corrective trimming and shoeing can help alleviate some of the effects of mild conformation problems in adult horses, and help correct some conformational defects in young horses who are still growing.

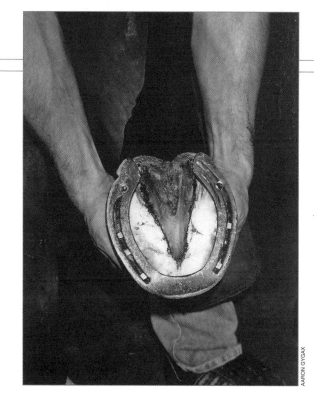

AARON GYGAX

The simplest, flattest shoe the horse can wear successfully is the best shoe for him.

The general rule is that *how* the horse's feet are trimmed and balanced, based on his conformation, is much more important than the quality of the forge work in making or shaping shoes. A corollary is that the simplest, flattest, and lightest shoe the horse can wear successfully is the best shoe for him. In this case, more (shoe) is not necessarily better.

Most horse owners consider shoeing to be a matter of course today, although some horses with exceptionally good feet can go barefoot while in steady work, and some light-use trail or pleasure mounts can go without shoes. Indeed, many farriers recommend pulling a horse's shoes for the winter, or whenever a horse is not going to be worked very hard, to help strengthen the hoof and give it a "break" from shoeing.

Does *your* horse really need shoes? Bare feet tend to be healthier and stronger and afford a horse better traction on paved roads and snow than do shod feet. If you keep your horses in a group turnout situation, horses whose hind feet are barefoot will cause less damage if they kick a pasture mate. If your horse goes from stall to paddock to bluestone-based arena, to sandy trails, and back again, going shoeless may be advisable. And, as is true in many instances with horses, there are often benefits to adhering as close to a "natural" existence as is practical. (You will save money as well.)

There's been a movement within the horse community in recent years toward leaving horses barefoot and trimming their hooves to replicate those of wild horses. Barefoot or "natural" trimming proponents feel that shoeing is unnatural, unnecessary, and causes damage to the foot, leading to many of the lamenesses seen in working horses. They assert that even competition horses can go barefoot if allowed time to acclimate and develop stronger hooves. Various methods of barefoot trimming are taught in certification courses, and farriers who specialize in barefoot trims are found around the country.

This movement is a significant departure from traditional hoof care. While there's no doubt that many horses can and do go barefoot successfully, other horses may not be suited for going without shoes while doing any kind of significant work. Since this theory of hoof care is relatively new, most of its practitioners have less than a decade's worth of experience with it, and many have much less.

If you'd like to try allowing your shod horse to go barefoot, consult with both your veterinarian and your farrier and ask for their professional opinions on how your horse might fare, taking into account the inherent qualities of his feet and how you ride him. If he's not comfortable being barefoot, or if his feet start to chip, crack, or show effects of an underlying problem, he'll let you know.

As long as your horse seems happy and comfortable, whether he's barefoot or shod, there's no reason to feel that you "should" change.

Remember, most of what we do with our domestic horses is not "natural"—riding, trailering, veterinary care, deworming, and shoeing are *all* foreign to horses who are truly living naturally. It's important to understand how the horse is designed and what his natural instincts are, and it's certainly ideal to replicate his natural environment when possible.

We urge caution, however, if you are considering doing your own trimming. The horse's hoof is a complex structure, and without significant training—more than you can gain in a weekend seminar or by reading instructions in a book or on a website—you should not attempt to maintain your horse's feet on your own. An unskilled and untrained person should never trim a horse's feet. Most horse owners who trim their own horses never get enough practice to become good at it, so their horses are always poorly trimmed.

A Balanced Hoof

To the uneducated eye, a hoof is a hoof—each one looks pretty much the same as the next. But when you know what you're looking at, you see vast differences that can have a significant impact on the horse's soundness (or lack thereof). Far too many horse owners just trust that their farriers are doing a good job without taking a critical look for themselves, simply because they have no idea what to look for.

The overarching concept of proper farriery can really be summed up in a single word—balance. A balanced foot is not subjected to undue stress on any one portion. It supports the horse's weight optimally because the weight is distributed properly.

When you look at a horse with balanced feet, everything should look symmetrical. Stand in front of the horse and look at his legs straight on, drawing an imaginary line down the center of the leg. It should bisect the knee and the fetlock and continue straight on down through the hoof, dividing the leg into two equal parts. A balanced hoof is divided exactly in half, with the portions from each side of the imaginary line being the exact same size. The coronet band should be parallel to the ground when viewed from the front, and the hoof should look like a trapezoid, with both sides sloping away from the leg at the same angle. Both front feet and both hind feet should be symmetrical.

Now, facing the horse's rump, pick up the horse's foot, tucking your head under the horse's body so that your head is directly over the hoof itself, and look down at the exposed bottom of the foot. Draw an imaginary line from heel to toe. The line should divide the hoof into two equal

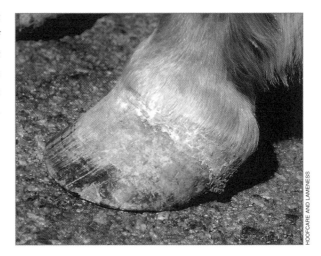

An overlong but normal foot: the hoof is not deformed, but the toe is just long enough to possibly interfere with normal weight bearing.

HOOFCARE AND LAMENESS

portions roughly semicircular in shape. If one side is flatter or rounder than the other, the hoof is not balanced. You also should be able to draw a line across the foot, from side to side at the widest point, which should divide it roughly in half. If the line is closer to the heel than the toe, or vice versa, the foot is not balanced.

Finally, view the horse from each side—you're not looking at balance here, but rather at the alignment of the horse's pasterns and hooves. The slope of each pastern should match the slope of the front of the corresponding hoof. There is no such thing as perfect conformation, and many small conformational flaws are acceptable and cause no problems to the horse. It is well recognized that trying to correct such natural imperfections by shoeing leads to lameness and shortens the horse's useful life.

The balance of the hoof needs to be correct whether or not the hoof is shod. With a shod foot, you also want to look at the placement of the shoe: it should be just a touch longer than the foot is in back to support the horse's heels. (If it's too far back, though, a front shoe is in danger of being grabbed and pulled off by the horse's hind foot.)

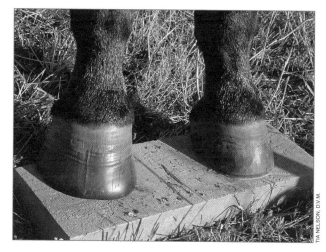

The newly trimmed front foot is on the right; the untrimmed foot is on the left.

A shoeing job should look neat and tidy, although you don't want your farrier rasping the outside of the hoof any more than is necessary to smooth the clenches (the portions of the shoeing nails that protrude from the hoof wall). Chips or flares in the hoof wall should have been removed during the trimming, although old nail holes often remain. The clenches should be in a neat line, and the nails should all be on the half of the foot closest to the ground. Nails placed behind (toward the heel) the widest part of the hoof restrict the hoof's natural expansion in the heel area when it hits the ground.[61]

Your farrier should be shaping the shoe to the foot, not the other way around. Rather than rasping away hoof to make the shoe fit, he should reshape the shoe as necessary to accommodate a properly balanced hoof.

If something about your horse's shoeing doesn't seem right to you, ask your farrier about it. It may take several shoeings to change the balance of a horse's hoof, and you might be looking at a work in

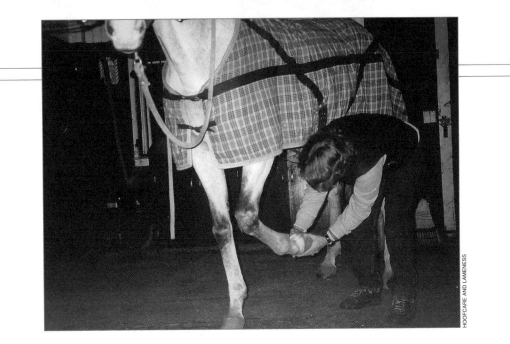

*Holding your horse's feet in your hands is a good way for him to learn to stand for the farrier.
(Restraining the horse in crossties is safer than looping a lead shank, as pictured.)*

progress. Remember, though, that some aspects of foot conformation can only be managed, not "cured."

If you're seeing consistent problems in your horse's hooves that are not improving, or if your horse is often sore after trimming or shoeing, it might be time to look for a different farrier.

Finding a Good Farrier

Farriers are not required to be licensed or certified. Anyone with an anvil and a rasp can hang out a shingle and claim to be a farrier. You should never choose a farrier by picking a name out of the phone book or just grabbing a business card off the bulletin board at your local tack shop without doing any other research. Your horse's hoof care is much too important to entrust to anyone other than a competent, experienced professional.

Several national farrier organizations offer voluntary certification at several levels. These certifications require passing a written as well as a practical exam. There are also many horseshoeing schools around the

This thrushy foot is also overgrown enough to make the horse lame.

country that teach farriery. If a farrier has some educational credentials, you have some assurance that the person is proficient at his craft.

Although education and certification are helpful, what really matters is how well the farrier does with real-life horses. Ask your veterinarian and/or trainer for recommendations, or call the large-animal equine hospital that serves your area. You may find that the highly recommended farriers in your area are so busy they can't take on new clients, but ask if there are other up-and-coming farriers in the area whom they would recommend. Most farriers do an apprenticeship before branching out on their own, so it's possible that an in-demand farrier has several protégés also working in the area.

A conscientious farrier is gentle with your horse, taking care not to unduly stress each raised leg or giving a stiff older fellow a break mid-trim if he needs it. If your horse does not stand well for trimming or shoeing, you need to work on this skill with him and train him to be a better "patient" for your farrier. If he is normally well behaved but suddenly

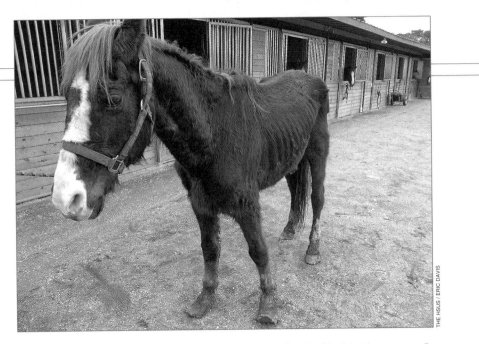

The terrible result of the failure to trim the hooves of a chronically foundered (and in this case starved)
horse is hoof growth abnormalities, often termed "elf slippers" due to the curled up toes.

objects to having one foot in particular worked on, he may be stiff or sore in that leg, or he may object to the way the foot is resting on the farrier's leg. Regardless, you want to have a well-mannered horse available for your farrier to work on. Otherwise, you'll quickly find that farriers do not return calls from owners whose horses tried to trample them on the last visit!

A farrier is in a very vulnerable physical position when working on your horse and should not be expected to tolerate misbehavior. Any discipline meted out should be appropriate, however. If you think your farrier is too rough or too harsh, or if your horse seems apprehensive about being shod, it might be time to look for a new farrier.

Routine Care

Although farrier care is extremely important, the owner's daily attention to a horse's feet is an equally integral component in a hoof care regimen.

Part of your routine should be picking out your horse's feet, removing any mud, gravel, or debris from each foot during daily grooming and after

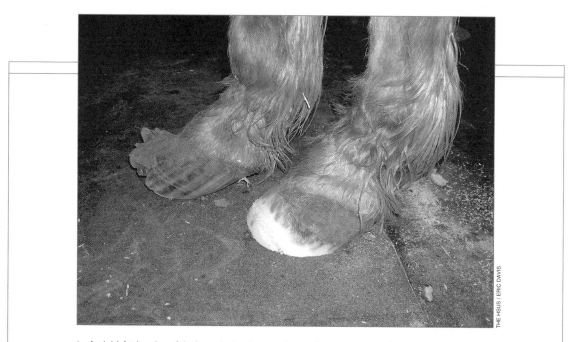

In the initial trimming of the horse in the photo on the previous page, some of the excess hoof has been removed from the near foot.

every ride. This is a good opportunity to inspect the bottom of each foot for any sponginess, malodor, or oozing of the frog (signs of thrush, the most common bacterial infection of the hoof); lodged stones; punctures to the sole; even skin lesions in the fetlock area (caused by fungi or bacteria and commonly known as mud fever, or "scratches"). Sometimes treatment is as simple as removing a stone wedged under the shoe or daily cleaning of the thrush-infected area with a stiff brush, followed by application of an anti-thrush preparation such as Thrushbuster or Kopertox. A puncture, however, requires immediate veterinary attention. Any injury or abnormality should be brought to the attention of your farrier or veterinarian.

This daily attention to your horse's feet is also valuable in teaching him to stand quietly for the farrier. Your horse will learn that standing on three legs for foot care is a necessary activity.

CHAPTER 12

Riding and Training

IT MIGHT SEEM ODD TO INCLUDE A DISCUSSION of riding and training issues in a book on horse care. After all, "care" is generally considered to be feeding, watering, grooming, medicating, cleaning, transporting, housing—everything that happens when you're *not* on the horse. It's the day-to-day minutia of seeing to your horse's physical needs.

But for most horse owners, riding is the reason you have a horse in the first place, and many aspects of your care for your horse are geared toward it. It likely affects where you choose to keep your horse, what you feed him, the vaccinations you give him, and more. Riding is also the cornerstone of the partnership for many horse-and-rider pairs; when you are astride your horse you experience some of the greatest highs, and perhaps some of the lowest lows, of your time together. That cooperative effort is the source of much pride in things accomplished, but it can be a source of frustration when things don't go well.

You may only spend an hour a day in the saddle, but that hour is very influential. Every ride is part of your horse's training, and one bad ride may require a dozen good ones to undo. How you ride your horse affects his soundness, his happiness in his job, and *your* safety. And just as in all other aspects of your horse's care, his comfort, safety, and well-being should always be at the forefront of your mind when under saddle.

Riding Skills

None of us is born knowing how to ride. We all start out bouncing awkwardly on the horse's back, inadvertently jerking his mouth with the reins as we struggle to find our balance, and committing all sorts of other riding sins. (Many of us probably have the cringe-worthy old home videos to prove it!) No matter if you're an Olympian or a weekend trail rider, you had to *learn* to ride—it's a process that every one of us goes through.

Fortunately for all of us, the world's sainted school horses and our own forgiving first horses usually tolerate new-rider-caused discomforts with patience. It's likely not until we've improved our riding or graduated to other mounts that we realize just what we put our "beginner horse" through!

Riding *looks* deceptively simple: if you can stay on the horse, you "know how to ride," right? But as you learn more about horses and riding, you start to recognize the differences between beginners and experienced riders. For example, you might observe the way green riders list from

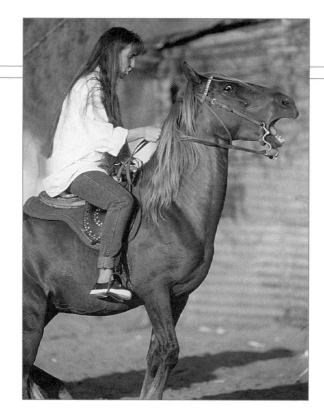

Poor riding skills cause your horse untold misery and put your life at risk. This horse's wide-open mouth, rolling eyes, and half-rear register his objection to the rider's too-tight reins, which are affixed to a long-shanked curb bit.

side to side on a horse, tip backward or forward as the horse accelerates or decelerates, or hunch over, drawing their legs up, trying to "will" themselves to stay on. Seasoned riders, in contrast, always seem to be in just the right place in the saddle—their upright, relaxed upper bodies and still legs seem unaffected by the horse's movement. The two move in harmony. It's one of the ironies of riding that it takes many hours of work in the saddle to develop the skills to make riding look so effortless.

A rider's balance (or lack thereof) in the saddle affects many other aspects of equitation as well. A common mistake among new riders is unconsciously using the reins to steady and rebalance themselves, pulling backward on the horse's mouth. They might clamp tightly with their legs if they start to list to one side, inadvertently cueing the horse to go forward…which likely tips them backward, leading them to catch the horse in the mouth. (You can see why "school" horses need to have limitless patience.) Watching beginning riders' lessons is typically an exercise in repetition, as the instructor shouts, "Heels down, shoulders

Although her riding position is not perfect (her lower leg and upper body are both too far forward and she has too strong a hold on her horse's mouth via his snaffle bit), this rider is doing some things right, since her horse nonetheless has an eager, confident, ears-pricked expression as he gallops forward.

back, eyes up!" over and over again, trying to correct the beginners' positions on their horses to maximize safety and effectiveness.

You'll notice, too, how horses speak up when the rider interferes with their way of going or makes them uncomfortable. They throw their heads up, wring their tails, grind their teeth, pin their ears, and generally use all the body language they possess to say, "Hey! That hurts!" When a rider is balanced and can cue the horse through consistent hand, leg, and body signals (called aids), the horse responds with a pleasant expression, pricked ears, and relaxed, fluid movement.

Your horse will do his part to tell you when you're making riding mistakes, if you take the time to listen. And, of course, you can learn by reading books, watching videos, and observing others. But you're likely to find that those methods work best when used in conjunction with riding lessons from a qualified instructor.

An instructor provides "eyes on the ground" and can help you address problems that you might not even know existed, fixing them before they become entrenched habits. One of the basic tenets of riding across almost all disciplines is that an observer should be able to draw an imaginary vertical line from the rider's ear through the hip to the heel when sitting upright (see the photo on page 258). This alignment places the rider in a balanced position that does not interfere with the horse.

It's one thing to read that information in a book or to see pictures in a magazine and another to try to replicate it on your own. There's no substitute for having someone on the ground who can put your body in the correct alignment until you learn what "correct" feels like and can find it more easily yourself. When you're riding on your own later, you can make a point of mentally checking your own position several times during your ride, and making adjustments if necessary. And then, at your next lesson, your instructor can assess your progress and let you know if you've improved.

A good instructor helps you progress in a safe, logical, and constructive manner. He knows how to introduce new concepts in a way that sets you and your horse up to succeed and have a good experience. A good instructor challenges you without overfacing you and helps you and your horse gain confidence in yourselves and in each other.

Instructors, like horses, come in all shapes and sizes and have an almost limitless number of views on the best way to train a horse. They all believe their way is the best. Your challenge is to find the one who is best for *you*. You should listen to both your horse and the instructor as you try to find someone who makes you a better rider and your horse happier about being ridden. An instructor who talks about "showing the horse who is boss" is going to have a different view of the horse-and-rider relationship from one who talks about "having a conversation with the horse." Some instructors may ride well and have a string of accomplishments to their credit, but if their horses are lifeless or intimidated, or even worse, fearful or traumatized, such people are to be avoided.

There's no shame in being a beginner, but it's important to recognize that, as a new and inexperienced rider, you're going to make some mistakes. Perhaps the most important function of a competent instructor is to help mitigate the effect of those mistakes on your horse, who's a good-natured partner along for the ride on your learning curve. For example, if your hands are not steady, an instructor makes sure that you're using a mild bit or shows you how to use a neck strap (a stirrup leather buckled around the horse's neck to give an unsteady rider a "handle" to grab onto for balance, if need be). Your instructor can tell you when you're ready for more advanced movements, like asking your horse to canter from a walk. Doing so when your legs are not yet effective in delivering cues can cause you to snatch the horse in the mouth with the reins or rush him forward when he is off balance. Your instructor can help you clarify your cues so your horse doesn't become confused by what you're asking him to do.

Experienced riders often joke about the reactions they get from non-horsey friends or family when they talk about taking riding lessons: "But, I thought you *knew* how to ride!" Riding is a lifelong learning process: every new horse can present new issues or problems, and even the most experienced riders work with coaches who can offer observations from the ground, where the view is often different.

When you're in a consistent lesson program, it shows that you're committed to becoming the best rider you can be, which is perhaps the greatest service you can do for your horse. You'll enjoy each other's company more if you're communicating effectively and working in harmony as a team, and you'll progress farther and faster, and accomplish more.

If you don't have an instructor but are interested in taking lessons, you can follow the usual course of action when looking for any kind of horsey professional: ask for recommendations from others in your local equestrian community. There's no mandatory certification program for riding instructors, so anyone can decree herself a "trainer" and start teaching lessons. Recommendations from others in the area will help you sort out the skilled instructors from those who are less effective teachers. You want an instructor who has experience teaching students

Karen O'Connor's strong, effective equitation helps the 14.1 hand Theodore O'Connor fly over this daunting fence at the 2006 Jersey Fresh three-day event. Karen's well-positioned lower leg gives her a secure base in the saddle, and her supportive rein retains contact with Teddy's mouth (via his snaffle bit) while in no way restricting his all-out jumping effort. Teddy's "work ethic and passion" made Karen and Teddy gold medalists at the 2007 Pan Am Games.

at your skill level, and if you're interested in pursuing a particular discipline, you want your instructor to be well versed in that sport.

Find an instructor who's knowledgeable and whose teaching methods mesh well with your learning style. See if you can watch a potential instructor teach a lesson or spend some time watching the warm-up arena at local shows, where you can watch several different instructors in action. Perhaps try a few lessons with a couple of different people and see who works best for you. Keep in mind that an instructor should help you make steady progress and build both your and your horse's confidence. If you seem to be regressing, if your horse is developing problems the instructor seems unable to fix, or if punishment is the "solution" for every riding problem, it's time to find a different instructor.

Dealing with Problems

It happens to every rider, regardless of experience. One day, seemingly out of the blue, your horse objects to something he never had an issue with before—stopping at jumps, for example, or refusing to pick up the left lead. He might start communicating in a novel way, such as bucking every time you ask him to pick up a lope, or throwing his head up and evading the bit. He might have had what seems to be a complete personality change, bolting or rearing when he never has before.

Such behavior can be confusing, frustrating, unnerving, and even dangerous. Suddenly you seem to have a completely different horse. It leaves riders scratching their heads and wondering out loud to their horses, in a tone of exasperation: "What the heck is *wrong* with you today?"

When you reach that point, you've reached what is perhaps the defining test of true horsemanship. You need to pull out your crystal ball, warm up your psychic powers, and try to figure out what in the world is going on in your horse's head. Is he misbehaving and being obstinate? Are you, the rider, inadvertently creating this issue? Is it a training problem? Does the horse not understand what you're asking him to do? Is the horse in pain?

Any of the above might be logical explanations. To remedy the issue, the rider must become a detective and ferret out the source of the problem.

Is It the Horse's Fault?

The tendency is easy to understand: when the horse is suddenly acting out or declining to perform tasks he's done before, it seems as if the blame should rest with him. Especially among young or inexperience riders, it seems as though this conclusion is the one reached first: after all, *he* did it (buck, rear, refuse, bolt), didn't he?

Certainly there are horses who willfully challenge their riders. A horse might be able to discern the weaknesses in his green rider and exploit them to evade work. For example, if a playful buck unseats the rider one day and the riding session suddenly ends (thereby rewarding the horse, in the horse's mind), the horse might try bucking again the next ride so he can end that session, too. If plain old misbehavior is the culprit, swift corrections are in order to teach the horse that such outbursts aren't appropriate.

With time in the saddle and maturity, however, comes the realization that situations are often more complex than they might appear at first blush. Any longtime rider or trainer can recall an instance during which he thought a horse was challenging him and disciplined the horse appropriately, only to discover later that there was a physical reason for the horse's misbehavior. A bolt might have been caused by a bee sting, for instance, or a burr under a saddle pad could be to blame for a buck. And there's little more mortifying to a horseman than to have disciplined a horse who didn't willfully do anything wrong.

There's a delicate balance in these situations. The rider must not allow the horse to dictate the terms of the partnership (because this isn't good for the horse), but also must exercise caution and be sure there are no other explanations for the horse's behavior.

Is It the Rider's Fault?

No one likes to admit mistakes. Often the horse is the unfortunate scapegoat for rider errors. Imagine watching a horse and rider in an amateur jumper class. As they approach the first fence, you can easily see several things the rider is doing wrong: pulling on the reins, cutting her line to the jump too short, and asking the horse to jump from a spot much too close to the obstacle. The horse, being a game and kind soul, jumps the fence anyway. But as the pair proceeds to the next jump and the next, the rider makes the same errors, and the horse's generosity runs out: he refuses a fence. The rider, oblivious to her own mistakes as she negotiated the course, hits the horse repeatedly with a crop as punishment for refusing. Meanwhile, spectators all around the ring are muttering, "Poor horse," as it's obvious to all that the rider bore the blame for the refusal. In *Talking of Horses*, author Monica Dickens recounts a similar round by a inept child rider who disgustedly leaves the show ring complaining, "This rotten whip is no good."

The situation doesn't have to be quite that blatant, of course. It can be a subtle error on the rider's part, such as not cueing the horse for a movement correctly or not recognizing poor saddle fit.

It's part of the rider's responsibility to the horse to become aware of her own mistakes and shortcomings. No rider is immune to errors, and it's important to shoulder the blame for them when they happen, rather than shifting it to the horse. If you watch televised equestrian competitions, whether horse racing or World Cup dressage, you almost always hear riders acknowledge *their* errors during their interviews and seldom blame their horses. If the world's top riders can do it, so can you.

Here's where having a regular instructor comes in handy. It's the instructor's job to spot these mistakes on your part and to help you correct them. There's no more humbling feeling than, after struggling with a problem for several rides on your own, having your instructor recommend a tiny change that instantly solves your problem! Your horse jumps confidently and eagerly; he picks up the canter on the right lead as if by magic; he stops on a dime. Your horse knew what to do once you found out what *you* were supposed to do. Often small changes really do make a tremendous difference. You are communicating, not dominating—an improvement for both horse and rider.

Is the Horse in Pain?

It's a sad irony that a horse who is hurting is often mistaken for one who is misbehaving. In many instances, it's only after the horse has been repeatedly punished for the "misbehavior" (with no improvement) that you discover he was in pain all along. (And punishment for misbehavior makes the problem worse, not better, since it can't "teach" a horse to ignore pain.)

When a horse is in physical discomfort, the symptoms can manifest themselves in a number of ways. He may not be overtly "lame" but might find certain movements or tasks to be very painful or uncomfortable. A horse who's sore-footed might refuse to walk across a gravel driveway, for instance, while one who has a sore left hock might not want to pick up the left canter lead. A horse who is backsore might pin his ears and wring his tail when being saddled up, while one who has Lyme disease might just feel exceedingly lethargic, stiff, and unwilling to move forward.

Pain isn't due to physical ailments alone; it can be caused by ill-fitting tack, an often-overlooked source of equine misbehavior, as well. A saddle that does not fit a horse's particular body shape can cause back soreness that may lead to bucking, while a bit that is the wrong size or is adjusted improperly can cause a horse to toss his head and evade contact (acceptance of the physical relationship between the horse's mouth and the rider's hands). (Teeth that are overdue for floating can cause similar symptoms.)

A properly fitted saddle distributes the rider's weight evenly across the horse's back. When the saddle doesn't fit correctly, it distributes too much weight in some areas and not enough in others. If there are dry patches amid the sweat marks on your horse's back when you remove the saddle, it's a telltale sign that the saddle is not coming into contact with his back in that spot. Areas on the back that are painful to the touch or develop white hairs (which occur with scarring) also indicate that the saddle does not fit correctly.

If a horse is usually a good-natured and willing fellow but suddenly experiences a drastic personality change and starts acting out under saddle, pain may be the most logical explanation for the behavior, and a call to your veterinarian for a work-up is probably in order. Have a trainer or experienced mentor check your tack fit as well, or call a professional saddle-fitter to see if your saddle needs adjustment to better fit your horse. Sometimes symptoms must be tracked through trial and error, even by equine professionals. Internet veterinary forums have helped some horsemen find others whose horses have had a similar array of baffling symptoms and their eventual diagnoses. Such detective work can point the horseman, farrier, or veterinarian in new directions to solve behavioral mysteries.

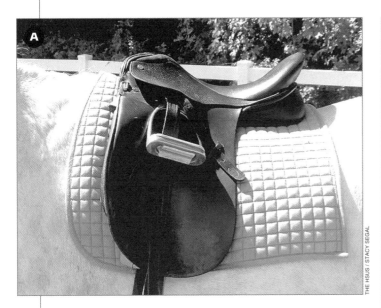

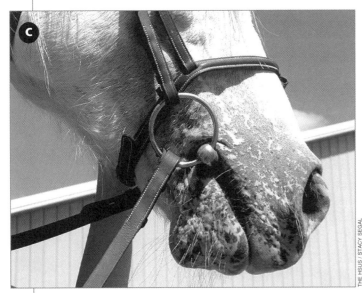

(A) Proper fit and placement on the horse's back can minimize the possibility of the saddle causing him discomfort. (B) The girth should be snug but not too tight. (C) A snaffle bit should rest high enough in the horse's mouth to create no more than one or two wrinkles at the corner of the mouth.

Is the Horse Unhappy in His Work?

If you've exhausted all possibilities and still haven't been able to resolve under-saddle issues, it may be that the horse is using his only available method to communicate to you that he's not enjoying his job. A jumper who continually stops at fences, a reiner who resists doing his maneuvers, a trail horse who stops dead at the property line and refuses to leave: they all may simply be trying to say as plainly as they can, "Enough!"

Just like the parents who desperately want their child to be a doctor and ignore his pleas to take art classes instead of biology and chemistry, riders can become oblivious to their horses' protestations when they're not happy with their work. We get the idea that our mount is going to excel in gaited classes, or event, or star in competitive trail riding, because that is what we want to do, sometimes neglecting to evaluate whether the horse enjoys those pursuits.

If a horse seems to have soured on his job, you can try offering more variety—get out on the trail if you normally work in an arena, add some galloping and conditioning work, or incorporate trotting poles or small jumps into your rides (assuming you don't jump regularly already). Sometimes a change in routine is enough to help a horse learn to enjoy his "regular" job again. But if you have your heart set on one particular sport and your horse seems to be better suited for another, it's not fair to either of you to try to force a square peg into a round hole. Instead, consider whether you'd both be happier with new partners in your equestrian endeavors, or whether you would be happy in a new discipline.

Training and Discipline

We tend to think of "training" as a formal process, conducted by an equine professional, with a particular set of goals in mind. But training actually happens every day and every time you work with your horse. Chances are, you've taught your horse lots of things without even trying to. He likely knows what the crinkle of a peppermint candy wrapper means as well as the clang of the grain bin being opened. He knows what time to expect

This Western rider is balanced over his horse's center of gravity with his arms high, giving his
horse ample rein and allowing him to move out with a calm, closed-mouth expression.

breakfast and dinner. When you pick out his feet in the same order every
day, he likely has the next foot poised for you to pick up as soon as you
put down the one you just cleaned. He knows his name. He may even
know the sound of your car.

Horses are quite intelligent and very trainable, perhaps not quite on
the same level as dogs, chimpanzees, or dolphins, but still very capable
of learning simple tasks or cues, sometimes without their owners even
knowing they have done so.

The most famous example is Clever Hans, a horse in Germany who
achieved worldwide fame in the early 1900s for his mathematic abilities.
His owner had trained him to "answer" math problems by tapping out the

correct number with his hoof. Hans's abilities regularly astonished crowds of spectators and attracted the attention of scientists as well. A special commission assembled to study the horse could not find any evidence of fraud on the owner's part, and so determined that Hans was legitimately answering the questions.

Psychologist Oskar Pfungst finally solved the mystery after realizing that Hans could only respond accurately when his *questioner* knew the answer. Pfungst determined that Hans's human observers were giving him inadvertent and almost imperceptible cues—they grew tense as he approached the correct number and then relaxed when he reached it. Hans had not learned to add or subtract but rather to read body language and facial expressions. (Perhaps a sign of even greater intelligence!)

An owner's challenge is to teach the horse the *right* things, in a humane and constructive way, while minimizing inadvertently teaching the wrong things.

How Horses Learn

When you examine the things horses learn on their own, without humans purposely trying to "teach" them, the simplicity of the equine learning process is revealed. They learn to associate an action with a reward through repetition. For example, a horse notices that the crinkle of the peppermint wrapper precedes the offering of a tasty peppermint. The next time he hears the crinkle, he looks for a peppermint, and lo and behold, one appears again. From that point forward, the distinctive wrapper crinkle equals a peppermint in his mind (and heaven help you if you try to unwrap a cough drop in his presence instead).

Horses make these associations quickly and easily, often well before their humans realize what they've just "trained" their horses to do. Unfortunately, this is also the case with more undesirable behaviors. Imagine a pony who innocently trots under a low-hanging tree branch, inadvertently removing his little rider. The ride abruptly ends, the pony is untacked, then turned out to eat grass. In the pony's mind, removal of rider via tree branch now equals the end of the ride and a rewarding meal of grass. Pity the poor child who next rides that pony anywhere near a tree!

We use this basic learning formula to our advantage all the time. We reward desired actions with positive reinforcement and then repeat the exercise until the horse learns to associate the two. If you give your horse a treat when you catch him in the field, he learns to associate being caught with something yummy to eat. You're rewarding the horse for allowing himself to be caught, rather than letting him make a negative association between being caught and having to go work.

The process also works in reverse. When a horse does something undesirable, we offer negative reinforcement. For example, if your horse crowds you when you walk into his stall with his grain bucket, you firmly push him back with a sharp word or a growl and withhold his grain. Once he is standing quietly and patiently outside of your space, you reward him by stepping back and allowing him to go ahead and eat. The horse learns that one behavior has negative consequences, and the other positive.

Every time you ride, you're using these principles. You make the desired action easy and rewarding for the horse, while the undesirable action is difficult or uncomfortable. Most horses, like most human beings, are "one-sided"—right- or left-handed. Say your horse doesn't like to pick up the left lead (the leg that strikes out first in the change from walk or trot to canter). When you ask with your leg and hand aids, he offers his more natural right lead. You immediately bring him back down to a trot and then ask again with firmer aids. You may repeat the process until he finally gives you the left lead. You exclaim "Good boy!" and give him a hearty pat on the neck, let him canter once around the arena, then pull up and end the ride.

In this example, every time the horse picks up the incorrect lead, he receives negative reinforcement: he is immediately asked to trot and try again, which is hard work. When he finally offers the correct lead, it's instantaneous positive reinforcement: a pat and a verbal reward; then he's finished with work for the day. He learns that he must work harder when he picks up the wrong lead. For the horse, the *end* of the ride is the greatest reward. Drilling a movement performed correctly, while it may be fun for the rider, is perceived by the horse as "punishment." He loses his interest in performing correctly and his desire to please his rider.

Training Happens Every Day

Literally *everything* you do around your horse teaches him something, whether you intend it to or not. You need to be aware of the habits you're instilling in your horse so you don't inadvertently teach him something undesirable. It's very easy to teach a horse something the first time: to "unteach" it later on is infinitely more difficult.

The day-to-day training is where your horse learns ground manners and respect for his human handlers. You need to teach rules for your horse's behavior and enforce them consistently. Your horse can't be allowed to nuzzle your barn shirt pocket for a peppermint but be jerked away by the bridle when he tries the same thing on your office or show clothes. He won't understand—it will seem to him that you're punishing him for no reason, and the only thing he learns is to be distrustful.

Too often, however, owners don't establish clear boundaries for their horses, thinking that they're being kind. Unfortunately, it's just the opposite. Allowing a horse to be unmannerly makes him difficult to work with, and veterinarians, farriers, and barn managers won't want you as a client. If you ever decide to rehome your horse (or circumstances force you to do so), you'll have a much harder time if your horse is pushy or spoiled. What you find acceptable the next owner or rider may punish severely. You're doing your horse a potential disservice if you don't teach him what is considered standard good manners in the horse world. You may be dooming your horse to a life of constant discipline and stress and taking away her chance of sharing a life with a devoted owner. Many horses who end up in equine rescues or sanctuaries do so because no one ever taught them good manners, encouraged positive experiences with human beings, or discouraged behaviors such as biting or kicking.

A well-trained horse who cooperates with even the smallest rider or handler is admiringly termed "kid safe."

NICOLE LYNCH

A bad-mannered horse can be outright dangerous. Horses are twelve hundred-pound animals who can seriously injure or even kill a human, whether by accident or on purpose. In tolerating rude behavior, you're endangering yourself, equine professionals who work with your horse, and innocent bystanders, including other horses.

Certain dangerous behaviors should never be tolerated, including aggression (baring the teeth or threatening to kick) and refusing to respect a handler's personal space (crowding the handler while being led; crowding/menacing the handler in the stall; or kicking out in the handler's direction while being turned out to pasture or paddock). A horse who exhibits these behaviors should be corrected swiftly, every single time. If such behavior continues, you should seek professional training help to break your horse of these habits, because they should never be allowed to continue.

The kindest thing you can do for your horse is to teach him—consistently and gently, but firmly—where the lines are that he may not cross. In doing so, you'll create the kind of horse who is a joy to work with and easily wins friends instead of making enemies. Everyone adores a horse who stands quietly for the farrier, cooperates with the veterinarian, leads well, and is polite to all of his handlers, even small and inexperienced ones.

Discipline

Horses are individuals, and some are much more sensitive than others. Think of your own group of friends and how some are likely to be much more sensitive to criticism than others: one person might burst into tears at the mere suggestion that he's done something wrong, while all but the most strongly worded criticism might go unheeded by another. Horses are no different.

There are two important principles involved in disciplining the horse. One is known as the "three-second rule"—your reaction must come within three seconds (preferably one or two seconds) of the behavior you're trying to reprimand. Otherwise, the horse won't associate the behavior with the reprimand and will think he's being punished for no reason. The other is to mete out *appropriate* correction in a controlled, dispassionate manner.

Correction can take a number of forms. A vocal reprimand is often very effective: you can growl the horse's name in a low tone or make a sound that you only use only to mean, "Hey, stop that now!" Since most horses are trained to know that the drawn-out "o" sound of "ho" or "whoa" means stop or stand still, you should avoid using "no" as a vocal reprimand—your horse isn't able to distinguish the difference and will just become confused. Horses are very attuned to the sound of your voice. If you remember the tone your mother took with you when you were just about to get into serious trouble, that's the tone you want to use with your horse!

Another method of discipline is to make the horse do something unpleasant. If your horse is "walking all over" you while being led, you can give him a vocal reprimand and then ask him to back up for several strides. Backing up is a submissive posture, and it's also relatively hard work for the horse, so you're reinforcing your authority and also teaching the horse that he makes life easier for himself when he behaves.

Unfortunately, discipline often becomes synonymous with physical punishment, and it's very easy for people to go too far in the name of "disciplining" their horses. Because of the horse's size, speed, and power, his sudden misbehavior can frighten or intimidate you. Your fear can lead to overreaction—and to too much punishment for what may have been an instinctive or spontaneous reaction. Unfortunately, you can go to almost any barn or horse show and sooner or later see equine misbehavior punished by an inappropriate use of whip, spurs, chain lead shank—or worse. There's a big difference between discipline and outright brutality. It's a responsible horse owner's job to control his emotions and know the difference.

Physical discipline is not without its place, but it must always be used judiciously. It should never be undertaken in anger or retaliation. If a horse threatens to bite, for example, a swift open-handed slap to the shoulder with your hand, accompanied by a disapproving, "Stop that!" warns the horse that the behavior will not be tolerated but does him no real harm.

Any time you reprimand a horse physically, you risk making him fearful of you. Such discipline should be reserved for dangerous or aggressive behavior, such as biting or kicking, and should never be more than a single open-handed slap that is designed to surprise, not hurt, the horse. (If you are uncomfortable with discipline, remember that horses nip or kick to communicate to each other acceptable behavior—although we don't recommend you try either.)

Such methods should be used very, very rarely. If you have a horse who frequently exhibits inappropriate behavior, you need to seek professional help, rather than try to solve the problem on your own. Some horses, especially those who have suffered abuse in the past, may not handle this sort of discipline well at all. You need to experiment with alternative man-agement methods (for example, feeding a horse who guards his feed tub from outside his stall until you are able to win his trust, or limiting who has access to the horse), or otherwise keep him and others out of harm's way.

The horse should never be hit anywhere on the head—not only is it inhumane, but it also leads to the horse becoming head-shy and resistant to handling. You can head off a horse's aggressive advances by keeping him respectful of your personal space.

The danger with physical discipline is that it's often used to punish, not train, the horse, and is more often a reflection of the owner's frustration than of any legitimate training goal. How often have you seen a rider fall off a horse, then spend several minutes trying to catch the horse, only to jerk on the reins or repeatedly slap the horse with a crop? By this point, the horse has no idea what he's done to incur punishment. (If anything, he'll think the punishment is for allowing himself to be caught.) The rider isn't trying to teach the horse anything; he is letting emotions get the best of him and is simply seeking revenge for being dumped in the dirt. What's worse is that, in many instances, such falls are the result of rider error and have nothing to do with the horse at all.

We're all capable of losing our patience or acting in anger. It's something to face up to, take responsibility for, and make every effort not to repeat. There may be times when you simply need to dismount, hand your horse to someone else or put him in a stall, and give yourself a few minutes to regain a cool head. You may be able to think through your problem by walking beside your horse or giving yourself a short talking to about who is supposed to be the more intelligent member of this team. Strangely, singing a verse of some silly tune may break the tension and reassure the horse that he is not engaged in a battle. There will be rides where one problem leads to another, horse and rider are both on edge and upset, and frustrations are building, with no resolution in sight. In such cases the smart thing to do is to simply find a good note— *any* good note, no matter how minor—upon which to end the ride, get off, give your horse a pat (no matter how insincere), and try again with a clean slate on another day. Do not let a problem turn into a battle of wills; such battles typically yield nothing but losers.

Discipline of any kind should always be a small part of a larger positive experience for the horse. It should be used judiciously and sparingly, along with copious rewards for good behavior. Remember, the goal is to make the correct choice the easiest and most pleasant one for the horse. If he has to back halfway down the barn aisle for getting into your space, but gets a treat when he stands politely, his choice will be easy.

Listen to what your horse is telling you. If he is becoming upset or fearful, or if your methods do not seem to be solving his behavioral issues, it's time to reevaluate your methods or seek professional guidance.

Finally, don't allow others to treat your horse in a way that makes you uncomfortable, even if they are "experts" or are in a position of authority. *You* are your horse's guardian and have final say over how he's treated. Just because an individual is a trainer or an advanced rider with a tack room full of ribbons does not mean that person is immune to bad decisions and mistakes. Success does not always equal humaneness in the horse world, as in many other environments. If you have concerns about a trainer's actions, ask questions and listen to the answers. If it seems as though every horse in the barn is hit, jerked in the mouth, or spurred for every infraction, described as a "piece of junk," or worse— go elsewhere.

Above all, pay attention to your horse. He should be confident, relaxed, and happy in his work. The proof of any trainer's methods is in the finished product. If your horse is not improving or progressing in his training—and most especially if he is regressing—then that particular trainer's methods are not working, and it's time to find a new trainer.

Spurs, Whips, and Gadgets

Whips, spurs, and gadgets have a limited but helpful role in training and riding when used appropriately. Due to their chronic misuse, these items of equipment are sometimes rejected outright as inherently cruel by those outside the equestrian community who don't understand that they can be used appropriately (that is, judiciously and only with great restraint). Whips, crops, and spurs have detractors inside the horse world as well. They may be lumped together with a wide assortment of training gadgets—side reins, draw reins, longing "systems," tie-downs, and more—that are perceived as artificial and harmful shortcuts used in place of correct training.

When used with restraint, whips and spurs can be an effective way of communicating with a horse. A crop can be used to teach a horse to move forward by reinforcing the rider's leg cues. Spurs are often used by upper-level dressage riders or reiners because they can administer a more precise cue than can the leg alone. These items of equipment should never be used in place of less aggressive forms of communication or to inflict pain.

Under no circumstances should any training aid cause harm or injury to the horse. Of course, using a crop should never raise welts, and using spurs should not cause raw skin or draw blood. A touch with the whip or spur is akin to someone poking you in the ribs with a finger. It's designed to produce a reaction, not to cause pain.

It's also important to recognize that a tool may be suitable for use by one rider, but not another. If you don't have a steady leg, you are not yet advanced enough to use spurs correctly. Many devices can be very harmful if not used correctly; it's preferable to use them only under the guidance of an instructor or trainer. Any piece of equipment, no matter how benign, has the potential to be misused. Many sports have rules defining "excessive" use of the whip or spurs, and you can be disqualified for violating them. Whips and spurs are designed to be used sparingly, for a specific purpose, by educated hands.

Natural Horsemanship

"Natural horsemanship" is a relatively new method of training that uses language—both human and equine—to achieve a better relationship between horsemen and their equine partners.

Natural horsemanship is a philosophy, a training method, and an outlook on our relationship with horses that combines old and new ideas. It stresses working with horses in a way that recognizes their natural behavior, instincts, and personality and incorporates those traits into a program intended to achieve maximum trust and cooperation and minimum fear, resistance, and conflict.

Natural horsemanship involves reading your horse's body language and communicating with him in a way he instinctively understands.

Behavioral reinforcement replaces punishment and force used in many traditional methods of training, resulting in a calmer, happier, and more willing partner in the horse.

Theory of Natural Horsemanship

Horses naturally fear human beings, whom horses consider to be predators. Horses are prey animals. The skills learned in natural horsemanship teach them that they needn't fear human beings, but trust them, instead. This is accomplished by communicating with the horse on his level—in his language.

Horses have a unique communication system based primarily on body language. In natural horsemanship, the goal is to learn, emulate, and use that language to communicate with them.

Horses have personalities and a hierarchy that determines who leads and protects the herd and helps it survive. People want horses to let people be their leaders. Some horses are looking for a leader and are more willing to perceive humans in that role. Others are naturally more dominant, and human beings need to earn horses' trust and respect before expecting their cooperation.

How do horses interact in the herd? Watching them in the wild or in your pasture will teach you a lot. You'll see them challenge each other for position and status. Human beings must understand this herd dynamic and each individual horse's personality to incorporate this behavior into their training program.

The lead mare uses body language to control the other horses in the herd: they yield to her, and she disciplines any who don't submit to her authority. They respect her and look to her for guidance, even the stallions. Proponents of natural horsemanship strive to emulate the lead mare's behavior. Once they have the respect of their horse, they have a foundation of trust on which to build his training.

How does your own horse behave in the pasture with other horses, with you in the barn, or out on an unfamiliar trail? Is she dominant or subservient? Bold or fearful? Bored or interested? Having this knowledge will help establish the framework for your training with your horse.

How Does It Work?

Natural horsemanship uses human body language to emulate horses' body language and relay cues that convey the desired response to the horse. Horsemen learn how to use the placement and parts of their body, their tone of voice and other tools that help hone their communication with horses. These cues and tools exert subtle pressure, and the horse is rewarded for responding to requests by a release of that pressure, just like a rebellious young colt finds relief from the lead mare's admonitions when he agrees to toe the line.

As with many other training methods, there are two types of reinforcement used in natural horsemanship:

- Positive reinforcement is offered when a desired behavior is acknowledged with a reward, such as when a horse is led to a trailer and asked to walk in, then fed a treat when he complies willingly.

- Negative reinforcement, used to encourage desired behavior, is removed when the horse complies; for example, applying pressure to ask a horse to move his body in a certain direction. Removing the pressure once the horse moves serves as a reward for correct behavior.

Who "Does" Natural Horsemanship?

Horse trainers, clinicians, and backyard amateur owners worldwide use natural horsemanship to improve their horses' behavior and performance. Pleasure riders benefit from the increased trust their horse places in them during rides on unknown trails or on windy days. Competitors in many disciplines, ranging from dressage to reining, find it improves their training, communication, and results. There are even competitions in natural horsemanship that allow followers to show off their skills and talents from the ground and under saddle in a way never before rewarded.

Natural horsemanship has become increasingly popular in the past two decades, and many resources are available, including books, websites, and at-home video training programs, that you can view and then practice with your horse.

A number of famous practitioners have developed and teach their own versions of natural horsemanship. Each has his own style and method, but they all practice within the same general philosophy.

Several offer clinics in various locations and certify instructors who can assist followers in their local areas should they get "stuck" on a concept or task.

No Magic Wand

As with a foray into any new equine sport or discipline, natural horsemanship converts must make an initial investment in both time and money. Some programs require purchasing specialized equipment designed to enhance and improve natural communication methods, buying books and videos, and attending paid seminars.

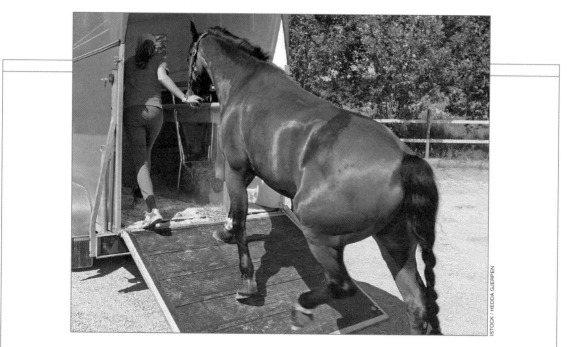

This horse is loading calmly and willingly into a bumper-pull-style trailer.

Natural horsemanship takes time, patience, and persistence. It is not a shortcut or gimmick, or a quick cure-all for every type of negative equine behavior. Many problems can be solved and doors opened with natural horsemanship, but there is no such thing as a quick fix program for "troubled" horses.

Trailer Loading

As a final footnote to our discussion of humane training, we'd like to touch on an issue that can be a cause of consternation to many horse owners: trailer loading.

It can be a familiar scene at the end of a competition or group trail ride. It's been a long day, it's starting to get dark, and everyone is ready to go home, but there's one lone horse who absolutely refuses to get on the trailer. Despite cursing and cajoling, he stands steadfast at the bottom of the trailer ramp, legs planted like tree trunks. His exasperated handlers are getting more and more impatient, and tempers are getting shorter and shorter.

Another valuable skill is teaching the horse to tie to the trailer itself. The lead rope or trailer tie should be attached to a halter (never to a bridle), long enough and high enough to allow the horse access to his hay bag and water bucket, but short enough to prevent him from backing into the towing vehicle.

This is a situation in which it's easy to lose patience and tempting to resort to methods you'd never consider in other areas of training. The result is often exhaustion, frustration, and a terrible experience for both horse and human—and, typically, a horse who will be even more determined not to get into a trailer next time.

Loading into a trailer is an extremely unnatural situation for a horse, one that his instincts scream is very dangerous—he's in a very confined space with no route of escape. Teaching a horse to load should be a slow, careful process, designed to allay the horse's fears and convince him that nothing bad will happen to him. It's work that should be done at home, where the horse feels secure, and at a pace the horse dictates.

Of course, when you're an hour from home, and the horse forgets those earlier lessons, you're in a tight spot. It's not as if you can just revisit the issue another day; you need to get home!

Unfortunately, such situations do not lend themselves to cooperative horses. You're in a strange place and you're rushed; you may be frustrated and angry at your horse for being obstinate. All of these factors conspire to create an atmosphere that is likely to make the issue worse, not better.

No matter how frustrated you are, or how late, or how tired, the "rules" of good training still apply. Trying to force the horse onto the trailer quickly is likely to exacerbate the situation (and prolong the ordeal). Go very slowly, be patient, and use appropriate positive reinforcement when the horse steps toward the trailer. If the horse is misbehaving or not listening, quietly ask him to back up or otherwise make him work and pay attention to you. It's imperative that everyone remain calm and avoid picking a fight. If you proceed very patiently, you should be able to convince the horse to load.

Obviously, before you trailer your horse again, you need to have several trailer-loading sessions at home to re-establish good habits in this area.

CHAPTER 13

Competition

WE HUMANS ARE A COMPETITIVE BUNCH. IT'S not hard to imagine that, shortly after the first horses were domesticated, the first horse race took place when one rider said to another, "I'll bet my horse can beat yours to that tree!"

For as long as horses and humans have partnered, there have been horse races, chariot races, pulling contests, jumping competitions, and the like. The competitive arena has given equine superstars a public stage on which to display their talents, giving legions of fans the chance to enjoy the athletic prowess of horses such as Brentina, Gem Twist, Hollywood Dun It, Wing Commander, and Winsome Adante.

The American Horse Council Foundation estimates that more than 2.7 million horses are involved in competition in the United States every year.[62] The vast majority of riders don't have Olympic or World Championship ambitions, however; they just want to compete for the fun of it and for the satisfaction of achieving personal goals. On any summer weekend, you can find horse enthusiasts around the country putting their skills on the line in an array of competitions, from informal backyard shows to officially sanctioned championships.

The Benefits of Competition

We all carry with us poignant memories of time spent with our favorite equines—a quiet moment of affection shared in the stall late at night or a lazy trail ride through beautiful scenery.

If you've spent much time competing, your mental memory book likely also includes a snippet of a moment full of possibility—standing at the entrance to an arena with your horse, looking ahead at the challenge that lies before you. It might be a show ring full of competitors, a trio of barrels, or a perfectly groomed dressage arena just awaiting your horse's hoofprints. It's a moment you've worked hard to reach: your horse is fit and confident, facing the test ahead with ears pricked. You are both perfectly turned out, with appropriate spit and polish, and stand ready to show the judge your best.

So much work goes into those brief moments of glory in the competition arena. Months, or even years, of preparation: lessons, daily practice, moving carefully up through the levels. Ribbons and prizes may come along the way, but the greatest reward often is simply the partnership you experience with your horse. You meet the challenges of competition together, trusting in each other's skills and sharing in the satisfaction of your accomplishments, as well as the disappointment of defeat.

There's something truly special about this aspect of the equine-human partnership, which perhaps explains why so many amateur riders find themselves drawn to competition, even though most have no illusions about ever reaching their sport's highest levels. These riders happily take time off from work, travel long distances, and spend hard-earned money on show fees, just for those opportunities to shine in the arena, even though they may last only a few minutes. That test is what motivates many horse people to improve their riding and horse-management skills, thereby indirectly benefiting their equine partners.

Competition (sometimes) provides its own rewards to the rider, in the form of ribbons, prizes, and recognition. There's nothing so satisfying as working toward a goal, matching the skills you've learned and your horse's talents against your fellow competitors, and being rewarded for it. While ribbons and prizes are wonderful, many other benefits are equally important, even if you can't hang them on the wall or put them in a trophy case.

Organized equestrian sport provides a ready-made ladder up which one can progress. Let's say you've decided to start out eventing at Beginner Novice. You're introduced to the basic concepts of the sport, where the challenges are achievable for good riders who are capable of an introductory level of competition. The dressage test rewards obedience and accuracy, but doesn't demand perfection. Cross-country allows the horse and rider to learn how to "gallop" (a nice canter is perhaps more accurate) and navigate simple natural obstacles in the open. Show jumping provides a final test, but with a very forgiving and elementary course.

As you move up the levels, more concepts are introduced. The dressage includes more difficult movements, and judges expect a higher degree of self-carriage from the horse. Cross-country courses begin to include water, ditches, or banks—small and easy challenges at first, but gradually becoming more difficult. Show jumping begins to demand that the horse be agile and careful.

The rules for each level spell out not only the height and width of fences, but also the degree of difficulty. You will easily sense if your horse is enjoying the challenge as much as you are. (If not, it is your responsibility to do what's best for him—even if that means scaling back your goals or finding an alternate activity that allows him to thrive.)

This logical progression is set forth by the governing associations for every sport. Judges, trainers, riders, and other experts determine what should be required and when to allow horses and riders to progress safely, learn the skills they need, and enjoy their success. The progression through the levels provides a built-in set of goals that doesn't necessarily revolve around placings. Winning doesn't need to be your only objective (and it definitely doesn't matter to your horse—your approval is his reward); it can also be advancing up the levels while still remaining competitive. There's a great sense of satisfaction in starting out at the lowest levels with a green horse and gradually moving up as the horse gains confidence.

Of course, there's nothing wrong with embracing that competitive spirit, if you do so with respect for the horse and your fellow competitors. On those rare occasions when all the pieces come together, and both you and your horse perform to the absolute best of your abilities, you *do* deserve to be rewarded with a ribbon or cooler or first-place check. They're rewards for your hard work and your skill—enjoy them!

Your placings serve another important function. They can help you measure how well you're meeting the criteria for your sport. Winning should never be "the only thing," but it certainly is a good gauge of how well you're doing.

For example, if you participate in endurance rides, and your horse consistently finishes among the "best conditioned," you can feel pretty confident about tackling some tougher or longer rides. If dressage is your sport, and you're consistently placing near the bottom of your classes, you're probably not ready to move up to the next level, as you haven't shown mastery of your current level. You should keep working on the skills required for the classes you're showing in, perhaps seeking guidance from a trainer or instructor who can help you pinpoint where you're lacking.

By nature, a competition pits you against your peers and fellow equestrian enthusiasts, as you're all trying to best each other for the top prize. But the horse world is rather small, and in most sports, your adversaries in competition are also your friends. You all attend the same competitions throughout the year, and perhaps even ride at the same barns or with the same trainers. You may even have grown up together in Pony Club or 4-H!

While there are exceptions, most equestrian competitors are friendly and cheer each other on. They offer hearty congratulations when you perform well enough to win, but they are also there to help you up and dust you off when things don't go quite so well (and catch and load your horse into the trailer, if need be).

Perhaps the supportive atmosphere is due to the fact that horses have such a way of humbling their human partners. Even the best of riders falls off occasionally or deals with horses who don't feel like being cooperative on a given day. An otherwise perfect effort can be marred by a spook, a buck, or an act of God. When your athletic partner is a species that can be stricken with panic at the sight of an umbrella, you have to be prepared for things not to go your way. The more you compete, the more such humbling scenarios, best met with sportsmanship and good humor, fill your memory book.

Winning is great fun, but for every success is a disappointment, and it's the ability to accept these gracefully, pat your horse, and return to ride another day that is perhaps the most valuable thing you'll gain. This may be the greatest contribution that competition can make to a horseman's education—sportsmanship.

The Drawbacks

Although taking part in competition has many benefits, it also has its downsides. Competition is hard work, for both horse and rider, and it's important to be cognizant of the effects the additional stress and mileage will have on your horse.

Imagine that you've traveled to a multiday hunter/jumper show a couple of hours from home. It's a warm summer day, but your horse stayed comfortable and cool in an airy trailer with a full haynet to keep him busy. You get to the show and hand-walk your horse around the grounds so he can stretch his legs and see all the sights. You find your stall in the temporary stabling area: it's smaller than you would like, but you've bedded it deeply.

You arrive at the showgrounds at 4 A.M. the following day to braid your horse's mane and tail and tack up for a quick school in the main arena. Then it's back into the stall for your horse, where he can munch on some hay while awaiting your early-afternoon hunter classes.

After lunch, you tack up again and head to the schooling area to warm up for your first class. The footing isn't the best and the ring is very crowded. You warm up well and head over to the main ring, where you and your horse lay down a beautiful round in your first class. Unfortunately, your second class is delayed by a medical emergency in the ring. You return to the schooling area to re-warm up, since your horse has now been standing around for half an hour, and then have another lovely round in your second class.

It's now mid-afternoon—it's hot and there's no shade. You have one more ride, in an under-saddle class, but it will be delayed for half an hour by two riders in your division who first must complete the over-fences class. You remount and head back to the schooling ring for another quick warm-up, ride in your last class, then finally untack for the day.

This hurry-up-and-wait routine is repeated on days two and three of the show. By the third day, your horse is a little stiff from being stuck in that small stall with no turnout, so you try to hand-walk and graze him several times a day. On the final day, it rains. The arena footing is deep, sloppy mud, and your horse slips on the approach to a fence and slides to a stop. Fortunately, he's not hurt, but the refusal means you are out of the running for the division championship. Nevertheless, you pack up for the long trip home feeling like it was a successful outing.

Over the course of this hypothetical show, your horse was ridden and jumped much more than normal, over sometimes-suspect footing and in summer heat. His routine was disrupted, with daily early-morning braiding and meals coming at different times, depending on class schedules, and he didn't have the benefit of his usual turnout time.

Even with a conscientious owner who doesn't enter an excessive number of classes, warms his horse up sparingly, and provides lots of supportive care (liniment baths, standing wraps overnight, lots of hand-walking), showing is a lot of work for the horse. He has the mental stress of being away from home in a new place with a new routine, and the physical stress of extra work in sometimes less-than-ideal conditions. If you show many weekends, that stress is multiplied.

Most veteran competition horses know their jobs and settle into a show routine easily. If a horse doesn't enjoy it, he'll let his rider know. Conscientious riders do their best to minimize the mileage on their horses and won't hesitate to withdraw from competition if they feel the weather is too hot or cold or the footing is too hard or too sloppy. "Save him for another day" is a mantra you hear often around caring competitors.

Unfortunately, the adrenaline of the show ring and our own competitive natures can sometimes drown out the voices of our inner horsemen. For professional riders and trainers, competition isn't just for fun, it's how they make their living, and their paying clients want top placings. When a client's expensive new horse isn't progressing as quickly as anticipated, or doesn't seem to be quite so talented as was expected, there can be tremendous pressure to rush the horse or resort to extreme methods to squeeze a higher level of performance from him. And in the heat of competition, when a top ribbon or prize is on the line, there's always the temptation to take unacceptable risks or to push the horse dangerously close to, or beyond, his limits.

Even for amateurs, there's a great deal of self-imposed pressure. Going to competitions requires a lot of time, money, and preparation. Understandably, those who compete hope to do well. Spending hundreds of dollars in entry fees, getting up in the wee hours to braid or bathe the horse, eating terrible horse show food, and riding in the oppressive heat or drenching rain is much more tolerable when you have a blue ribbon at the end of the weekend to show for your efforts! End-of-the-year awards in many state equestrian associations are based on cumulative points, rewarding those who compete in show after show, a scenario so common it is called point chasing.

The struggle we all face is how to balance our competitive ambitions with our stewardship of our horses. If a Western pleasure mount is clearly tired and souring on showing but is just a few points shy of qualifying for the World Championship show, should the rider give him a vacation or just try to make it through another one or two shows first to qualify? What about a barrel horse who is having some aches and pains, but is sound with a little Bute—should the rider continue to point toward the national shows or finish the season early? The humane horseman makes these decisions in favor of his horse: his horse's needs, desires, and preferences matter, too.

In many sports rules are in place to address these issues. But many decisions about the horses' welfare are entirely up to the owner. She decides how frequently to show, at what level to compete, how many classes to enter, what conditions to ride in, and what amount of medication (within the confines of the rules) she is willing to use. The competitive horse world presents a never-ending series of small ethical dilemmas that constantly challenge us to rein in our own competitive desires and do what's best for the horse.

There are unscrupulous individuals in every sport, however, who are not troubled by ethics. Or rules, for that matter. Or even laws. For them, winning at any cost is the priority, and the horse is just a means to an end. They have no compunction about using drugs or abusive training methods, as long as they think they can get away with it.

Such individuals are fortunately a small minority in the competitive equestrian world. But their actions show how the relentless pursuit of ribbons or prize money without conscience can eclipse the original purpose of equestrian competition—to enjoy and showcase the incredible athleticism of the noble horse.

Finally, consideration must be given to the fate of the athletes when their competitive days are over. What happens to horses—those who are successful and those who aren't—when they can no longer compete?

Our equine athletes give fully of themselves, often experiencing wear and tear on their bodies that will eventually limit their usefulness for sport or even casual riding. A severe injury may convert a relatively young horse into a pasture ornament, leaving the owner with the prospect of caring for an unrideable horse for many years.

Horses are not just "sports equipment," like bats or balls, to be used up and discarded. They are living beings and our willing partners in sport. Humane horsemen commit to taking care of their horses for life or making sure that someone else will do so.

Competing with a Conscience

If you find yourself torn between the thrill of good-natured competition among peers and the stress on your horse and the risk of injury, you're not alone. Many of those who compete do so very conservatively. They're *not* aiming for the Olympics or even year-end awards; they just want to have fun and test their skills in a safe and constructive way. Ribbons and prize money are an added bonus.

It takes a special disposition to be at once competitive and also a guardian of the horse's welfare. In fact, even among the most highly regarded and accomplished riders and trainers, there are individuals who readily admit they've made errors in the past. Perhaps they pushed a horse to competition too soon or past his natural capabilities. Maybe they showed a horse when there was a nagging feeling that he wasn't quite "right," or kept showing a tired horse against their better judgment.

We're all human, and we all make mistakes. (And the more experience we gain, the more obvious our past errors become to us, so if you think you're immune, just wait!) There's one litmus test that should be applied to every decision you make: what's best for the horse? The answer should not depend on whether you're in last place or first, or whether prize money or points are at stake. Lost time and money are regrettable, but your horse's health and soundness are irreplaceable. There are always other competitions.

Your considerations for your horse's welfare should not be confined solely to his physical well-being; it's also important to consider his mental attitude toward competition.

The best show horses truly love their jobs. They "light up" when they get into a ring in front of a crowd, and they enjoy putting their talents on display. They can feel the electricity in the air at a big competition. Many even respond to the roar of applause when they finish their performances, giving a playful buck and head-toss that seems to be the equine equivalent of shouting "Whoo-hoo!" and pumping a fist in the air.

Such horses are the product of careful training and preparation. They're fit and confident and ready to perform to the best of their abilities.

But that's not true for every horse you see in the competition arena. Some seem to be saying quite clearly that they'd prefer to be somewhere else. They voice their displeasure in the only way they can—by refusing or running out at jumps, resisting, misbehaving, or acting out.

If moving up a level seems to be a struggle for your horse, reconsider whether he's prepared or truly capable of what you're asking him to do. Keep in mind that there is no set schedule for how you or your horse should progress. Competing at a certain level for a period of time does not automatically mean you're ready to move up to the next level.

In fact, you don't *have* to move up at all; if you're comfortable at your current level and want to stay there, that's okay, too. It can be difficult to prepare for upper-level competition sufficiently when you have other responsibilities in life, such as a full-time job or a family. Many amateurs keep their ambitions modest, planning to advance only as far as their limited availability allows.

When you ask your equine partner to join you in your sporting endeavors, you are acknowledging that he risks being injured by doing so. Most injuries are minor, and many horses are able to recover and return to the same level of competition. More severe injuries may mean that your horse might not compete at the same level again or has to move to a less stressful sport. In some instances, injuries are career-ending, although the horse can recover to be pasture sound and still live happily for many years to come.

Your responsibility to your horse doesn't end when he ceases to be useful for your chosen sport. Whether he sustained his injuries while acting as a willing partner in your competitive ambitions or via a pasture accident, he deserves to be cared for and valued regardless of his usefulness as a competition mount.

Fortunately, riders from all levels of competition recognize this covenant. Many Olympians have fields full of retired former partners who graze away their remaining days in pampered comfort. Many lower-level riders who can only afford to keep one horse change sports or forgo competition altogether if they must, to care for their horses in the manner to which they're accustomed.

Whether you keep your former competitive partner yourself, rehome him with a rider who doesn't require him to carry a very heavy workload, or pension him to a retirement farm, you owe it to your horse to ensure that, whether as a therapeutic riding mount or pasture puff, he is just as treasured as he was when winning ribbons at the highest levels.

CHAPTER 14

Stewardship

THE OWNER HAS A PAT LINE READY WHENEVER someone makes the inevitable comment about how good her twenty-something horse looks for his age—"Don't look at his hocks!" she'll say with a laugh.

Under the long, woolly coat, the signs of many miles logged in the competition ring are surely evident. There are a few windpuffs and splints, spavins in the hocks, and the general creakiness of a body that's worked hard for many years. But most people don't notice. Instead they see the mischievous spark in the gelding's eye, the glint to his coat, and the way he puffs himself up when he's been bathed and trimmed, as if he's headed back to the show ring. They see the way he bosses around the other horses in the pasture, exuding an air of "Don't mess with me, kid—I've seen everything."

The owner sees these things, too, but is also accustomed to looking past them with a critical and caring eye. She makes a mental note to increase the gelding's joint supplement when he seems stiffer than usual or to talk to the farrier about rounding off his toe more when he starts to stumble. She notices that his hearing isn't what it used to be and that he spooks more easily, probably because his eyesight is fading. She keeps a careful eye on his weight, knowing how quickly an elderly horse can get thin under a winter coat and how difficult it can be to put weight back on him.

It can be a lot of work and worry to care for an older horse, but the owner figures it's her chance to return many previous favors. She remembers all the times she got him to a fence too fast, too slow, without enough impulsion, crooked in the approach and he jumped it anyway, even though he had every right to refuse it. She remembers her first clumsy attempts at treating his wounds, nursing him through colic and dealing with lamenesses, and marvels that he survived it all. And she remembers all the silly (and stupid) things the horse good-naturedly endured because she was a teenager who didn't know any better—giving pony rides to dozens of friends, parading on the Fourth of July between "horse-eating" floats and marching bands, carrying the "Headless Horseman" on Halloween....

She owes this horse a great deal. He kept her safe. He taught her how to ride. All of her skills were honed on him, and he often suffered through the "error" part of trial and error before she got it right. Any horse she owns in the future will benefit from the kind, yet firm, way she handles horses on the ground; the soft hands and independent seat she has developed; the ability to read the subtle physical signs a horse shows when he's sick or sore. She learned all of this from the elderly gelding.

More than anything, they are old, good friends. A quiet moment shared in the stall late in the evening, his graying head pushed into her chest, speaks volumes—things that can't, and don't need to, be expressed in words.

This horse had five owners in the first ten years of his life. The sixth owner has owned him as long as all the others combined. She will care for him until the end, because she feels he is owed that. He gave her what she wanted, the chance to learn and compete. Now he gets what he wants—the chance to eat and sleep his days away in lazy retirement, secure in the fact that his every remaining need will be met. What more could a horse want? What more could an owner give?

Owner, Steward, Caregiver

If your role as keeper of your horse came with a job title, what would it be?

Most horsemen probably refer to themselves as their horses' "owners": after all, under the law, that's what we are. Pets and livestock are considered property; they're bought and sold just like a car, a couch, or a bag of carrots.

One hopes that a horse merits more care and attention than a car or a couch, and that despite the legal definition of the horse as property, ownership means much more. Ownership implies a certain level of responsibility and an inherent value. When you own something, it's your job to take care of it and handle its upkeep and maintenance to protect your investment.

We horse owners know there's more to it than that, of course. Technically, horses are our property, but in reality, they're also our friends and companions.

The term "caregiver" might be more appropriate. It suggests that there's more involved in this relationship than just ownership; there's a level of custody as well. But it still doesn't quite convey the true depth of the partnership between a horse and his human. For those of us who really cherish our horses, there's an emotional investment in addition to a monetary one. We're not just responsible for meeting our horses' physical needs, such as food, water, shelter, and veterinary care; we're also charged with ensuring they're happy and enjoy their lives and their jobs. We care about them and their well-being. So let's consider the concept of "stewardship" instead.

The role of a steward is probably more similar to that of a parent than an owner or caretaker. Legally, a parent's obligation ends when a child turns eighteen, but that certainly doesn't mean a parent stops caring. We maintain relationships with our parents throughout our lives, still seeking their advice and guidance long after we're physically and financially independent.

Yes, of course, a steward is still responsible for a horse's care and is still his legal owner. But stewardship invokes an ethical responsibility that transcends simply being financially or legally responsible for a horse's care. It's an obligation that doesn't end when a horse reaches a certain age or when a rider moves on to other things.

Grow Old, Go Away?

When you adopt or purchase a puppy or a kitten, you're making a commitment to care for that animal for the rest of her life. You'll enjoy the adorable antics of kitten- or puppyhood and teach your pet to be a well-behaved canine or feline citizen. As middle age settles in, you'll have a well-trained companion with whom you hope to share many years of adventures and close friendship. Old age will eventually encroach, and you'll care for your elderly friend conscientiously through his twilight years. And when the time comes, your faithful buddy will either pass on naturally or be helped along by euthanasia in your final act as a responsible pet owner.

Imagine the outcry from your pet-loving friends, though, if you decided to sell your dog because he is not good at fetching balls or give your cat away because she has gotten too arthritic to jump up on the sofa like she used to. It's simply not done, except in the most extenuating circumstances. Taking ownership of a pet is supposed to be a lifetime commitment.

With horses, though, it has been accepted—and even expected—that an animal will have many owners throughout his lifetime. Horses are usually working animals, and they have a job and a purpose. Just as most people don't spend their entire careers working for the same company, a horse may be best suited for jobs with a variety of owners throughout his "career."

Buying or selling horses isn't inherently wrong if circumstances demand it. Under the right circumstances, it can work out wonderfully for all involved. After all, if horses weren't bought and sold, most of us wouldn't be able to enjoy the experience of horse ownership!

But the buying-and-selling process can go terribly, terribly wrong. Take a walk around the crowded pens at an auction and look at the equine castoffs and see former show- or racehorses who once commanded five-figure prices, ponies who were once cherished childhood friends, and strong, staid draft horses who have spent their entire lives working hard for their owners. At some point in their lives, these horses had perceived "value" and probably had owners who treasured them and cared well for them. Yet at the end of their days, their only value is the price per pound they can command from the slaughter buyers.

Things depreciate. State-of-the-art computers quickly become obsolete. New cars rack up mileage. No matter how high the number on the original price sticker, the monetary value of these objects dwindles over time until it essentially reaches zero. Ten years later, that state-of-the-art computer is a glorified doorstop, and that new car is a junker.

But here's where the concept of stewardship comes in. Unlike inanimate objects we might own, a horse's value should not be pegged solely to how much money someone is willing to pay for him. Other factors influence his worth—memories of a spectacular trail ride through the foothills in autumn, for instance; a wall lined with ribbons the two of you earned together; the feel of his lips and whiskers tickling your hand in search of a treat; the way he nickers softly at you every time you pass his stall.

A horse's monetary value eventually reaches zero. It may happen when he's two or when he's twenty, but it will happen. The significance of being your horse's steward as opposed to "just" his owner is that his value to you doesn't necessarily equal his price tag.

To Sell or to Stay Together

Hey, we're realists— plenty of horse-and-rider combinations are not the stuff of fairy tales. There are practicalities and priorities. Life has a way of rudely intruding and quashing even the best of intentions. Storybook romances end in divorce. The underdog team loses at the buzzer. Bad guys win, and good guys lose.

Selling a horse has traditionally been an accepted part of the horse world and part of the machinery that keeps the horse industry moving. Many horse owners find it emotional and difficult, but they're told this is the way things are done and to follow the advice of traditional "old timers" in the horse world.

If you're reading this book, you're likely to be someone who feels a sense of responsibility toward your horse. You have a deep appreciation for that equine magic, that sense of partnership you get from riding a well-trained horse or the sense of accomplishment you get from learning and progressing in your riding.

There's another level to the connection between horse and human that many owners miss out on, however. Most companion animals don't live nearly as long as their human caretakers. You're lucky if you enjoy a few years with a fish or a hamster. Cats and dogs often live a decade or more, but that's still a pretty short period in human years. Horses, though, routinely live into their twenties, thirties, and beyond. If you choose an equine partner wisely—and with an eye toward the future—your abilities, skills, and talents will complement each other and allow for a long and productive career together. The unique sense of partnership you feel with your equine friend is only heightened the more time you spend together.

There's great satisfaction in being able to reap the benefits of the most productive years of a horse's life—whether those benefits are ribbons or the pleasure and education found through hours in the saddle—and then give something back to that horse as he enters his golden years. But, sadly, it's an aspect of horsemanship that many miss out on completely, even though it's one of the most rewarding.

But by being a responsible steward for your horse, you can minimize the chances that unforeseen circumstances will force you to sell. And if you open your eyes to alternatives other than selling, you might see another level of horsemanship that doesn't involve skill in the saddle.

When the Partnership Is Over

Irreconcilable Differences

Chapter 13 touched on the importance of assessing whether a horse is happy in his work. If it becomes apparent that a horse simply isn't suited to a particular job (whether that job is as an upper-level competition horse or a "babysitter" mount for a young rider), a career change is in everyone's best interest. Neither the horse nor his human is well served by stubbornly trying to fit a square peg into a round hole.

Sometimes, too, the partnership between horse and rider just never solidifies—the two simply don't "click." It's normal for a new horse-and-rider combination to spend a few months getting to know each other and working out the kinks in their relationship, and sometimes professional training can be a great help in solving misunderstandings and communication issues. But in some cases, the two just plain might not be a good match. Riding is supposed to be fun and enjoyable for both horse and rider. If it's not, something needs to change.

But here's where it gets tricky. If you were to sell a car that no longer suited your needs or give an old couch to Goodwill after redecorating, what happened to the car or the couch once it was out of your possession probably wouldn't matter much to you. You took care of it while it was yours, but if the new owners aren't as conscientious…well, it's their loss, not yours. Right?

Your horse is property under the law, and you're certainly within your rights to sell or give him to someone else. However, he isn't a car or a couch; you're responsible for his well-being. Once you hand his lead rope to someone else, his fate is out of your control.

It may not seem practical to suggest that all horse owners consider their commitment to a horse to be the same kind of lifetime commitment they'd make to a cat or a dog. Horses are large animals that are expensive to keep. Some people don't have the resources to turn a young, healthy horse out to pasture to live out the rest of his days. (Many horse owners can afford only one horse; they must face the terrible dilemma of "retiring" along with their unsound horse or finding a way to keep riding without him.)

A mismatched horse and rider can be downright dangerous, both to themselves and to others. It's not fair to a horse to ask him to perform in a capacity for which he's not suited, and riding is too expensive and time-consuming to pursue if you don't absolutely love it. Sometimes, certain horse-and-rider partnerships are just better off ended.

So what then?

Selling

Perhaps the Quarter Horse mare you hoped would be your trail-riding companion hasn't settled into the bombproof buddy you thought she would. On a cool and windy day, she likes to express her enthusiasm for life with a few "oh-I-feel-so-good!" bucks that leave you clinging to the saddle horn. Her outbursts are never malicious and probably wouldn't bother a stronger rider, but they erode your confidence until you no longer feel safe riding out on the trail—or riding at all.

In this case, selling the horse may be the right option. This *isn't* the perfect horse for you, but she might be the perfect horse for someone else. In a new home and a new career, your horse might enjoy her work more and really shine. Selling her will also give you the funds to buy a replacement that might be better suited for your goals and what you want to do.

Once you sell a horse outright, though, you no longer have any control over how she's kept or treated. Her new owners could keep her in conditions you wouldn't approve of or ride her harder than you think appropriate. They could be rough, or even abusive. And eventually they could sell her to someone else, so you might lose track of your old friend completely.

Frankly, no matter how careful you are, selling a horse is a risk—once the horse is out of your control, anything can happen. But there are steps you can take to minimize the chances that the horse you once cherished will end up in an unfortunate situation.

Vetting Goes Both Ways

We've already covered the horse-buying process from the buyer's side. It's time to focus on this transaction from the seller's point of view.

You should approach selling your horse as a sort of interview process for potential owners. It is your responsibility to ensure your horse is going to a home of which you approve, and you may want to include this criterion in your ad.

Be prepared with a list of questions for potential buyers. Ask about their riding experience and whether they have a trainer or other knowledgeable person they can go to for advice. Ask where they plan to keep the horse, and whether he'll get turnout and how much. If possible, visit his potential new home. Ask about the prospective buyer's riding goals and plans. Ask for references.

Pay attention to how the prospective buyer interacts with your horse, both in and out of the saddle. You know your horse's quirks: do you think the buyer will be able to handle them effectively? The buyer might not be able to assess her own riding skills very objectively, but you can.

Also, be as honest with the buyer as you possibly can. Misrepresenting your horse's temperament or abilities isn't the way to find him a home where he'll be a good fit; it's just setting him up to be sold again when that partnership doesn't work out. Be up-front about any health or training issues he's had, his level of experience, how difficult he is to ride, and his competitive record. You're not doing your horse any favors by pumping up his résumé and putting him in a situation for which he's not suited.

Don't be afraid to seem nosy or distrustful. Above all, don't be afraid to follow your gut. Your horse will thank you for it.

Letting Go…But Not Completely

If the stars are properly aligned, you'll find a buyer for your horse about whom you're actually excited, someone you feel will take excellent care of your friend. Ideally, you'll be happy, not apprehensive, when watching your former horse head down your driveway in his new owner's trailer.

Keep in touch with the buyer and be sure he always has your current contact information. Let the buyer know that you care about this horse and ask to be contacted if things don't work out, or if the buyer ever needs to find the horse a new home.

Many sellers try to work this into their bills of sale by either including a buy-back clause or a right of "first refusal." The first contractually "forbids" the new owner from selling the horse and requires that he be sold only back to you. The second merely reserves the owner's right to have "first dibs" on the horse if he should ever be offered up for sale.

Both methods are a great idea in theory, but, in practice, they're difficult to enforce and shouldn't be relied on. The new owners may pick up and move without notice to you…if not after the first move, perhaps after the second or third relocation. Neither a buy-back clause nor a right of first refusal will do anything to help you track down your horse if the buyer sells him without informing you.

A New Lease on Life

After all this, does the idea of selling your horse make you apprehensive? It should. There's really no way to ensure that your horse won't find his way into a bad situation. The only way to be sure your horse is always cared for in a manner you find appropriate is to maintain ownership of him.

However, there are ways you can find your horse a new situation for which he might be better suited and still remain his owner.

Leasing a horse allows you to maintain ownership but gives another rider certain responsibilities and privileges. As we said in chapter 4, some leases entail a fee—a rider pays the horse's owner specifically for the opportunity to ride *that* horse, usually a very talented individual with a top show record. (The rider pays the horse's expenses—including show expenses—in addition to the riding fee for the opportunity to compete on a horse he could not otherwise afford.) More common is a "free lease," or "expenses-only" lease, which requires that the lessee pay only certain expenses, such as board, feed, and farrier and veterinary care.

In some ways the lease can be the best of both worlds if you want to be a responsible caretaker. You're still your horse's legal owner and are ultimately in charge of his fate, but your horse is partnered with someone better suited to his talents or abilities.

To ensure that a lease works out as intended, be sure to draft an ironclad written lease agreement that spells out each party's responsibilities. Screen potential lessees as carefully as you would screen potential buyers—and stay involved. If the horse is stabled at a different facility from where you board or live, call the lessee for frequent progress reports and stop by the facility to make sure your horse looks as happy as you want him to be.

As important as a written lease agreement is, it isn't worth the paper it's printed on if you don't keep in touch with your lessee. If you don't, you could discover he has sold the horse without your permission or, after a few unreturned phone calls, eventually find the lessee and horse are long gone. In such cases (and they do happen), you have very few practical options available to you. It is much better to stay in frequent contact with the lessee and inspect your horse in the flesh on a regular basis.

Donation

For some people, leasing can be rather labor-intensive. Finding the right lessee may take a long time, or you might not find one at all. In cases of partial (or part-time) leasing, you're still shouldering some of the financial burden. If leasing is not feasible for you, but you don't want to sell your horse outright, donating the horse might be a viable option.

Many organizations accept donated horses for use in various programs—mounted police, therapeutic riding programs for the handicapped, and intercollegiate equestrian teams are a few of the most common. In most cases, you have to cede ownership to the organization, but many groups will agree to keep you informed about your horse and give you the opportunity to buy him back or reclaim ownership if he's no longer able to participate in their program. Most do not guarantee that they will keep him once he is no longer useful to their program, however, so if you don't make arrangements for his return to you, he may be sold to the highest bidder when that time comes.

Research the organization thoroughly before signing your horse over to it. Ask for references and ask local veterinarians or trainers for their opinions about the group. Visit the group's facility and speak to the person in charge of caring for the group's horses. Ask about deworming, vaccination, and shoeing schedules. Look at the type and quality of feed offered. Cast a critical eye over the other horses under this group's care; do they look healthy and happy?

Make sure you'll be welcome to visit your horse at any time, and do so. Keep in touch with the people actually caring for him: make sure *they're* aware that you'll take your horse back if he's no longer appropriate for their program.

If you're lucky, an organization in your area with a long-standing, gilt-edged reputation will love your horse, and you can rest assured that your horse is going to a proven good home.

Donation is often a good option for horses who might not be particularly easy to sell to the right buyer. One horse may have great athletic prowess but also have management or riding issues that will put many buyers off, such as a stable vice or a quirk that requires a certain level of rider skill to deal with. Another may have age and physical issues that don't affect him now but do make him less appealing to buyers who don't want to gamble with potential physical problems down the road.

An organization that accepts donated horses is more willing to work around these issues. College programs may be interested in talented-but-complicated horses since they want to challenge their students' riding skills. Therapeutic riding programs can be a wonderful choice for horses nearing the end of their useful riding careers, because the horse is rarely required to move faster than a walk. In fact, slightly creaky older gentlemen and ladies are in high demand for such programs because they're so quiet and sensible!

Your donation is usually tax-deductible, so you'll enjoy that as a benefit, as well as the knowledge that you're helping a worthwhile program. It's a good feeling to know that your horse is introducing children to the joys of riding or helping a handicapped adult overcome a physical disability.

Nothing Good Lasts Forever

Holding Things Together

Good veterinary care—especially preventive care—helps to keep an equine athlete working comfortably well into middle age and beyond. As a horse gets older, your veterinarian will likely become one of his closest friends! Many therapies and nutritional supplements can help keep a horse sound and comfortable and allow him to continue in his job.

It's not unheard of for horses to continue competing into their late teens, or even early twenties. In 1998 eleven-year-old Megan Moore was a divisional national barrel-racing champion at the Great Lakes Nationals on her horse Deckem Lilly Bug, who, at twenty-eight, was by far the oldest equine winner in the competition. That kind of longevity is unusual, but plenty of horses are comfortable and happy being ridden—and even being in competitions—into their golden years.

In the previous chapter we discussed how riders have to be careful not to let their horses' welfare suffer at the hands of their competitive spirits. Likewise, we have to be cautious that we don't exploit veterinary advancements to the point that a horse becomes Humpty Dumpty: constantly "breaking" and being pieced back together again. If you start to feel as though you're holding your horse together with the veterinary equivalent of duct tape, something is amiss.

Horses are notoriously accident-prone and fragile; if you own any individual horse for any length of time, he's highly likely to sustain a few injuries that require a period of being laid up. It can be something as innocuous as a hoof abscess or as serious and career-threatening as a bowed tendon. Even under the best of care, horses get hurt.

There's a difference, though, between the accidents and injuries that "just happen" (inevitably the week before a show) and an ongoing string of wear-and-tear injuries or repeated flare-ups of chronic conditions.

Pain and injuries are the body's way of forcing us to slow down and take it easy. If your horse's body is speaking up that loudly, listen.

As the person responsible for your horse's well-being, it's up to you to make decisions about his treatment and work/competition schedule. Here's where a good, trusted veterinarian is an invaluable ally, because you need someone to help you understand the full extent of any injury, the horse's prognosis for recovery, and his overall condition. You should explore all treatment options, as well as routine maintenance (such as anti-inflammatories or joint supplements), that can help your older fellow continue to feel comfortable and enjoy his job.

Many older horses do well on maintenance-level doses of anti-inflammatory drugs, such as aspirin or phenylbutazone (Bute). These drugs are usually safe and well tolerated, although they can cause gastric upset and ulcers in some horses, even at low doses.

Such drugs can help alleviate the aches and pains that aren't serious but are common among older horses. They shouldn't be administered except on the advice of a veterinarian, though, and should be given at a low dose, so the pain-relieving effect isn't so high that it masks pain from a serious injury.

You don't want to medicate your horse to the point that his pain is dulled and then keep riding him as if nothing is wrong while a chronic injury worsens.

When One Door Closes, Another Opens

If it doesn't seem that your horse can physically hold up to the rigors of his current job, or if he simply isn't enjoying his work anymore, it might be time to change his job description.

This doesn't necessarily mean it's time to pull his shoes and turn him out to pasture, although that's certainly something to consider. But exercise is actually quite good for older horses, and it's a good idea to keep them at a constant level of light to moderate fitness as long as possible.

Lightening his workload may be enough to keep him happy and comfortable. Make his daily workouts less strenuous—take more walk breaks and don't ride quite so long. Take more long, lazy trail rides as an alternative to concentrated work in an arena. If you jump, don't do it as frequently, lower the fence standards a hole or two, and cut down on the jump efforts significantly.

Retirement

Some horses are able to be ridden throughout their lives, right until the very end. But for others, there may come a point when they truly cannot hold a "job" anymore. Your horse might incur an injury that makes him permanently lame, or founder, or suffer an illness that makes him unable to perform regular work—even light riding.

As an owner, you must be prepared for this to happen at any point in your horse's life. A well-placed kick from a pasture mate, for example, can lead to a career-ending injury for a horse of any age. But if you own an older horse, the end of your horse's riding life should be at the forefront of your mind.

Horses who are no longer ridden become purely companion animals (albeit very large ones). Keeping a horse solely as a pet has its challenges—horses can be expensive to house and feed. But when a horse has spent a lifetime in service to humans, a proper retirement is his due.

Your horse will tell you if this is what he wants and needs, if you listen carefully. You'll notice that he's ever stiffer when being led out of the stall in the morning. He won't dance at the ends of the reins as you lead him to the mounting block in anticipation of a fun-filled ride. He won't puff himself up with pride when he does something well under saddle: on the contrary, it'll seem that the quality of his performance is on a constant backslide. His performance may seem labored, the joy gone.

You know your horse better than anyone, and he'll tell you quite clearly when he no longer enjoys his work.

Green Fields, Blue Skies

Most retired horses do best with as much turnout as possible, so they can get plenty of leisurely exercise. You need to decide for yourself if your horse would enjoy twenty-four-hour turnout, or if he'd rather be brought in for a few hours a day, either away from heat and insects or out of windy, icy conditions, based on his eagerness to be brought in. Horses are more affected by heat and cold as they age, so if your horse is turned out full time, keep a careful eye on your friend in extreme weather conditions, particularly if access to shelter is limited.

A horse out in a field by himself is hardly ever happy. If you're not fortunate enough to have your own farm, you may find it necessary to change your horse's living arrangements when he takes on his new role as a lawn ornament. Since you're no longer riding him, you might be able to find a boarding facility that provides good care but fewer rider-oriented amenities (after all, why pay a premium price to board at a barn with well-groomed riding arenas you'll never use?) or is less conveniently located for daily visits.

Sometimes a retiree can find a new job as a companion horse. You might ask your horse-loving contacts (including veterinarians and farriers) if they know anyone with a single horse at home who wants a buddy.

There are many farms advertised as retirement facilities for horses around the country, and they do sound idyllic. Your horse can while away his days in a large green pasture with a number of other old cronies. Be sure to check out any such places thoroughly.

You still want to see your retiree regularly, of course. He'll need someone to groom him and doctor his cuts and scrapes. You should also keep a vigilant eye on his body condition, so you're aware of any changes in his health. His teeth may need more regular examination by the veterinarian or equine dentist, due to age-related wear and loss. He may be able to go barefoot, perhaps for the first time in his adult life, but he will still need regular farriery. His vaccination schedule may change if he is not traveling to shows, trail rides, and clinics any longer, but the likelihood of age-related chronic problems (such as Cushing's disease) will increase. Your retiree will never complain, but you will want to stay an engaged, observant owner, whether he is in your backyard or a huge field, as he ages through the years, then slips into decline.

The Final Good-bye

When It's Time to Euthanize

There may come a time when you have to make that final, difficult decision in your horse's best interest. He may sustain an irreparable injury that leaves him in constant pain. He might develop any number of disorders that plague older horses—Cushing's disease, thyroid problems, chronic founder—that are likely to lead to a constant worsening of his physical condition.

As the stewards of our animals, we shoulder the responsibility for making this difficult, yet kind, decision on our animals' behalf. It's a daunting burden to hold a life in your hands, and if you've never had to make the decision before, you might wonder how you'll know when is the right time.

Longtime pet or horse owners will tell you that you'll know when the time is right—you'll just *know*. If a horse stops eating, cannot rise

Your old-timer will let you know when it is time to say good-bye.

AMY KOLZOW

or move about comfortably, if he no longer interacts with his herd-mates or seems unresponsive to the ebb and flow of daily life, or develops an illness requiring invasive treatment with little hope of real recovery, take heed. Trust your judgment. Listen to your horse. Ask for the candid advice of a trusted veterinarian. Usually, the answer will be clear. While the decision to euthanize is difficult and fraught with sadness, without a doubt, it's also the kindest decision you'll ever make on your horse's behalf.

The Long Sleep

The preferred method of euthanasia for horses, recommended by The Humane Society of the United States, is administration of a lethal dose of barbiturates in combination with a sedative. These are federally controlled substances administered via intravenous injection by a licensed veterinarian.

Your veterinarian will give the sedative first, and then an overdose of sodium pentobarbital. The barbiturate depresses the central nervous system and leads to respiratory and cardiac arrest; the sedative minimizes the horse's reaction and, ideally, allows the veterinarian to "lay the horse down" without violent thrashing.

The process can be difficult to watch, especially if you're seeing it done for the first time on your own beloved horse. A horse is a large animal who doesn't always fall gently. The horse may exhibit some thrashing, kicking, or twitching, but this is an automatic response and not a sign that he is experiencing pain. Other than inserting the intravenous needle, the process should be painless. You may want a trusted friend, one with whom your horse is familiar but who has less of an emotional attachment, to help the veterinarian in this role—in exchange for your promise to do the same for him.

Although euthanasia by barbiturate overdose is more expensive than other options, since it requires a veterinarian to be present, it is the accepted humane method. You assume financial responsibility for your horse when you purchase him, and this final expense is his just due.

You will also have to make arrangements for disposal of your horse's carcass after euthanasia, which usually entails a separate fee paid to a livestock disposal service. With prior notification, the service will send a truck to the euthanasia site to haul the body to a rendering facility. Your veterinarian can help you make this arrangement. Many horse owners prefer not to witness the removal of the body, and with prior payment of the fee and clear directions to the driver, this can be accomplished.

If local ordinances permit it, and you have—or can hire for a reasonable fee—the heavy equipment required, you can bury your horse on your property. (Note, however, that this now is illegal in some states.)[63] You can also have your horse cremated. Veterinary colleges usually perform this service. (Pet cemeteries with crematories typically cannot handle a body the size of a horse's.) Composting, although not legal in all states, is considered an inexpensive and environmentally sound method of carcass disposal, when undertaken correctly. Landfills may also be an option; each landfill operates under its own policy, and delivery to the landfill also has to be arranged.

An Unacceptable Alternative

Although horsemeat is not consumed in this country, U.S. slaughterhouses historically have processed horses for human consumption overseas. These facilities were often where lame, unwanted, or elderly horses met their end; their owners were more concerned about wringing a few last dollars out of them than with giving their horses a humane end.

From 2000 to 2007, up to one hundred thousand horses were slaughtered in the United States annually, according to the U.S. Department of Agriculture (USDA), which oversees this industry and enforces the laws that regulate it. Thousands more were slaughtered in Mexico and Canada, outside USDA's jurisdiction.

Most horses come to slaughterhouses from livestock auctions and sales, where "killer-buyers" purchase them for just a few hundred dollars apiece. These horses are from all walks of equine life—racehorses, children's ponies, show horses, broodmares. Many obviously had loving owners at one point in their lives but have been sold so many times that a caring owner might be a distant memory; others are in such sorry shape that it seems they've never been shown any kindness at all.

There are many humane and ethical concerns regarding the slaughter of horses, and over the past several years, public consciousness and legislation has caught up to what some in the horse world have known for a long time—that many of this country's horses meet their end not at the hands of a veterinarian or peacefully in a field, but at a slaughterhouse.

One of the primary concerns about equine slaughter is the fact that the horses must often be transported long distances to the slaughter facility. A horse sold for slaughter in Florida, for example, historically had to endure a thousand-mile trip crowded into a stock trailer with strange horses before reaching his final destination in Texas. The horses often fight and injure each other en route.

Legislation has been enacted that was meant to ensure these horses are treated more humanely during their final journey. USDA's regulations require that horses be fed, watered, and rested at least every twenty-eight hours en route, and the use of double-decker trailers to transport horses was outlawed in 2006. Although the legislation was meant to help end some of the abuses horses face in transport, the regulations still leave a lot to be desired and are seldom, if ever, enforced.

Once at the slaughter facility, horses are "stunned" by use of a captive bolt—a gun that shoots a metal rod into the horse's brain, rendering the horse unconscious. (Horses who are euthanized by barbiturate overdose cannot be safely consumed by humans, so the captive bolt is used instead.) After stunning, the horse is hoisted by one leg from a chain, and his throat is cut. He subsequently bleeds to death and his carcass is processed.

Improper use of the captive bolt during slaughter means that horses may often endure repeated blows with the device and may be improperly stunned as they proceed through slaughter.[64]

Although having a horse euthanized on the farm will likely cost the horse owner a couple of hundred dollars, administering a quiet and humane end should be worth that. Horses who go to slaughter endure a strenuous trip under horrific conditions, and their last moments are filled with fear. For those reasons alone, no conscientious owner should allow a horse for whom she is responsible to go that route.

On an ethical level, caring horsemen simply shouldn't stand for the idea that it's acceptable for horses who have spent their lifetimes as servants and companions to humans to be slaughtered for human consumption, and the voices proclaiming that are growing louder and louder.

Federal legislation has been introduced (although not yet passed) that would ban the slaughter of horses for human consumption *and* their export for slaughter. Six states have already outlawed the practice—

California was the first, enacting legislation in 1998; since then, five others have followed suit, and more states are considering a ban.

Slaughter for human consumption is not the same as rendering (which is the process of using the carcasses of dead horses for pet or animal food, or fertilizer). Rendering facilities only accept carcasses (usually animals who have either died of natural causes or have been euthanized with a barbiturate overdose, which makes them unfit for human consumption), not live animals.

Conclusion

As horsemen, we all owe a great debt to the horses on which we've learned and practiced our skills. For some of us, that list of equine partners is very long; for others, it may only contain a few names. Regardless, we all have certain horses whom we remember fondly— that first lesson horse, the first horse you owned, an exceptionally talented horse, or one who was especially kind.

We get nostalgic and reminisce about rides on those horses, and the tricks they pulled or the lessons they taught us. If we have put his fate in the hands of others, we muse aloud, "I wonder whatever happened to him."

The hope, of course, is that those old friends are continuing to thrive at their jobs, teaching new generations of riders, and living to a ripe old age. When their riding days are over, we hope they're living like the horse in the example that began this chapter—simply enjoying being horses after a lifetime of hard work, with a conscientious human looking after them.

A horse may have several owners throughout her lifetime; if just one of those owners is lacking in compassion or a sense of responsibility, that horse's life may suddenly deviate in a direction most of us don't want to think about. She could end up starved or abused. She could be pushed to keep working when she's lame or sore. Her final days might not be spent snoozing in a sunny pasture but crammed into a truck with a dozen other horses, headed for a slaughterhouse in Mexico. Her final, ignoble end could be on a dinner table in Belgium.

In 2003 it was learned that Ferdinand, the winner of the 1986 Kentucky Derby, likely died at a slaughterhouse in Japan in 2002 after a career at stud. The bright chestnut Thoroughbred won almost $3.8 million on the racetrack and was the fifth leading money-winner of all time. He certainly had earned his keep, but even his stellar accomplishment wasn't enough to prevent his last owner, a Japanese horse dealer, from sending him to slaughter.

The fact that even a superstar like Ferdinand isn't guaranteed a happy ending only reinforces the importance of stewards for the "mere mortal" horses whose names aren't enshrined in history. Fame and competitive success aren't enough, nor is a cute face or a sweet disposition. Horses rely on people to secure them the final days they deserve.

CHAPTER 15

Activism

AFTER ABSORBING ALL OF THE ADVICE SET forth in this book, you're amply prepared to care for, ride, and compete your own horse in a humane manner befitting the trust your horse places in you, and the responsibility you feel toward him. Both your horse's health and his well-being will be the better for it.

But all horses are not so lucky. There are individuals within the horse world for whom equine health and well-being are not important considerations; they're more interested in the glory of competitive success or running a prosperous business. To some, horses are little more than commodities or equipment to be used and disposed of by any convenient or financially beneficial means. Although it may be difficult to fathom for those of us who care so deeply for our horses, some people simply don't care at all. Horses are often the victims of neglect or abuse by owners who should know better.

It's a constant struggle to secure humane treatment for all animals, horses included. Ensuring the best of care for our own horses is, of course, where we all should focus our efforts, but it's also important to help elevate the care of horses as a whole. As admirers of the species, we owe it to these magnificent creatures to continue improving the situation of horses everywhere.

We're not all capable of running a rescue or leading a legislative battle, but there are myriad ways in which average horse owners can help make the world a better place for horses to live, even if it's just one horse at a time.

Speak Out Against Cruelty

The horse world is a diverse one, where well-meaning individuals often have very different opinions. But there's one issue around which all equine enthusiasts can unite: opposition to abject cruelty and neglect.

Unfortunately, it seems as though every few months a new case of abuse gains widespread publicity due to its severity—a farm where the owners simply stopped feeding the horses, leaving dozens of them to starve; a horse who is dragged to death behind a truck; kids shooting and killing horses for "fun."

Many times these are incidents perpetrated by mentally disturbed individuals whose actions are outside our realm of understanding. In other instances, the abuse is the result of a cavalier attitude toward animal life in general. In any event, such situations are a matter for law enforcement to handle, but it's often everyday citizens who sound the alarm and get authorities involved.

You can do your part simply by being observant and aware. Make a point of getting to know (if only by sight) the horses in your general area. Take note of any out-of-the-way horse properties you might pass while driving down back roads, or that might be visible from the trails while you're riding, and observe how many horses there are and their general condition. (You should never trespass, however; simply make mental notes of what's visible as you pass by.)

In some instances of abuse, horses exist on a property in very poor condition for months or even years, simply because there are no watchful eyes around to see and report them. Being on constant alert for abuse and neglect might allow you to be the one person who notices the too-skinny horse in a secluded paddock off a dead-end road, and can get him the help he needs.

If you spot horses who look to be in very poor condition, or if you notice a deterioration in the condition of horses with whom you're familiar, you can notify local animal-control authorities and ask them to investigate. (You can do so anonymously, if you wish.) Provide them with as much detail as you can about the situation—the address of the farm, the number of horses on the property, and what you noticed about their condition and the care being provided. For example, if you can see that the horses' hooves are curling up at the toes, that's a telltale sign of neglect, as are untreated wounds.

If you feel comfortable doing so, you can simply approach the owner with an offer to help. Many times neglect springs from ignorance or poverty, and the owner might be grateful for someone to guide him to options that will help him provide better care.

Know the laws regarding animal neglect in your state and what constitutes a sufficient level of care—in most instances, horses must be provided with food, water, veterinary care, and shelter (although in some jurisdictions, a stand of trees may qualify as "shelter"), but specifics vary. If there are obvious violations, such as failure to provide shelter, include that information with your complaint. Let the animal-control officer know that you are an experienced horse person so the officer will know your assessment is an educated one. (These officers are also called on by those who are less knowledgeable to investigate "dead" horses who are simply napping in the sunshine, or "blindfolded" horses who are wearing fly masks, so they are likely to appreciate knowing that your report is based on actual knowledge of proper horse care.)

The attitudes and helpfulness of local animal-control officials range widely. In some jurisdictions they may not take such reports very seriously, or they may be so severely understaffed that they have a large backlog of cases. (Animal control may not exist as a separate agency but be the responsibility of the sheriff's department, or be handled by a volunteer investigator from a nonprofit agency.) Keep an eye on the horses in question and follow up with animal control, especially if it seems that the animals' condition fails to improve. If you're not satisfied with the response from animal control, ask for help from your elected officials or contact equine rescue organizations or local humane societies in your area and see if they can help you light a fire under the proper authorities.

Keep in mind that there are legitimate reasons for horses to be in poor shape, so don't automatically assume the worst. Elderly horses often have a very difficult time maintaining their weight, despite the best efforts of their owners, and may be unthrifty, shaggy, and sway-backed, even if they're in decent health for their age. A horse who has been ill or injured may lose considerable weight that takes time to gain back. Perhaps the horse in question is a rescued animal in the process of being rehabbed. When animal control investigates such complaints, the officer should be able to discern easily whether it's a case of abuse or neglect or if there are reasonable explanations for why a horse is in poor condition. He may check for available food and water on the premises or ask to see the owner's feed-store receipts. Officials can also check back after a period of time to ensure that animals are improving.

Less Obvious Forms of Abuse

Lack of food, water, and shelter are not the only abuses to which horses are subjected, unfortunately, nor does abuse happen only on secluded private properties, out of the sight of passersby. Often abuse occurs in front of witnesses or at public facilities, such as horse show grounds, and may be perpetuated by so-called equine professionals in the name of "discipline" or "training."

If you're familiar with the concept of diffusion of responsibility, you know that, when there are more people around to observe a situation, it's often less likely that someone will speak up or intercede, simply because everyone assumes someone else will do it. You see this principle played out in real life in the warm-up arena of an equestrian competition. Perhaps a frustrated rider is jerking her horse in the mouth, jabbing him with the spur, or walloping him repeatedly with a crop, the punishment getting more out of control as the horse's behavior (understandably) doesn't improve. Other riders steer clear to avoid upsetting their own horses, and trainers warming up their students in the ring seem oblivious to the meltdown in progress. Spectators along the rail avert their eyes, muttering, "That horse is a saint," or "What a shame," to one another.

Rarely does anyone speak up or attempt to stop behavior that is clearly inappropriate. No one wants to offend fellow riders or competitors or challenge those deemed more experienced or accomplished. People allow the abuse to continue because they don't want to be perceived as rude or make a scene during an otherwise enjoyable day. This "see no evil" strategy damages everyone who participates in every organized equine activity. It is tacit acceptance of, and complicity in, bad behavior.

No matter what your discipline, a sanctioned competition always has some sort of official whose job it is to enforce the rules, including those that govern abusive behavior. If you witness a situation you feel crosses the line between appropriate and inappropriate treatment of a horse, find that official immediately and insist that she accompany you back to the horse and rider in question. In most cases the official actually must witness abuse to take action against a competitor; she cannot simply rely on eyewitness accounts from bystanders.

Even if the official doesn't witness the abuse first-hand and can't sanction a rider under the rules, she is likely to have a stern word with the abuser and let the person know she is being watched. Perhaps this action alone will prevent similar outbursts from this rider in the future or cause the rider to reflect on her behavior and realize it was out of line.

There are times, however, when there are no officials available to help, and it's up to individuals to step in and speak up. If you witness behavior you believe is abusive—at a private facility where you're a visitor, or perhaps at the barn where you board—approach the individual in a firm, but non-threatening way, if you can. Sometimes simply drawing attention to the fact that the incident has been noticed—that witnesses are present—will change the behavior. At other times, a private but subtle criticism ("Trainer Smith, I'm uncomfortable with how hard you are on Midnight. It seems to me he is frightened, not 'just being an idiot.'") will at least force the rider/handler to justify behavior that is unacceptable to students and onlookers.

Your "interference" may not be received well. Someone who is upset enough to mistreat a horse is obviously not in a frame of mind open to criticism. Expect defensiveness, even hostility. Such a response is telling in and of itself. Do what you can without risking your own safety. At least by stepping forward and speaking up, you may have inspired others—grooms, working students, horse-owning novice parents—to summon the courage to do the same.

Educating Others

Although many cases of abuse or neglect are premeditated, purposeful, and can have no legitimate excuse, there are instances in which horses suffer because their owners simply don't know any better. Those who don't have much horse knowledge might not recognize when a horse is too thin or might not know the difference between hay (feed) and straw (bedding). An owner might not realize the importance of regular hoof or dental care. Or an individual might simply be overwhelmed by the work—and cash—involved in caring for horses and find herself caught in a downward spiral of neglect from which there seems to be no escape.

Individuals have a responsibility to be educated about the animals in their care and to provide for them. But not all ignorant people are inherently careless or unkind; they are not necessarily lost causes.

If you make the effort to get to know your horsey neighbors and other horse owners in your community—the folks whom you pass on the trails or meet at the tack or feed stores—and become involved with others at the local level, you can sometimes spot dangerous situations developing and make yourself available to help.

Perhaps your next-door neighbor has an older horse who has gotten progressively thinner over the course of the summer and fall, and winter is fast approaching. Neighbor Jim is a well-meaning person, but he is not very knowledgeable about horses: he might not even have noticed that the horse was losing weight or might not know what to do about it.

Stop by his house to say hello. Compliment his barn paint job, dog, or garden, then casually mention that you noticed old Stormy was looking a little thin: has the neighbor tried a particular brand of feed that worked well for your older horse? Would he like the number for your equine dentist, who did such a great job helping your older fellow?

It's certainly not unheard of for horse people to tell a few white lies to help effect a solution. You might just happen to have a few bags of senior feed sitting in your feed room that you're not going to use (*because you bought them for the neighbor's horse*)—would he like to try some? Or you might coincidentally have the equine dentist coming over to float your horses' teeth next week—would he like to join in on the appointment?

Well-intentioned but uneducated horse owners can be helped, if someone takes the time to do so (and they're amenable to being helped). In such cases, small efforts on your part can make a big difference for the horses, and can perhaps turn around what otherwise could have developed into a very unfortunate situation.

Vote with Your Wallet

In any local area, you're likely to find some professionals (trainers, barn managers, and the like) with wonderful reputations as consummate horsemen, nearly universally recommended by others in the area.

But there are a whole lot more whose reputations are decidedly mixed. You might hear of a trainer who many say has worked wonders with their horses, but he has also been suspended several times by the governing association of his sport for rules violations. Another might be that rider you saw losing her temper with her horse in the warm-up arena.

Rumors can often run rampant, of course, and it can be difficult to confirm or debunk what you hear about others. But even if only half of what you hear in any given local horse community is actually true, it's enough to make your hair stand on end.

For some individuals, all that matters is that a professional gets them results—whether it's ribbons or a horse sold or a training problem solved—even if the methods are questionable. They dismiss previous transgressions and are willing to look the other way if rules or ethical covenants are broken. If the trainer helps Suzy win the championship at this year's big show or runs the glitziest barn in town, they choose to ignore the fact that horses in his "program" seem to last only a few years before being broken down or sold off, or that he was suspended for showing a horse that tested positive for cocaine.

Unscrupulous individuals are kept in business by those who are willing to put ethics aside for their own personal gain, and unfortunately, the horse industry has a healthy contingent of such people.

If the humane treatment of horses is important to you, you should support equine professionals who share your beliefs. Vote with your wallet, and give your business to those in the industry who have demonstrated that they believe in putting the horses first. Avoid those who are known for bending the rules (and even the law) when it suits them. Rules violations are usually a matter of public record. (For instance, the USEF, which governs saddle seat, show hunters and jumpers, eventing, dressage, and reining, among other organized sports, publishes all rules violations in its monthly members' magazine.)

When enough people decide that they're not willing to financially "enable" the horse world's less savory characters, the horse world becomes a much less attractive place for the unsavory to do business.

Educate Yourself About Welfare Issues

Over the last hundred years, great strides have been made in ensuring humane treatment for all animals, including horses. It used to be that animals were considered a person's property, and owners could do as they chose, regardless of the effects on the animal. Today, the humane community views all animals as entitled to basic standards of care and protection from abuse, whether they're pets, farm animals, or animals used in research. The humane treatment of animals is an established part of our culture, and, although many serious issues persist, progress is being made all the time.

These changes didn't occur overnight and wouldn't have been possible without substantial pressure from concerned citizens, those who demanded laws to protect animals, and those who worked to educate the public and change perceptions about how animals should be treated. That work continues today, both in the United States and in developing nations, where much remains to be done to ensure protection for animals under the law and to educate the general public.

As a horse owner, your first focus (and rightfully so) is your own horse, managing his care and simply enjoying his company. But as equine enthusiasts, we also have an appreciation for the entire species. And some horses are not fortunate enough to have owners like you who care so diligently for them. Who looks out for those horses?

By becoming educated about the welfare issues facing our equine friends, we can help spur discussion of these concerns within the equestrian community and use our collective expertise to develop solutions. Visit The HSUS at its website, *www.humanesociety.org*, to find out how you can help us combat cruelty.

How Horse Lovers Can Help

Although the issues facing horses can seem vast and insurmountable, progress is being made all the time, thanks to horse-loving individuals who get involved. Equine enthusiasts come from widely varying backgrounds—from the cowboys of the West to elite show riders of the East—but what all should have in common is a reverence and respect for the horse. When riders from across disciplines come together and speak in one voice, much can be accomplished.

The protections our horses have now were not quick in coming, and the horse lovers who preceded us had to work hard to secure them. Solutions to complex problems are rarely perfect, but such problems can always be improved over time. Although we may never live in a society where all animals are safe from mistreatment or neglect, it's certainly a noble goal to strive toward.

We can't all be Anna Sewell, whose *Black Beauty* almost single-handedly made animal welfare a popular cause more than a century ago, or Velma Johnson ("Wild Horse Annie"), who campaigned to obtain federal protection for free-roaming mustangs and burros on the western plains. But individuals can take many small actions that, cumulatively, can make a big difference.

Be an Example

As an individual horse owner, one of the most valuable contributions you can make is to be a good example. When your own horse is happy and supremely well cared for, it sets the standard for other horse owners around you and raises the overall level of care. When you don't tolerate callous attitudes toward buying and selling, or when you disavow abusive training practices, it encourages others to do the same. And when you compete in a conscientious manner, embodying the ideas of putting the horse first and engaging in good sportsmanship, it shows others how things should be done.

You can actively help your friends, neighbors, and barn-mates to learn about the welfare issues that affect horses. Some may view their horse activities as an escape from "real-life" problems and *want* to hide from the dark side, but others are simply so involved in their own small corner of the horse world they may unaware of what goes on elsewhere.

Support Legislation

All the good examples in the world won't encourage certain individuals to change their practices—they need to be forced to do so by legislation. In recent years, state and federal legislation has addressed the slaughter of horses for human consumption, equine transport, and fraud in horse sales. New legislative efforts are always emerging, from local ordinances to federal laws, that can either be a boon or a detriment to humane horse care.

Take the time to educate yourself on such issues, and then make your opinion known. Call or write your elected officials, tell them what you think, and encourage others in your local equestrian community to do the same.

Familiarize yourself with the existing laws regarding equine welfare in your state. As welfare advocates have become frustrated with lax enforcement and paltry punishments for heinous crimes against animals, there's been a push to change such laws from misdemeanors to felonies. Forty-three states now have some sort of felony-level penalties for animal cruelty, and twenty-nine of those were enacted in just the last ten years. Take a look at your state's laws and see how they compare. Do they apply to first-time offenders? Do they include provisions for stiff fines and prison time? If not, make your voice heard and press your legislators to toughen the laws that protect animals.

Laws are only useful when they are enforced, however. How seriously does your local law enforcement take animal-related crimes? Is your local department of animal control effective and responsive to complaints? Animal-control departments are quite frequently underfunded and understaffed. If this is the case in your community, lobby for improvements that will help these local officials pursue cases of abuse and neglect more effectively.

Get Involved

Did you know that many states, and even some cities and counties, have their own horse councils? These non-profit membership organizations represent all equine interests in their areas, from such big businesses as horse racing to individual horse owners. They monitor legislative efforts that affect the ownership and use of horses, such as changes in zoning laws, including access to trails and public lands. And they provide an information clearinghouse tailored to local interests, information on disease outbreaks, alerts about stolen horses or tack, lists of boarding facilities, and so on.

With the modest dues you pay to these organizations, you help support educational initiatives and ensure that local government hears the opinions of your community's horse owners. You'll also be firmly plugged into your community's equine network, more aware of the local issues facing horse owners, and better able to help resolve them.

There are national and local equine organizations that represent particular organized disciplines. If you're an active competitor, you're likely already required to be a member of the national organization, but consider joining a local one, too. It will help you connect with other enthusiasts in your area. Even if you're not an active competitor, national and local memberships help to support your sport. They give you a chance to become involved in your sport's governance and lobby for rules that help protect the horse's welfare.

Volunteer and Donate

There are hard-working equine rescues in many communities whose volunteers are on the front lines of the battle for humane treatment. Whenever a large-scale case of abuse makes the news—the discovery of a farm with dozens of starving horses, for example—these groups take in the rescued animals. They're equipped to deal with severe cases of starvation and abuse, everything from putting horses who are too weak to stand in slings to help them recover, to expert trimming and rehabilitation of horribly neglected and overgrown hooves.

These groups take in the unwanted and the abused and nurse them back to health, then either make them available for adoption or provide them with a permanent, safe home. They also offer valuable educational opportunities for the local community and help raise awareness about the welfare issues that affect horses.

These groups rely on horse-knowledgeable volunteers—from beginners able to handle a pitchfork and a feed scoop to experienced hands able to work with problem horses. If you have time to give, it will certainly be well spent helping out at a reputable horse rescue in your area. It can be heartbreaking work, seeing horses who have often been horrifically neglected or abused, but it is also incredibly rewarding to see them learn to trust humans, gain weight, and blossom once again into beautiful animals.

If you have an empty stall at home, you might also consider fostering a rescue horse. You typically provide feed, housing, and perhaps some basic training until a horse can be placed in a new, permanent home. Putting horses in foster care helps them get more individualized attention and frees up space at a rescue facility for emergency cases.

In addition to giving your time, you can support these groups with monetary and equipment donations. Many rescues accept used tack, horse blankets, riding clothes, and other items, either to use in their programs or to sell to raise funds.

HSUS Director of Equine Protection Keith Dane comforts one of the Miracle Horses rescued in 2007.

Rescues aren't the only groups that can benefit from volunteers, however. If you have a local Pony Club or 4-H, consider helping out in an educational capacity. You can lend your expertise to help shape young equine-loving minds, ensuring that sound horse-management practices and a concern for equine welfare are passed on to the next generation.

Join Up

Finally, consider becoming a member of The Humane Society of the United States (*www.humanesociety.org*) and other equine advocacy organizations. Doing so will help keep you abreast of the welfare issues that affect horses in this country and around the world. You'll add your voice to the hundreds of thousands of others calling for change when it's necessary.

Your monetary contributions also help lobby for new legislation that protects horses, and the continued enforcement and strengthening of existing laws. Since its founding in 1954, The HSUS has worked to prevent animal cruelty, exploitation, and neglect through education, advocacy, and public policy reform. The HSUS has been a major force in pushing for the ban of equine slaughter for human consumption, educating women about Premarin, and advocating for stricter anti-cruelty laws.

There are also many other non-profit groups with a more specialized focus that may match your own interests. Some organizations work to transition racing Thoroughbreds, Standardbreds, and Quarter Horses to new pleasure or sport careers. Others specialize in providing veterinary care for working horses in developing nations and educating their owners about proper harness fit and horse-management practices.

Whatever issues matter to you most, you're sure to find an organization out there dedicated to addressing them. By lending your moral and financial support, you can help further the cause of humane horse care beyond your own stable or local community.

Notes

Chapter 1

[1]Karol Wilson (director of member services and regional administration, United States Pony Clubs), e-mail message to author(s), March 5, 2007.

[2]Luann Ulrich (assistant manager of communications, American Quarter Horse Association), e-mail message to author(s), March 1, 2007.

Chapter 2

[3]International Museum of the Horse, "The First Horses: Hyracotherium" (2007), *http://www.kyhorsepark.com/museum/history.php?chapter=7*.

[4]*http://horses.about.com/od/understandinghorses/a/horsesleep.htm*.

[5]Katherine Albro Houpt, *Domestic Animal Behavior for Veterinarians and Animal Scientists* (Ames, Iowa: Iowa State University Press, 1991), 90–92.

[6]Ibid., 90–92.

[7]U.S. Department of Agriculture, *National Animal Health Monitoring System Equine Study* (Washington, D.C.: USDA, 1998), n.p.

[8]Houpt, *Domestic Animal Behavior for Veterinarians and Animal Scientists*, 46–53.

Chapter 3

[9]Elwyn Hartley Edwards, *The New Encyclopedia of the Horse* (New York: Dorling Kindersley, 2000), 28–29.

[10]International Museum of the Horse, "Early Attempts at Riding: The Soft Bit and Bridle" (2007), *http://kyhorsepark.com/museum/history .php?chapter=14*.

[11]International Museum of the Horse, "Harnessing the Horse: Riding Comes to the Near East: 1350 BCE" (2007), *http://kyhorsepark.com/ museum/history.php?chapter=17*.

[12]Edwards, *The New Encyclopedia of the Horse*, 2000, 93.

[13]International Museum of the Horse, "The Classical World, 700 BCE: Xenophon: The Father of Classical Equitation" (2007), *http://kyhorsepark.com/museum/history.php?chapter=23*.

[14]Edwards, *The New Encyclopedia of the Horse*, 38–39.

[15]International Museum of the Horse, "The Roman Empire: 27 BCE–476 AD: The Circus Maximus" (2007), *http://kyhorsepark.com/museum/history .php?chapter=26*.

[16]Edwards, *The New Encyclopedia of the Horse*, 68–69.

[17]International Museum of the Horse, "Return to the New World: Colonial Horses" (2007), *http://kyhorsepark.com/museum/history.php?chapter=56*.

[18]Edwards, *The New Encyclopedia of the Horse*, 295.

[19]Ibid., 257.

[20]Emily R. Kilby, "Demographics of U.S. Equine Population," report prepared for The Humane Society of the United States (2006), in Deborah J. Salem and Andrew N. Rowan, eds., *The State of the Animals IV: 2007* (Washington, D.C.: Humane Society Press, 2007), 176.

[21]Staffordshire Past Track, "Coal Mining in North Staffordshire: Support Systems" (2007), *http://www.staffspasttrack.org.uk/exhibit/coal/support%20systems/lastpony.htm*.

[22]Ascot Park Polo Club, "A Short History of Polo" (2007), *http://www.polo.co.uk/polo_history.htm*.

[23]National Jousting Association, "The Medieval Tourney" (2007), *http://www.nationaljousting.com/history/medieval.htm*.

[24]International Museum of the Horse, "Origins of the Blooded Horse: The Fox Hunt" (2007), *http://kyhorsepark.com/museum/history.php?chapter=61*.

[25]Edwards, *The New Encyclopedia of the Horse*, 14–15.

[26]International Museum of the Horse, "Medieval Horse: 476–c.1450: Overview" (2007), *http://kyhorsepark.com/museum/history.php?chapter=34*.

[27]Edwards, *The New Encyclopedia of the Horse*, 216–217.

[28]Kilby, "Demographics of U.S. Equine Population," 183.

[29]American Horse Council, "National Economic Impact of the U.S. Horse Industry" (2007), *http://horsecouncil.org/economics.html*.

Chapter 6

[30]Kilby, "Demographics of U.S. Equine Population," 193.

[31]International Museum of the Horse, "The Horse in Nineteenth Century American Sport: Caprilli's Forward Seat Revolutionizes Equitation" (2007), *http://www.kyhorsepark.com/museum/history.php?chapter=92*.

[32]U.S. Dressage Federation, "Description of Dressage for Olympic Media Guide," *http://www.usdf.org/AboutUs/DescriptionOfDressage.asp*.

[33]North American Trail Ride Conference, "Frequently Asked Questions" (2007), *http://www.natrc.org/faq.html*.

[34]National Reining Horse Association, "About the NRHA" (2007), *http://www.nrha.com/about.php*.

[35]American Quarter Horse Association, AQHA World Championship Shows (2007), *http://www.aqha.com/showing/guidetoshowing/worldshows.html*.

Chapter 7

[36]Arabian Horse Association, "AHA Basic Facts" (2007), *http://www.arabianhorses.org/AHAfacts.asp*.

[37]American Quarter Horse Association, "Horse Statistics" (2007), *http://www.aqha.com/association/pdf/annualreport_horses.pdf*.

[38]Edwards, *The New Encyclopedia of the Horse*, 230–231.

[39]It must be observed that the AQHA has its political side as well and has been criticized by groups such as The Humane Society of the United States for its opposition to a ban on horse slaughter.

[40]American Saddlebred Horse Association, "Breed History 1800's" (2007), *http://www.asha.net/Breed-History-1800*.

[41]Edwards, *The New Encyclopedia of the Horse*, 232–233.

[42]American Morgan Horse Association, "Frequently Asked Questions" (2007), *http://www.morganhorse.com/*.

[43]International Museum of the Horse, "Horse Breeds of the World: Thoroughbred" (2007), *http://www.kyhorsepark.com/museum/breeds .php?pageid=8&breed=94&alpha=Five*.

[44]The Jockey Club, "The Thoroughbred" (2007), *http://www.jockeyclub.com/thoroughbredHistory.asp*.

Chapter 9

[45]Changing Ration for Horses, Extention. *www.extension.org/pages/ Changing_Rations_for_Horses*.

[46]*The Horse* Staff, "Veterinarian's Input on Olympics Horse Events Has Had Global Impact," *The Horse* (October 16, 1998), Article #2209, *http://www .thehorse.com/ViewArticle.aspx?ID=2209&nID=7&n=Heat%20Stress&case=2*; Marcia King, "Cool Aid: Beating the Heat with Working Horses," *The Horse*

(July 1, 1999) Article #350, *http://www.thehorse.com/ViewArticle.aspx?ID=350*; Ray Geor, BVSc, Ph.D., Dipl. ACVIM, "Chilling Out after Exercise," *The Horse* (July 1, 2001), Article 897, *http://www.thehorse.com/ViewArticle.aspx?ID=897*; Nancy S. Loving, D.V.M., "Heat Stress," *The Horse* (July 1, 2003), Article 4492, *http://www.thehorse.com/ViewArticle.aspx?ID=4492*.

[47]Erin Ryder, "Eating Like the Joneses," *The Horse* (December 4, 2006) Article #8327. *http://www.thehorse.com/ViewArticle.aspx?ID=8327&nID=12&n=Grains&case=2*.

[48]American Horse Rider and Horses and Horse Information, "Sweet Horse Feed Recipes with Added Molasses (i.e., Sugar) May Contribute to Underlying Equine Health Conditions," 2007, *http://www.horses-and-horse-information.com/articles/0203_how_sweet.shtml*.

Chapter 10

[49]Karen Briggs, "Vaccination Essentials: Rabies, Tetanus, and Botulism," *The Horse* (February 2005), n.p.

[50]University of Kentucky Cooperative Extension Service, "Rabies in Horses" (2007), *http://www.uky.edu/Ag/AnimalSciences/pubs/asc125.pdf*.

[51]Karen Briggs, "The Ever-Present Threat," *The Horse* (April 2005), n.p.

[52]U.S. Department of Agriculture Animal and Plant Health Inspection Service, "Questions and Answers About West Nile Virus" (2003), *http://www.aphis.usda.gov/lpa/pubs/fsheet_faq_notice/faq_ahwnv.html*.

[53]U.S. Department of Agriculture Animal and Plant Health Inspection Service, "Equine Herpesvirus Myeloencephalopathy: A Potentially Emerging Disease" (2007), *http://www.aphis.usda.gov/vs/ceah/cei/taf/emergingdiseasenotice_files/ehv1final.pdf*.

[54]University of Minnesota College of Veterinary Medicine, "What Is Potomac Horse Fever?" (2007), *http://www.cvm.umn.edu/img/assets/9385/Potomac%20Horse%20Fever.pdf*.

[55]Cynthia A. McCall, "Monitoring Your Horse's Vital Signs," Alabama Cooperative Extension Service. ANR-808 (reprinted February 1999). *http://www.aces.edu/pubs/docs/A/ANR-0808.*

[56]Nancy S. Loving, "Impaction Colic: Blocking the Way," *The Horse* (May 2006), n.p.

[57]Erin D. Malone, "Colic: Public Enemy #1" (2007), *http://www.extension.umn.edu/horse/components/factsheets/colic.htm.*

[58]Christy West, "Foot X Rays: A Crystal Ball?" *TheHorse.com*, *http://www.thehorse.com/ViewArticle.aspx?ID=9805&kw=founder.*

[59]Christy West, "The Quest to Conquer Laminitis" (May 1, 2007), Article # 9471. *http://www.thehorse.com/ViewArticle.aspx?ID=9471.*

Chapter 11

[60]Henry Heymering, "Who Invented Horseshoeing?" (2007), *http://www.horseshoes.com/advice/invtshoe/winvhrs.htm.*

[61]Scott McKendrick, Patricia Evans, and Clell Bagley, "Proper Basic Hoof Care" (2006), *http://extension.usu.edu/files/publications/publication/AG_Equine_2006-03.pdf.*

Chapter 13

[62]American Horse Council Foundation (AHCF), "The Economic Impact of the Horse Industry on the United States," (Washington, D.C.: American Horse Council Foundation, 2005).

Chapter 14

[63]Erika Street, "After Goodbye" (July 2004). *Thehorse.com.*

[64]Veterinarians for Equine Welfare. *www.vetsforequinewelfare.org/jin/php.*

Glossary

4-H—A youth agricultural organization

Aids—Cues used by the rider, either natural (hands, seat, voice, and leg) or artificial (whips or spurs)

Board—V., to keep a horse at a facility owned by someone else; n., the fee paid for keeping a horse at a boarding facility

Breeches—Riding pants

Bronky—untamed, as a wild bronco

Bute—The common name for phenylbutazone, an anti-inflammatory drug

Canter—A three-beat gait (also called the lope) in which the outside hind leg strikes first, followed by the diagonal pair of the inside hind and outside front, and, finally, the inside front. In the left canter lead, the left front leg strikes out slightly farther than the right, and vice versa for the right lead.

Catch riding—Riding a horse for someone else

Clench—The portion of a horseshoe nail that protrudes from the horse's hoof wall and is flattened down to fasten the shoe to the hoof

Coffin bone—The bone at the bottom of the leg column, contained within the hoof capsule

Coggins test—A routine blood test that screens for antibodies to the equine infectious anemia virus

Colic—All-encompassing term for any sort of digestive upset in the horse

Conformation—The way in which a horse is put together and all the various body parts relate to each other, including the straightness (or lack thereof) of legs, angles of joints, and the overall proportions of the horse's body (see chart on page 343)

Coronet band—The line formed where the hoof joins the leg, also called the coronary band

Cribbing—A stable vice that involves chewing wood or sucking air

Curb—A bit that acts via leverage on the horse's poll

Cushing's syndrome—A disease, usually seen in older horses, caused by a benign tumor in the pituitary gland that leads to hormonal imbalances; horses with Cushing's often have excessively long coats and are at increased risk for laminitis

Dam—A horse's mother

Digital pulse—The pulse in the digital arteries, which are found on the inside and outside of the fetlock joint; a pounding digital pulse is one symptom of laminitis

Discipline—A particular sport or type of riding, such as dressage, Western pleasure, etc.

Draft—The large, heavy breeds of horses traditionally used for pulling large loads (also spelled draught)

Draw reins—Special reins that run from a rider's hand, through the ring of the bit, and attach to the girth, giving the rider additional leverage; also called running reins, they are almost always used in conjunction with regular reins that attach directly to the bit, and should be used by experienced riders only.

Easy keeper—A horse who is easy to care for and has no trouble maintaining his weight (the opposite is a hard keeper)

Esophagus—A muscular tube that connects the horse's mouth to his stomach, through which food passes

Euthanasia—The act of humanely ending a horse's life with veterinarian-administered drugs

Farrier—An equine professional who trims and shoes a horse's hooves

Feedlot—A facility where horses are held before being shipped to slaughter

Flat—V., to ride without jumping, as in "to flat in front of a judge"; n., riding a horse when not jumping, as in "on the flat"

Floating—Filing down the rough edges on a horse's teeth

Foal—A horse or pony under the age of one year

Founder—The sinking of the bony column of the horse's leg as a result of laminitis

Gelding—A castrated male horse

Get—offspring

Green—Inexperienced (either horse or rider)

Groom—A person who provides daily care for a horse, perhaps including grooming, tacking up for the rider, feeding, etc.

Grooming—The daily process of cleaning a horse, usually including brushing, picking out hooves, and/or bathing

Halter—Show ring classes where a horse is judged on appearance and conformation; also the piece of equipment encircling the horse's head by which the horse can be led or tied (above)

Hand—A unit of measurement that equals four inches, used to measure a horse's height at the withers

Hard keeper—A horse who tends to lose weight easily

Head-shy—A term used to describe a horse who is fearful of having his head touched or handled

Hoof abscess—An often-painful infection and swelling in a horse's hoof

Horse dealer—An individual who buys and sells horses

Hunt coat—A blazer worn in the hunter show ring

Impaction colic—Digestive discomfort caused by an obstruction in the intestine

Impulsion—The horse's energy and desire to move forward

Insulin resistance—A syndrome in which the horse's tissues do not respond normally to insulin, leading to an abnormally high level of glucose in the blood

Jodhpurs—Riding pants worn with short jodhpur boots

Joint flexions—The process of individually flexing and stressing the joints of a horse's leg (usually during a lameness or pre-purchase exam) to exacerbate and detect any lameness or pain in the joint

Joint injection—The process of injecting medication directly into a joint to combat arthritis

Lameness—Any physical ailment that prevents the horse from bearing full weight on a limb or using the limb normally

Laminitis—A disease of the laminae (supporting structure) in the hoof, also called **founder**

Lead—Term for one of two variations of the canter gait; when going to the left, the horse should be on the left lead, and vice versa for the right. See also **canter**.

Ligament—A band of tough, fibrous tissue that connect bones to other bones

Longe—To exercise a horse in a circular pattern from the ground by means of a longe line (a long nylon or cotton line)

Mare—A female horse

Mucking—The act of cleaning a stall to remove soiled bedding
and manure

Mustang—A free-roaming feral horse, usually referring to horses
on the Western plains of the United States

Overface—to ask a horse and/or rider to jump a fence too high or too
complex for his level of training, causing him to fail and subsequently
lose confidence in his ability to negotiate fences of any height

Pace—A two-beat gait in which the horse's legs move in lateral pairs
(as opposed to the trot, where they move in diagonal pairs)

Paddock—A fenced enclosure used for turnout, which may or may
not have grass

Pasture—A large area used for grazing, usually enclosed by a fence

Peristalsis—Waves of contractions in the muscles ringing the digestive
tract that move food along

Poll—the top of the horse's head, behind the ears

Pommel—The part of an English saddle that arches over the
horse's withers

Pony—An equine who stands less than fourteen hands two inches
(or 14.2) at the withers when fully grown

Pony Club—An individual chapter of the United States Pony Clubs,
a national youth equestrian organization

Posting—The process of rising in the saddle every other beat of the trot

Pre-purchase exam—An examination conducted by a veterinarian before a horse is purchased

Prospect—A horse, usually green or inexperienced, who is considered to have potential in a particular discipline

Rack—A high-stepping, four-beat gait performed by gaited horses

Rain rot—An infection of the horse's skin caused by excessive moisture; also called rain scald

Registry—An organization that records and tracks horses of a particular breed

Ringbone—A lameness characterized by arthritis or excessive bone growth (often in a ring around the area) in the lower pastern, often caused by poor conformation

Roughage—A term usually used to describe hay and grass or other feeds that are very high in fiber

Run-in—A shed or other building that a horse can enter and leave at will

Running walk—A variation of the flat walk, performed by gaited horses

Schoolmaster—A well-schooled horse who is very experienced and is often used to teach advanced skills to less experienced riders

Side reins—Special reins that run from the bit to a saddle, or surcingle, used when longing a horse to encourage flexion

Sire—A horse's father

Slow-gait—A four-beat gait performed by gaited horses

Snaffle—A bit that acts directly on the bars of the horse's mouth

Soundness—The quality of being free from lameness or injury

Spavin—Term for a lameness in the hock, either a bog spavin (a soft swelling) or a bone spavin (arthritis)

Splint—A hard swelling on the horse's lower leg, usually on the inside, but sometimes found on the outside; when new, splints feel warm and can cause lameness, but later they become cold and cease to cause the horse discomfort

Spook—The process of startling abruptly at a frightening sight or sound

Stall walking—A stable vice in which a horse repeatedly paces or circles in his stall

Stallion—An uncastrated (or "entire") male horse, sometimes also called a stud

Studbook—The listing of horses accepted in a particular breed registry

Supplements—Nutritional feed additives that improve joint health, protect a horse against parasites, address vitamin/mineral deficiencies, etc.

Tack—All-encompassing term for riding equipment, including saddles and bridles

Tendon—A cord of inelastic tissue that connects muscle to bone; flexor tendons flex a join, while extensor tendons return a limb to its normal unflexed state.

Tendon sheath—The sleeve that covers a tendon

Thrush—A bacterial infection of the hoof, often caused by not picking out a horse's hooves frequently enough

Trainer—A professional who trains horses and instructs riders

Tree—The wooden frame on which a saddle is built

Trot—A two-beat gait in which the horse's legs move in diagonal pairs; also called the jog

Turnout —1. A horse and rider's overall appearance (grooming, tack, etc.), especially at a show or competition. 2. A paddock in which a horse exercises

Turn out—To give a horse free access to a pasture or paddock to exercise and graze.

Unthrifty—thin, lacking bloom

Windpuff—Soft, fluid-filled sacs around the fetlock joint, often seen in young horses who are just beginning work; these are considered blemishes, rather than lamenesses

Yearling—A one-year-old horse

Parts of the Horse

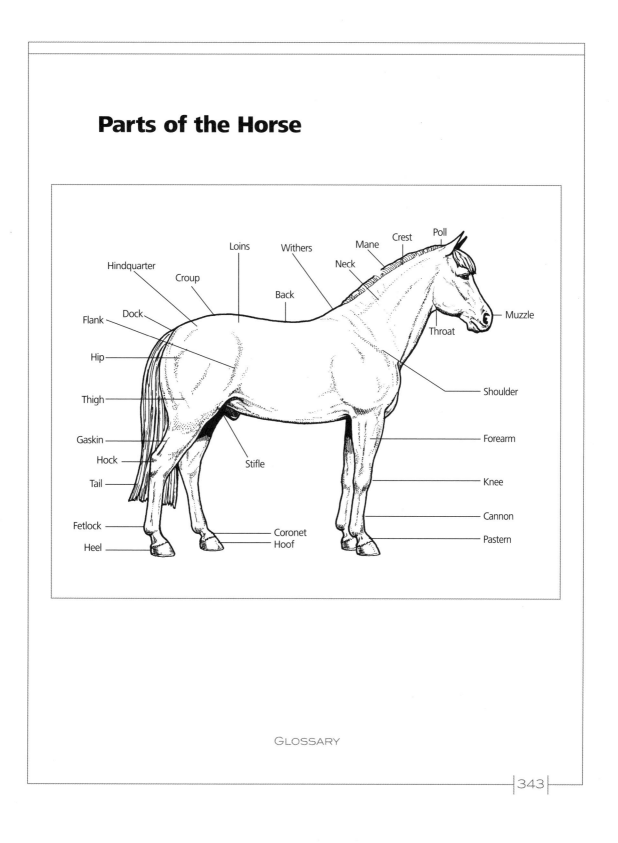

Index

Page numbers appearing in *italics* refer to tables and figures

G

Gaited horses. *See also specific breeds*
  breed-specific shows, 106
  description, 105–106
  saddle seat discipline and, 104
  soring issue, 106–107
Gas colic
  description and treatment, 211
Gastric ulcers
  description and causes, 27
Grain
  bagged, processed commercial type, 183
  easy keepers and, 183
  hard keepers and, 172, 178, 183
  multiple small amounts, 170–171
  overfeeding, 187
  pelleted form, 185
  rice bran, 187
  selection criteria, 186
  storage, 187–188
  sweet feed, 183–184
  unadulterated types, 185–186
  visually inspecting, 187
  wheat bran mashes, 187
  whole grains, 183
Grass hays
  description, 180
Greeks
  uses of horses, 39–40, 41

H

Habits
  horse's normal eating and drinking habits, 208
  noting changes in, 208–209
  pasture behavior, 208–209
  stall habits, 208
Hanovarians
  geographic derivation, 132
  movement and gait, 122

Hunting
historical background, 46–47

I

Impaction colic
description and symptoms, 210
treatment, 210–211
Internet
equine rescue listings, 76
horse-for-sale websites, 78–79

J

Jockey Club
Thoroughbred registry, 131, 132
Jumper classes
description, 100–101

K

Kopertox
thrush treatment, 243

L

Lameness
common causes, 215
conformation and, 215
description, 215
footing and, 216
head bobbing and, 217
horse's movement and, 217
leg and hoof examinations, 217–218
recognizing visually and by feel, 216–217
riding style and, 215–216
soundness and fitness relationship, 216
watching the horse on a longe line and, 217
Laminitis
acute type, 212
causes of, 212
chronic type, 212
coffin bone rotation and, 213
description, 211–212
emergency nature of, 213